Educational Practices in China, Korea, and the United States

A volume in
Literacy, Language, and Learning
Claudia Finkbeiner and Wen Ma, *Series Editors*

Educational Practices in China, Korea, and the United States

Reflections from a Study Abroad Experience

edited by

Chuang Wang
University of North Carolina–Charlotte

Lan Kolano
University of North Carolina–Charlotte

Do-Hong Kim
Augusta University

INFORMATION AGE PUBLISHING, INC.
Charlotte, NC • www.infoagepub.com

Library of Congress Cataloging-in-Publication Data

A CIP record for this book is available from the Library of Congress
http://www.loc.gov

ISBN: 978-1-64113-876-5 (Paperback)
    978-1-64113-877-2 (Hardcover)
    978-1-64113-878-9 (E-Book)

Copyright © 2019 Information Age Publishing Inc.

All rights reserved. No part of this publication may be reproduced, stored in a
retrieval system, or transmitted, in any form or by any means, electronic, mechanical,
photocopying, microfilming, recording or otherwise, without written permission
from the publisher.

Printed in the United States of America

CONTENTS

Introduction: Chinese, Korean, and American Education:
Foundations and Practices..ix
Chuang Wang, Lan Kolano, and Do-Hong Kim

PART I
INFLUENCE OF CULTURE, PARENTAL INVOLVEMENT, AND ECONOMY

1   How Culture Influences Gender Roles and Expectations
in Chinese Culture 3
Yolanda Kennedy and April Smith

2   Factors That Influence Parent Involvement in an Educational
Context in the United States, China, and South Korea:
Benefits and Barriers..19
Elizabeth M. Landon and Peter L. Johnson

3   A Comparison Study on the Effects of Parental Involvement,
Teacher Ability, and Socioeconomic Status on Academic
Achievement in the United States, China, and South Korea...........31
Kathryn Wagner and Lauren Schmidt

4   Education and the Economy: An Examination Into the
Effectiveness of Education in China, the United States,
and South Korea..49
Taylor Allen and Michelle Chen

vi ■ Contents

PART II
TEACHING AND LEARNING

5 Comparative Analysis of Instructional Texts and the Cross-Cultural Dialogue Between Teachers: Scenes From a Chinese and an American Classroom 73
Laurie Dymes

6 Comparisons of Teaching English as a Second Language in the United States and China 89
Kelsey Alvarez and Jessie Lay

7 English as a Foreign Language and Foreign Language Education in the United States, China, and South Korea 101
Jennifer James

8 Student Fitness Abroad: A Comparative Analysis of Physical Education in the United States, China, and South Korea 117
Jessica Kapota, Hongjun Qiu, and Gwitaek Park

PART III
NEW PEDAGOGICAL FRAMEWORK AND PRACTICES

9 Chinese and South Korean Education Reformations: Unrealistic Expectations in the Implementation of Western Pedagogy 133
Cory Alexander

10 How Smart Learning Is Defined: An Analysis of 27 Definitions by Korean Scholars 149
Kiran S. Budhrani

11 21st Century Classroom: Finding the Right Balance 175
Florence Martin

12 Culturally Speaking: Comparing Culturally Relevant Pedagogy in Chinese, Korean, and American Classrooms 189
Lori J. Williams

Contents ▪ **vii**

PART IV

CONCLUSION

13 Conclusion: Implications for Teacher Education 209
Lan Kolano, Chuang Wang, Michelle Pazzula,
and Do-Hong Kim

About the Contributors.. 221

INTRODUCTION

CHINESE, KOREAN, AND AMERICAN EDUCATION

Foundations and Practices

Chuang Wang, Lan Kolano, and Do-Hong Kim

Chinese students account for one third of all international students in the United States (Redden, 2018). China maintained its No. 1 position to send students to the United States by keeping an annual increase of 4% in undergraduate and 2% in graduate students, respectively. The number of students from South Korea (Korea hereafter), the No. 3 country to send students to the United States, dropped by 7% due to the improving quality of its own higher education system (Redden, 2018). The reasons for the recent shifts in the number of international students in U.S. schools are not the focus of this book; however, an understanding of the culture and educational philosophies in China and Korea will help U.S. educators better understand and serve international students in general and Chinese and Korean students in particular.

This book offers various facets of education in China, Korea, and the United States through reflections of a study abroad experience. Many of the chapters provide direct comparison and contrast in education between the

---

Educational Practices in China, Korea, and the United States, pages ix–xxii
Copyright © 2019 by Information Age Publishing
All rights of reproduction in any form reserved.

countries. The comparisons were based upon reviews of the literature, on-site classroom observations, and analyses of data collected during the study abroad experience. These comparisons and contrasts illustrate the differences and similarities, and the findings across the chapters provide not only a wide range of critical issues in comparative education but also important implications for educational policy and practices in the three countries.

We provide an overview about foundational issues of education and current challenges in education in China, Korea, and the United States in the following section. Our purpose is to find a way about how educators can learn from each other and how to teach students from these cultures. The introduction concludes with a summary of the major findings from each of the chapters in the book.

EDUCATIONAL FOUNDATIONS IN CHINA, KOREA, AND AMERICA

Both Chinese and Korean education are deeply influenced by its ideology, Confucianism, which holds distinct beliefs concerning teaching and learning. Philosophers in the east (e.g., Confucius, Mengzi, and Zhuangzi) were born not many years apart from western philosophers (e.g., Socrates and Aristotle). The feature that distinguishes the eastern philosophers from western philosophers is the focus of their teaching. While eastern philosophers try to understand the people–people relationships, western philosophers put their efforts into the investigation of the relationship between people and the world we are living in (Li, 2012). This difference drove the development of the eastern and western societies in two directions in the past 2000 years and contributed to the gap between the East and the West: Western societies are more developed in science and technology, whereas the eastern world is more sophisticated in human relationships.

Education in China and Korea

Confucianism has dominated Chinese and Korean minds for thousands of years. Confucius' greatest contribution to education is the pedagogy to teach students in accordance with their aptitudes, which is similar to individualized teaching in the United States (Liu & Ma, 2018). However, the values of modesty and community rooted in Confucianism and deeply embedded in collectivist societies of the East Asia contract sharply with individualism in western culture. For a longer time in history, both Chinese and Korean education, which are rooted in a Confucian-heritage learning culture, highlighted teacher-directed and content-based educational practices.

The hierarchical relations between teachers and students are still prevalent in Chinese and Korean education, which is very different from the decentralized and learner-oriented view in the United States (Ma, 2014).

High-stakes assessments are deep rooted in China and Korea (Brown & Gao, 2015; Kwon, Lee, & Shin, 2017). Competition and examinations are prevailing in China and Korea. Great power is embodied in high-stakes examinations because grades were used to select top students to serve as government officials in both China and Korea. For example, Keju in China started in the Sui dynasty (581–618) and was fully implemented for civil service in the Tang (618–907) and Sung (960–1279) dynasties (Elman, 1991). For centuries, pivotal assessments have determined future prospects for Chinese students, and education is seen by many to be the only option for upward social and economic mobility (Zhao & Qiu, 2012). In modern China, the Keju was replaced with the National College Entrance Examination (NCEE), which measures the academic performance and achievement of high school graduates. Similarly, the civil service examination known as *Gwago* in Korea started in the Goryeo dynasty (918–1392) to select high government officials (Kwon et al., 2017). After the Korean war (1950–1953), the government started to implement the high-stakes testing systems. Although the college admission system has been changed frequently since then, the national College Scholastic Ability Test (CSAT), also known as *Suneung* has been the determining factor for where students go to college. In both countries, students at all levels (from elementary to high school) study hard to prepare themselves for the college entrance exam in order to move up the social ladder; however, only a small fraction of them can be admitted into top-tier universities. In order to prepare students for these highly consequential assessments, traditional Chinese teaching practices revolved around rote learning methods such as knowledge reproduction and teacher-oriented classrooms (Liu & Feng, 2015; Tan & Chua, 2015).

Academic performance was highly valued in China and Korea due to its tight alignment with economic success (Kwon et al., 2017; Reitz & Verman, 2004). High-performing students in the college entrance exam and their families have been historically rewarded not only in family socioeconomic status but also in reputations among neighbors. This helps to account for the fact that parents in both countries invest heavily in their children's education and have high academic expectations of their children. Although the college entrance exam is a necessary assessment for college admission and placement of students, it brings students great pressure and burden and takes away quite a lot of joy of their childhood (Wang, Ma, & Martin, 2015).

With globalization, the world becomes increasingly culturally diverse. More and more Chinese and Korean students further their study in English-speaking countries. In the 2010–2011 academic year, China exported more students to the United States than any other country in the world.

Meanwhile, many American students study in China. For example, 13,674 American students were studying in China in the 2008–2009 academic year (Chen, 2011). Globalization presents Chinese and Korean education both opportunities and challenges. As described in Ma's research (2014), Chinese students confront great cross-cultural challenges in western countries in the following aspects: (a) language competency; (b) academic unfamiliarity; and (c) socio cultural intricacies. In spite of the differences, educators are trying to look for a more inclusive "middle ground" which incorporates the strengths of both eastern and western educational strengths.

Comparisons Between Chinese and Koran Education

Education in Korea is deeply grounded in Confucianism and highlights a hierarchical order in human relationships and gender stratification. Teaching is a very popular career choice in Korea, and only top high school graduates can realistically consider it as their possible career path (National Center on Education and the Economy, n.d.). This is mainly due to its competitive salary, long holidays, job stability, generous pension benefits, and nice working conditions. In Korea, the hiring process of public school teachers is strictly controlled by the central office at each metropolitan or provincial school district. Similarities between China and Korea in education are as follows:

1. Educational administration, legislation, and consulting systems are close. Similar to China, the Korean Ministry of Education is in charge of education at all levels: pre-school, elementary, secondary, and post-secondary education.
2. The 12 grade levels in both countries are six grades in elementary school, three grades in middle school, and three grades in high school.
3. The college entrance examination in Korea functions as a measure of the content knowledge in subject areas as well as the ability to adapt to college courses. The purpose of this examination is to assess students' ability to learn new knowledge in college. However, the purpose of college entrance examination in China is to select the top-performing students for college.

Education in the United States

Socrates' philosophy for the purpose of education is the same with that of Confucius: to prepare talented administrators for the country; however, his approaches in teaching were quite different. Instead of feeding the students with knowledge and skills, Socrates asked his students to answer his questions first and would not correct the students' wrong answers immediately. Instead, Socrates asked more questions to guide the students arrival to the correct answer themselves. This pedagogy has a deep influence on Paul Freire and was later known as the dialogue education that views learners as active learners and honors mutual respect and open communication between teachers and students (Vella, 2002).

Education in the United States was greatly influenced by the western philosophy to understand the relationship between people and the world (Li, 2012). Using rationalism and logic, people study the world to gain knowledge about the world and use the knowledge to serve their needs and control the world. Intelligence plays a significant role in western education because human beings use intelligence to construct knowledge and question what they see. A model of intelligence includes seven constructs: verbal comprehension, word fluency, number facility, associative memory, reasoning, spatial visualization, perceptual speed, and induction (Kaufman, 2009). Standardized tests were developed in the West to measure intelligence quotient (IQ), a total score that represents a person's intelligence. Despite the centuries-long debate about the heritability of intelligence (e.g., Devlin, Daniels, & Roeder, 1997; Turkheimer, 2008), IQ tests were used during World War I in the United States to screen men for officer training (Kennedy & McNeil, 2006). After the war, IQ tests were widely used in schools and industry to measure innate intelligence although the results of the tests were controversial and dubious because environmental factors were not considered and that the tests reaffirmed racism and nationalism (Kennedy & McNeil, 2006).

Curiosity, playfulness, and intrinsic enjoyment are valued characteristics for Western learners and American education. Private schools were established to educate White men, especially children from wealthy families (Monaghan, 1988). However, Horace Mann, an American educational reformer, challenged this and argued that all American citizens should have access to education through public schools (DeMarrais & LeCompte, 1998). Due to Horace Mann's efforts, compulsory education began to take shape in the United States. With more and more immigrants coming to the United States, the need to "Americanize" newcomers became stronger at the end of the 19th century, so public schools were charged with increasing patriotism (Durkheim, 1964). Scholastic Aptitude Test (SAT) college exam was also developed to replace IQ tests. Lock (2011) reviewed a wide variety of quotes about American education put forth by scholars and educators during the late 19th century and early 20th century, which is a period of transformation of American education, and urged us to learn from history to avoid the same traditional mistakes in education.

CURRENT ISSUES, CHALLENGES, AND OPPORTUNITIES FOR K–12 EDUCATORS

Education in China, Korea, and the United States are rooted in different philosophies and therefore have different beliefs and practices. However, the education in all three countries has experienced great changes to meet the challenge of the 21st century. For example, equity issue is universal. All public school systems need to provide adequate resources to the residents in the school districts but the gap between the haves and have-nots is enlarging in China, Korea, and the United States. In the United States, teacher salary is relatively low and school resources are based on local tax revenues. As a result, teachers in some districts are paid more than teachers in other districts and some schools have more resources than other schools, which has caused inequity issues in the United States (Gamoran, 2017). The American urban schools and their students are in a state of crisis due to overcrowding, scripted curricula, less experienced teachers, segregated schools, less per pupil expenditures, and few resources in addition to the pressure of state-mandated testing and tracking students into lower ability classes (Coleman, 1967; DeMarrais & LeCompte 1998; Kozol, 2005; Steinberg & Kincheloe, 2004). Weber (2010) provides an overview of the failing American urban schools and emphasizes the increased dropout rates, crime rates, and prison population that are afflicting urban students. Communities are greatly affected by the increase of high school dropouts, which in turn have enormous cost. For example, 68% of the Pennsylvania prison population were high school dropouts, and each prisoner costs $132,000 a year (Weber, 2010).

Large differences between schools and school districts are found in China as well, although teaching is a stable and respected career. Good schools provide incentives and high salaries to attract quality teachers so the gap between resources among schools is enlarging with all quality teachers moving to good schools. The teacher's salary in a top-tier school in China can be ten times more than that of a teacher's salary in a lower-tier school at the same level. The difference between rural and urban/suburban schools with respect to resources (e.g., technology, facilities, and teacher experience) is also big that migration and soaring prices for apartments near good schools have become big problems in China. The rural dropout rate is increasing due to poverty, poor academic performance in a competitive educational system, and rising opportunity cost (Yi et al., 2012). The desire for social mobility continues to fuel a population of Chinese students to work countless hours to achieve this goal. Zhao (2009) highlights the increased obesity rates, suicide rates, test stealing, and lack of creativity plaguing Chinese students due to test pressure.

While education equity has been an elusive quest for both Chinese and American schools, Korean educational system has shown the possibility to narrow educational inequality. For example, public school teachers in Korea periodically rotate the working school (i.e., every 5 years) to make sure that teachers with good quality work in both poor and rich areas. Since the Ministry of Education in Korea has set the teacher's salary schedule, differences in teachers' salaries are very small across schools and districts. Teaching is regarded as a lifelong profession, so teacher attrition or turnover is not a critical issue in Korea. Most teachers do not leave the profession before they reach their retirement age. Another attempt to the equity issue was the High School Equalization Policy (HSEP), which randomly assigns high school students to schools within their school district through a lottery-based enrollment system (Byun, Kim, & Park, 2012). Although there has been long standing debates on the pros and cons of HSEP, especially its effect on student achievement, HSEP has made a positive contribution to educational equity in Korea, especially to low-income students (Byun et al., 2012).

Another current issue faced by all three countries is testing (Wang, Hancock, & Campbell-Whatley, 2016). Education is valued and recognized as the path for social mobility and for a more successful life in all three countries. Testing is a measure to determine what has been learned and to predict future productivity. Educational policy-making in the United States has always been a state and local issue, and there was no national curriculum or national assessment (Flaitz, 2011; Pine, 2012). Recently, however, Common Core State Standards Initiative is driving the instruction and testing among most, if not all, states. Testing has become more centralized than before. In China, however, testing has become more decentralized recently due to the complaint of inequity issues (Zhao & Qiu, 2012). Some provinces in China (e.g., Zhejiang & Wuhan) have developed their own college entrance examinations to replace the NCEE and some top-tier universities (e.g., Zhejiang University, Tsinghua University, and Xi'an Jiaotong University) are piloting admitting students using their own assessment tools. In Korea, great efforts have been made to move away from relying on a single test in the college admission process, but instead implement a multiple assessment portfolio (Kwon et al., 2017). However, alternative routes into university have been criticized for widening the gap in college admission among social classes.

Recent educational reform efforts in China have attempted to shift instructional practice away from rote didacticism and encourage a more student-centered approach. Educational authorities in China are looking to western educational models and are borrowing several practices, including the use of formative assessments (Poole, 2016). Schools are being encouraged to implement formative assessment practices as part of their ongoing efforts to replace exam-oriented education with "quality oriented education" (Tan & Chua, 2015, p. 691). Although assessment reform is a focal

xvi ■ Chinese, Korean, and American Education

point of China's widespread efforts, many barriers to full implementation exist (Berry, 2001; Huang & Luo, 2015; Pham & Renshaw, 2015).

THE ORGANIZATION OF THE BOOK

This book features the experiences and perspectives of American educators of Chinese and Korean education. In addition to the Introduction, there are 12 chapters, clustered into three sections: (a) influence of culture, parental involvement, and economy; (b) teaching and learning; and (c) new pedagogical framework and practices, followed by a conclusion and discussion of implications to Chinese, Korean, and American education. Taken together, these chapters present a more holistic picture of Chinese and Korean education from the perspective of American educators in the United States across various disciplinary areas.

These chapters present, from an American educator's perspective, Chinese education in the disciplines of culture, gender, parental involvement, economy, curriculum, student fitness, English as a second/foreign language, smart learning, and educational reformations. Each chapter is situated within the current research literature, connect with classroom practices and innovations, as well as flesh out some of the larger theoretical/pedagogical issues between education in China, Korea, and the United States.

These chapters reveal salient similarities and differences in theoretical underpinnings, pedagogical principles, and classroom practices in China, Korea, and the United States. They also explore the larger conceptual/theoretical orientations between learning and learners in the three countries. These narratives add to a collective discourse about the difficulty, possibility, and promise for educators to bridge and transform seemingly opposing perspectives, which may broaden our thinking about how to bring out the best to form a more pluralistic pedagogical framework across the pacific shores.

Part I (Chapters 1–4) captures the equity issues in China, Korea, and the United States. Topics included differences in educational resources and career opportunity with respect to gender, parental involvement, teacher quality, and family socioeconomic status. Specifically, Chapter 1 utilizes qualitative inquiry to explore how gender roles and expectations influence women's educational and career aspirations in China. Through researchers' personal accounts and experiences of their immersive trip to Xian, China, this chapter seeks to compare the experiences of women in China and the United States. Findings suggest that gender roles do influence women's educational and career aspirations in China because of the historical view of women in Chinese societies. While this influence is more subtle than it has been in previous years, the observations and interactions with the women in China reveal that they perceive that their access to higher education and employment are still limited.

Chapter 2 looks at factors influencing parent involvement in the United States, China, and Korea. Chinese and Korean students in the United States are often lumped into the "model minority" category which touts higher levels of economic and educational success compared with other minority groups. The schools visited in both countries provide insight into how parents in affluent areas are involved in their children's education, namely through parent-oriented motivation and financial investment. This left the authors wondering about the implications for parents who cannot provide optimal conditions for their children's educational success, much like many of the parents of ESL students in the United States. The implications of this study point to the need for alternative supports for those students whose parents' involvement is limited by socioeconomic status, educational attainment level, work demands, and language barriers.

Chapter 3 examines the factors that influence students' experiences in schools, for example, parental involvement, teacher preparation, and school resources. Students from high and middle socioeconomic backgrounds are often afforded more academic opportunities for higher education. However, minority and non-English speaking students in the United States, and Chinese and Korean students with low socioeconomic status, a majority of whom live in rural communities, are the ones to feel the effects of an imbalanced educational system the most. This qualitative study offers a comparison of three facets of the educational systems in the United States, China, and Korea. More specifically, this chapter investigates how parental involvement, teacher ability, and student family socioeconomic status impact the academic achievement of students in each country.

Chapter 4 examines the effectiveness of education in China, Korea, and the United States. The Chinese dream involves going to college and getting a good government job. Although college entrance examination was successful in selecting the brightest students and giving them an opportunity to serve the country in Chinese history, successful students tend to be the ones whose family can afford to pay for specialized tutoring in modern China. As a result, significant changes are undergoing in China: emphasis on liberal arts education, collaborative activities, decentralized education, and more classroom assessment. Korea is also experiencing collaboration and creativity. The authors think that the American educational system is still the best in the world based on the facts that all the best companies are American. However, the authors were also concerned with recent changes in American education, which is becoming more and more centralized and focused on standardized testing.

Part II (Chapters 5–8) moves into teaching and learning in the three countries. These chapters examine how texts were selected in the textbooks

xviii ■ Chinese, Korean, and American Education

to provide a platform for students to engage in cultural dialogues. Topics included in this part also includes research-based teaching methods used frequently to teach English as a second language as well as physical education. Specifically, Chapter 5 examines instructional and cultural goals within a Chinese middle school and an American middle school through the respective Language Arts textbooks. The ten Chinese curriculum tenets were identified within the Chinese middle school anthology, using content analysis methods. Likewise, using a thematic analysis process for the American textbook, a table of the most common themes was created. Both the Chinese and American anthologies provided examples of thematic connections to the text selections and the respective cultures in which the anthologies were used. This study revealed that the adopted educational textbook allows a platform to engage in cultural dialogue. This close examination of cultural and instructional choices of text selection may be beneficial to gain insights into the goals of an educational system. Finally, these insights provided a gateway for international dialogue amongst international educators.

Chapter 6 compares strategies used to teach English as a second language in the United States and China. In the first section of the text, the authors describe different research-based teaching methods used frequently to teach English as a second language. In the results section, the authors compare the usage of these strategies in their own classrooms and in the classrooms observed in China. The research showed that these methods were used in both countries and can attribute to the successful rates of second language acquisition.

Chapter 7 creates an authentic picture of which foreign language pedagogical approaches, structural, functional, or interactive, are preferred in each country, and how these approaches compared with American trends in foreign language education. The author highlighted the benefits of the distinct approaches to second language learning abroad and examined how the attitudes of language teachers and educational officials in other countries could inform the training of foreign language educators in the United States.

Chapter 8 discusses the students' physical body, and how schools value and approach education incorporating it. The authors compared the United States, China, and Korea by examining their physical education in both planning and execution, and the cultural attitudes towards supporting these programs. This discussion is an overview of how physical education has developed and where it stands, according to both the experiences of the authors and researchers in the field. The authors discuss historical influence on the creation of policy, the implementation and success of those policies, and compare how they are received and supported by the community.

Finally, Part III (Chapters 9–12) presents a discussion of new pedagogies, classroom practices, and learning strategies in China, Korea, and the

United States. Specifically, Chapter 9 studies the trend of adopting education policies and pedagogies across borders, regardless of the disparity between the cultures. While the East has been currently undergoing numerous reformations of their traditional education system in order to more closely mimic that of the West, research reveals that these attempts at adopting foreign policies are not only moving slowly, but are reaping little benefit. Therefore, the theory is explored that a country's culture, history, and traditions inherently impact both the effects and types of policies successfully utilized in that particular society's field of education. The conclusion is that the power and influence of tradition and culture greatly overcome any deviations or attempts of change that are outside the characteristic of the culture. Rather than adopting policies that were bred in a completely different setting of values and history—such as the stark differences between those of the East and the West—it is argued that policies must instead root from and support the cultural norms from which they are founded in order for any restructurings to make an enduring impact.

Chapter 10 examines 27 smart learning definitions derived from literature by Korean authors/scholars between 2010 to 2016 in an attempt to better understand how they define or describe smart learning environments, smart pedagogies, and smart learners. Korea has established a nationwide shift from e-learning to m-learning and u-learning to "smart learning" as an education reform in 2011. Smart learning definitions have manifested the use of more advanced, intelligent, and adaptive technologies, but with emphasis on personalized and self-directed instructional strategies to foster thinking, communication, and problem-solving skills among learners. While Korean scholars have attempted to define and describe smart learning and its characteristics, no clear definition of smart learning exists to date. Utilizing the three elements of smart learning environments, smart pedagogies, and smart learners as predetermined coding categories, the 27 smart learning definitions were scanned for keywords that represent the three elements and tallied for rank order and frequency. Results show that the definitions of smart learning currently existing among Korean authors/scholars have placed more emphasis on smart learning environments and pedagogy over the skills associated to smart learners.

Chapter 11 reviews the characteristics of 21st century learners and classrooms in the United States (student-centered, technology-enhanced, performance-based and collaborative learning) and China (teacher-centered, technology for delivery, exam-based, and individual learning). Data were inductively analyzed to identify frequently occurring themes from observations, informal interviews during the trip, and follow-up interviews after the educational trip to China. Two elementary schools, one middle school, one high school and three universities in Chengdu and Xian in China were observed. Informal interviews were conducted during the trip with several students and teachers at each of these schools. Follow-up interviews were conducted with colleagues from China who currently live and teach in the United States. Twenty-first century skills (communication, creativity, critical thinking, and collaboration) that are essential to prepare 21st century learners are recommended at the end of the chapter.

Chapter 12 provides teachers with a comparative overview of how culturally relevant pedagogy is used in China, Korea, and the United States through an examination of the use of culturally relevant pedagogy within the context of K–16 schools. The data were obtained during personal observations and informal interviews with participants at schools and other settings in both countries. The findings conclude that the practical application of culturally relevant pedagogy is similar in many respects when comparing its use in China, Korea, and the United States. Additionally, the findings show that culturally relevant pedagogy can have a positive impact on student learning, and positively influence parental and community involvement. This chapter informs teachers and educational stakeholders about the benefits of using culturally relevant pedagogy in K–16 schools.

Finally, the conclusion summarizes and discusses on the central themes that emerge from all these chapters and echoes the introduction in the discussion of similarities and differences in educational theories, teaching practices, learning styles, and educational policies in China, Korea and the United States. In summary, the 12 chapters across the whole book reveal salient similarities and differences in theoretical underpinnings, pedagogical principles, and classroom practices in China, Korea, and in the United States. They also reflect on the larger conceptual/theoretical orientations between learning and learners in China, Korea, and the United States. These chapters contribute to a better understanding of not only the differences and similarities in educational thinking and practices in the three countries, but also the sociocultural reasons behind them. As such, the insight that emerges from this book may help the educational community in all three countries to integrate the divergent perspectives toward building a more pluralistic pedagogical framework required by the 21st century. The implications will be further discussed in the conclusion chapter.

REFERENCES

Berry, R. (2011). Educational assessment in mainland China, Hong Kong and Taiwan. In R. Berry & B. Adamson (Eds.), *Assessment reform and education: Policy and practice* (pp. 49–62). New York, NY: Springer.

Brown, G. T. L., & Gao, L. (2015). Chinese teachers' conceptions of assessment for and of learning: Six competing and complementary purposes. *Cogent Education, 2,* 1–18.

Byun, S., Kim, K., & Park, H. (2012). School choice and educational inequality in South Korea. *Journal of School Choice, 6*, 158–183.

Chen, Q. (2011). 中美历史教育交流的新篇章—记美国《社会教育》特刊 [*A New Chapter in the History of Sino–U.S. Educational Exchange*]. Retrieved from http://www.pep.com.cn/gzls/js/xsjl/xsdt/201108/t20110817_1064388.htm

Coleman, J. (1967). Towards open schools. *The Public Interest, 6*, 20–27.

DeMarrais, K., & LeCompte, M. (1998). *The way schools work: A sociological analysis of education*. White Plains, NY: Longman.

Devlin, B., Daniels, M., & Roeder, K. (1997). The heritability of IQ. *Science, 388*, 468–471.

Durkheim, E. (1964). *The division of labor in society*. New York, NY: Free Press of Glencoe.

Elman, B. A. (1991). Political, social, and cultural reproduction via civil service examinations in late imperial China. *The Journal of Asian Studies, 50*, 7–28.

Flaitz, J. (2011). Assessment for learning: US perspectives. In R. Berry & B. Adamson (Eds.), *Assessment reform and education: Policy and practice* (pp. 33–48). New York, NY: Springer.

Gamoran, A. (2017). Educational inequality in the United States: Can we reverse the tide? *Journal of Education and Work, 30*, 777–792.

Huang, J., & Luo, S. (2015). Formative assessment in L2 classroom in China: The current situation, predicament and future. *Indonesian Journal of Applied Linguistics, 3*, 18–34.

Kaufman, A. S. (2009). *IQ testing 101*. New York, NY: Springer.

Kennedy, C. H., & McNeil, J. A. (2006). A history of military psychology. In C. H. Kenney & E. Zillmer (Eds.), *Military psychology: Clinical and operational applications* (pp. 11–17). New York, NY: Guildford Press.

Kozol, J. (2005). *The Shame of the Nation: The Restoration of Apartheid Schooling in America*. New York, NY: Crown.

Kwon, S. K., Lee, M., & Shin, D. (2017). Educational assessment in the Republic of Korea: Lights and shadows of high-stake exam-based education system. *Assessment in Education: Principles, Policy & Practice, 24*, 60–77.

Li, J. (2012). *Cultural Foundations of Learning: East and West*. New York, NY: Cambridge University Press.

Liu, S., & Feng, D. (2015). How culture matters in educational borrowing? Chinese teachers' dilemmas in a global era. *Cogent Education, 2*, 1–15.

Liu, X., & Ma, W. (2018). *Confucianism reconsidered: Insights for American and Chinese education in the 21st century*. Albany: State University of New York Press.

Lock, C. R. (2011). *Foundations of modern school practices: A sourcebook of educational wisdom*. New York, NY: Rowman & Littlefield Education.

Ma, W. (2014). *East meets West in teacher preparation: Crossing Chinese and American borders*. New York, NY: Teachers College Press.

Monaghan, E. J. (1988). Literacy instruction and gender in colonial New England. *American Quarterly, 40*(1), 18–41.

National Center on Education and the Economy. (n.d.) *South Korea: Teacher and principal quality*. Retrieved from https://www.nnstoy.org/download/international-comparisons/NCEE%20%C2%BB%20South%20Korea%20%20Teacher%20and%20Principal%20Quality.htm

Pham, T., & Renshaw, P. (2015). Formative assessment in Confucian heritage culture classrooms: Activity theory analysis of tensions, contradictions and hybrid practices. *Assessment & Evaluation in Higher Education, 40,* 45–59.

Pine, N. (2012). *Educating young giants: What kids learn (and don't learn) in China and America.* New York, NY: Palgrave Macmillan.

Poole, A. (2016). "Complex teaching realities" and "deep rooted cultural traditions": Barrier to the implementation and internalization of formative assessment in China. *Cogent Education, 3,* 1–14.

Redden, E. (2018, November). New international enrollments decline again. *Inside Higher Ed.* Retrieved from https://www.insidehighered.com/news/2018/11/13/new-international-student-enrollments-continue-decline-us-universities

Reitz, J. G., & Verman, A. (2004). Immigration, Race, and Labor. *Industrial Relations, 43,* 835–854.

Steinberg, S. R., & Kincheloe, J. L. (2004). *19 urban questions: Teaching in the city.* New York, NY: Peter Lang.

Tan, C., & Chua, C. S. K. (2015). Education policy borrowing in China: Has the West wind overpowered the East wind? *Compare: A Journal of Comparative and International Education, 45,* 686–704.

Turkheimer, E. (2008). A better way to use twins for developmental research. *LIFE Newsletter, 2* (1), 2–5.

Vella, J. (2002). *Learning to listen, learning to teach: The power of dialogue in educating adults.* New York, NY: Jossey-Bass.

Wang, C., Hancock, D., & Campbell-Whatley, G. D. (2016). Data-driven formal and informal measures. In G. Campbell-Whatley, D. Hancock, & D. Dunaway (Eds), *A School Leader's Guide to Implementing the Common Core* (pp. 37–51). New York, NY: Routledge.

Wang, C., Ma, W., & Martin, C. L. (2015). *Chinese education from the perspectives of American educators: Lessons learned from study-abroad experiences.* Charlotte, NC: Information Age.

Weber, K. (2010). *Waiting for superman: How we can save America's failing public schools.* New York, NY: PublicAffairs.

Yi, H., Zhang, L., Luo, R., Shi, Y., Mo, D., Chen, X., & Rozelle, S. (2012). Dropping out: Why are students leaving junior high in China's poor rural areas? *International Journal of Educational Development, 32,* 555–563.

Zhao, Y. (2009). *Catching up or leading the way: American education in the age of globalization.* Alexandria, VA: ASCD.

Zhao, Y., & Qiu, W. (2012). Policy changes and educational reforms in China: Decentralization and marketization. *On the Horizon, 20,* 313–323.

PART I

INFLUENCE OF CULTURE, PARENTAL INVOLVEMENT, AND ECONOMY

CHAPTER 1

HOW CULTURE INFLUENCES GENDER ROLES AND EXPECTATIONS IN CHINESE CULTURE

Yolanda Kennedy and April Smith

Gender inequality is an issue that permeates political, social, and workforce cultures around the world. According to Hannum, Kong, and Zhang (2009), women have struggled globally to maintain equal status and employment with their male counterparts. In the United States, this inequity actuates gender disparities within the culture and influences major issues such as the underrepresentation of women in many occupations, political environments, positions of power, and leadership roles (Barreto, Ryan, & Schmitt, 2009; Conway, 2001; Pettit & Hook, 2009). More specifically, in the United States, the unequal representations of women in certain occupations reflect the gender inequities and biases in the American educational system (Jacobs, 1996).

This chapter utilizes qualitative inquiry to explore how gender roles and expectations influence women's educational and career aspirations in an

Educational Practices in China, Korea, and the United States, pages 3–17
Copyright © 2019 by Information Age Publishing
All rights of reproduction in any form reserved.

Asian country. During our time abroad our experiences in Xian, China drove our interest in this topic. Through a review of the literature focused on the historical factors of women's education, women's educational experiences, and the integration of culture and values in the educational system in China, we seek to explore how gender intersects with culture and influences how women choose their career path. The second portion of the chapter explores this topic through our accounts, observations, and interactions with the students in Xian.

LITERATURE REVIEW

Confucian Influence on Education

In the traditional Chinese culture, masculine principles were developed and taught for thousands of years. A large part of these teachings focused on the hierarchical order of a person as it relates to their role in society. This hierarchy was commonly referred to as the "five relations" or Wu Lun (Leung, 2003). The five relations consisted of: a ruler over those ruled; father over his son; oldest brother over younger brother; husband over wife; and friend with friend, which constituted as male friends. These male dominant relationships left women without authority and power. Women were seen as temporary members of their biological families and had no rights to property or inheritance (Leung, 2003). Only sons could provide their parents with security in their old age. When a daughter married, she had to leave her home and join her husband's household, and her husband's family norms became her norms for the rest of her life. Confucian ethics accepted the subservience of women to men as natural and proper because women were regarded as unworthy or incapable of education (Leung, 2003).

The historical emphasis of traditional Chinese culture plays a vital role in how Confucian principles influenced the way women gained an education. Around 500 BC, KongZi, also known as Confucius, was the first educational and political revolutionary in ancient Chinese times who developed Confucian (Chuang, 2007). His ideology has been essential in constructing Chinese culture, and while Confucian is not an organized religion, it influenced the paths of government, society, and families of East Asia. The ethical values of Confucian have been around for over 2,000 years, and these values remain in certain elements of the Chinese culture, for example, their educational systems.

China's educational history dates back for centuries; however, women were not part of the mainstream education system until the last 60 years (Liu & Carpenter, 2005). Under Confucian principles, women were restricted to an oppressed status which continued the resistance of women's education allowing for discrimination (Liu & Carpenter, 2005). The fundamental feature of the Chinese masculine structure in the gender division of labor is captured by one of the principles of Confucius (551–479 BC): "Men are primarily outside the home, and women are primarily inside the home." This principle meant that women sought to remain "inside" as "a spatial statement of virtuous femininity" (Rofel, 1994, p. 235) and that they were not allowed knowledge of the outside world.

The Confucian doctrine reflects, "Women and crooks are unteachable" (Lei, Chen, & Xiong, 1993, p. 13). This statement furthers the deep-rooted thoughts of the value of women in Asian Confucian influence. However, in the late 1800s, schools for females started to appear from a Westernized Christian ministry, and the Qing Dynasty approved an experimental school for females. This was the start of the transition for women to gain an education instead of only men.

As women started to accept lower paying jobs, their daughters or young girls usually sacrificed their education as well. Sometimes it was by choice and sometimes by request to alleviate the cost of education and help the family with housework (Liu, 1998). These situations were seen more in rural areas of China versus the urban areas. Some families in rural areas did not want their girls studying with boys because it was not part of their tradition (Asian American Satellite TV Station, 1997). Because of this, girls were being oppressed and made to feel inferior.

Education is important in the rural areas, especially for girls. Confucian beliefs minimize the importance of education for women and parents needed to learn how educating girls was beneficial to the family. As previously mentioned, the Confucian beliefs are deeply ingrained in rural areas through informal learning, and the family is a powerful economic and social unit in which the traditional cultural beliefs had not changed significantly. Gender roles of women were taught and mutually accepted by women (Tsai, 1996).

As we review this historical perspective of gender roles in Confucian and look at the educational system today, things have changed; and have become more like the socialist egalitarian model. However, the Confucian ideology still plays a pivotal role in the minds of many in East Asia.

Gender Inequality

Although some studies show that gender inequality in education is improving (Zeng, Pang, Zhang, Medina, & Rozelle, 2014), there is a plethora of research that highlights that gender inequality is still a major issue in China (Fincher, 2016; Glewwe & Kremer, 2006; Matthews & Nee, 2000). Without gender equality, women are at risk of lower social statuses within families and less economic growth. According to Glewwe and Kremer (2006), girls who receive an education improve their living conditions, social status, and promote a healthier economy not only for their families but the nation. Gender inequality is an issue that plagues many countries.

In China, there are different factors that influence gender inequality. One factor is the city type which compares urban areas versus rural areas. This system is referred to as the Hukou system. In urban areas, the family planning policy stated that each family could only have one child unless the firstborn child was a girl. The family planning policy was implemented because the government wanted to control population growth in order to improve citizen's quality of life (Tan, 2012). In rural areas, many ethnic minorities were exempt from the family planning policy and could have more than one child. This meant that if sons were born, they were more likely to get an education in comparison to their daughters. Rural families could not always afford to send multiple children to school because of fewer welfare resources and lower incomes. In 2015, the family planning policy became more relaxed, and not all families in China are held to the policy.

Because of an increase in GDP, China's economy has grown more than 10% per year since the 1970s (National Bureau of Statistics of China, 2010). The economy that was once being developed is now growing because of its market orientation (Brandt & Rawski, 2008). When businesses are being profitable, the owners or managers make the decisions on having an efficient business. Today, China is wealthier and able to invest more in its social services. As a result, the economy could provide more schools to increase the number of people educated. The ability to provide social services such as education has risen at all levels (Hannum, Behrman, Wang, & Liu, 2008).

Another factor that plays a role in gender inequality is ethnicity. The Han and non-Han populations have differences in their socioeconomic status and the setup of their employment cycle (Gustaffsson & Li, 2003). The non-Han, which is considered the minority group, has an unstable educational infrastructure. However, the Han language is widely used in the educational curriculum for examinations that students must take. Because the non-Han students are less familiar with the Han language, they are less likely to do well on examinations that include the Han language. This is an example of cultural biases within the Han and non-Han communities further suggesting why there are larger income and social gaps (Hannum, 2002; Hong, 2010). This type of cultural bias not only causes differences in the Han and non-Han societies but also biases amongst girl's access to education (Hannum, 2002; Zeng et al., 2014).

Education and Gender

Chinese women's education in the first half of the 20th century evolved from the severe struggles for survival and growth, and some women benefited from the westernized feminist movements. Some women were allowed to attend school, but for many women, the schools were preserving a gender-biased society where women were learning about being obedient wives and nurturing mothers. Women also received fewer years of education than men. The education of women was not controlled by women, it was controlled by men, and even into the mid-20th century, 90% of females remained illiterate in China (Wei, 1995).

The socialist egalitarian model portrayed men and women as an equal unit; however, it ignored the biological differences between the two genders. The historical unequivocal status of women and the biases they held were ignored; allowing sexism to surface in the masculine system (Hannum, 1999). Because of this bias, females were limited to certain positions in the workforce like nurses, elementary school teachers, and clerks. These biases were also perpetuated in school settings. For example, the teachings in the schools that girls attended did not have books that had women in them before 1990 which further portrayed a male's place in education versus a woman's place (Hannum, 1999).

It can be argued that because women in education were not always receiving the same type of education as men, it was a way to discourage them from even wanting to attend school. For those women who were able to have better-paying jobs, they suffered from legitimized discriminatory practices such as high layoff rates (Davis, 2009). This layoff practice discouraged women from accepting higher paying jobs. Therefore, women started to accept lower-paying jobs due to the bias employment practices. Women with higher levels of education were not able to utilize the hard work they had put in through gaining an education.

Research on Gender Education and Employment

Confucianism influenced societal norms that impacted the hierarchical structure in China and the gender roles and expectations of Chinese women. Gender equality in China was not heavily studied until the late 1970s. Before the 1970s, there was little evidence of gender inequality regarding barriers of discrimination. Furthermore, there was little data to support the claim (Cheung, 1997). The interdisciplinary gender research program was established for this reason at the Chinese University of Hong Kong in 1985. Since then studies have emerged examining the role gender plays in education and the workforce.

8 ▪ Y. KENNEDY and A. SMITH

In earlier studies, gender discrimination was found in both education and the workforce (Au, 1993; Cheung, 1997; Cheung, Lai, Au, & Ngai, 1997). Cheung et al. (1997) present a chapter in their book about gender identity and stereotypes in Hong Kong. In an earlier study, Ho, (1983) analyzed newspaper recruitment articles and found that women applicants were preferred in wholesale/retail, export, and hotel/restaurant industry, and men were preferred in manufacturing, public utilities, financial, transport, communications, and storage sectors. In a study conducted by Au (1993), findings suggest that gender stereotypes associated with different occupations reflect differential attitudes towards the abilities of men and women. These attitudes created biases that were reflected in the treatment of both men and women in entry-level positions.

These biases were also observed in the educational materials provided for students in primary school. Gender roles were presented in school textbooks and streaming in school subjects divided along gender lines (Cheung, 1997). Cheung (1997) discussed the differences in expectations for girls and boys in primary schools. Girls were encouraged to develop more in arts subjects, while boys were encouraged towards science subjects.

In another study Bauer, Feng, Riley, and Xiaohua (1992) examine gender inequality and the position of women and men in urban China. They argue that even though the participation of women in the Chinese workforce dramatically increased from 1949 to 1988, the type of positions and power that women obtained did not support the claims of an "equal" society. Bauer et al. compared the gender inequality in the Chinese workforce to that found in western countries, a stratified labor market; the study focused on two major life course events in China: education attainment and employment. These events are noted as "among the most important for individual women as well as men in a modern society" (p. 334). They are also described as interconnected, because of the strong relationship between education and employment. Educational attainment influences social status, employment opportunities, and occupational status in Asian countries.

Bauer et al. (1992) examined China's 1987 One Percent Population Survey to document the change in female education and labor force participation. They examined the differences in occupational participation in the workforce after joining the labor market and found that women's disadvantage is most evident in their severe underrepresentation in the more powerful, political, positions even after controlling for education and experience. Bauer et al. argued that the enormous increase in the level of female labor force participation has not necessarily been accompanied by gender equality.

Similarly, gender inequalities of education have been emphasized over the last couple of decades by Wang and Staver (1997); Zhou, Moen, and Tuma (1998); and Hannum et al. (2009). Wang and Staver (1997) discussed the difficulties of placing female college graduates in the workforce and creating job placement opportunities in the early 1990s. Many colleges and universities raised their admission scores for women and imposed quotas on female students. In their 1993–1994 urban survey, Zhou et al. (1998) found an increasing gender gap in senior high school and college enrollments. Currently, the minimum test scores required for entrance to senior high schools and colleges are published in newspapers, making gender-selective admission difficult. However, even among those with a college education, it is more difficult for women than men to obtain high-paying jobs.

Hannum et al. (2009) investigated the gender gap in education. In this study, they discussed parental perceptions of abilities and appropriate roles for girls and boys and parental perceptions of labor market outcomes for girls' and boys' education. In contrast to earlier studies, Hannum et al. (2009) found that girls rivaled or outperformed boys in academic performance and engagement. However, over the course of 7 years, boys had attained just about a third of a year more schooling than girls, a finding that was not explainable through parental perceptions or academic achievement.

In the interviews with the parents in Hannum et al.'s (2009) study, parents expressed high aspirations for both their boy and girl children, and although some parents viewed boys as having a greater aptitude, they described girls as having more dedication. Findings suggest that in this rural Chinese province, parental educational attitudes and practices toward boys and girls are more complicated and less uniformly negative for girls than generally portrayed.

Similar to Western societies, gender inequality is still present in the educational system and workforce in China. Even though the Chinese government has made significant progress in increasing the representation of women in the workplace, more recent research is needed on how these changes are affecting the societal views of women.

The experiences that will be shared in the next section of this chapter will reflect on our personal experiences with the educational system in China and how we explored the issue of gender inequality in the educational system in Xian.

METHOD

For this explorative inquiry, we utilize our personal experiences, interactions, observations, conversations, and interviews during our visit to an urban Chinese city, Xian. We utilized autoethnographic techniques to gather the data during our 10-day stay in Xian. Autoethnography is described as a qualitative research methodology. According to Chang (2008),

"Autoethnography is an ethnographic inquiry that utilizes the autobiographic materials of the researcher as the primary data" (p. 1).

Setting/Participants

During our stay in Xian, we observed primary, secondary, and students in postsecondary education. We were able to have conversations with the students, teachers, and faculty about their educational system. We also visited culturally rich historical exhibits in this country, and will also include our interactions with residents of Xi'an as well as experiences at cultural events throughout the city.

Data Collection

This data was collected from our experiences, observations, and interactions with an average of 10–40 students from five different schools in Xian, China over the course of a week. We were fully emerged in multiple schools observing and talking with the teachers and their students. There were some group discussions with students where questions were asked to the students. During that observation, notes were taken to capture words spoken by the students. Some discussions took place as a 1 on 1 (i.e., student and observer), or 3 to 1 or 2 (i.e., students and 1 or 2 observers). In those discussion groups, we would interact with each other during lunch or a tour.

Data Analysis

To analyze the data we utilized the techniques similar to Ronai's (1995) approach by comparing and contrasting our personal experiences with existing research. We also analyzed our field notes and utilized thematic coding to the data collected from the interviews with cultural members (Tillman-Healy, 2003).

RESULTS

During our stay, we had the opportunity to observe students at all three levels in the educational system: primary, secondary, and postsecondary. Each morning before we arrived at the school, a local guide would give us information about her personal experiences as a Chinese woman living in Xian. She explained a lot of the culture and the mind-set of how Chinese viewed the Americans. The idea of having big eyes, a slender nose, and thin lips was seen as beautiful and is also a trait of European Americans. I remember observing only European Americans on billboards and in commercials while in China. This could be viewed as women are only symbols of beauty as is portrayed in the Confucian teaching.

We also learned from our tour guide that even though free education is provided for children until they reach middle school, the free public school system is of low quality. She said, "Generally people pay about $200 per month for their children to go to a semi-decent school, and the wealthy spend a lot of money on their children's education. The better (more expensive) schools are for the children of the wealthy and well known." These conversations led to discussions about the impact income have on educational opportunity and access.

China was a fascinating place; at our very first school visit to a primary school in Xian, the principal highlighted the importance of historical culture within the curriculum. One of the major goals of the school was to embed these values before the children reach the age of 13. These values included things such as morals, etiquette, family, and love; how their values were built on Confucianism and Darwinism (yin and yang) and how these principles are embedded in the school. One thing that stood out during this conversation is the importance of preserving the culture. The principal talked about how everything is influenced by Western culture that sometimes it is hard to maintain Chinese tradition.

The amount of orderly conduct displayed in the primary schools, particularly kindergarten, was intriguing. We watched 4- and 5-year-old children listen to instruction from their teachers with their hands behind their back. I remember thinking, "These students know how to listen before starting on their activities." Most of the little girls in the class wore uniform skirts or little dresses, and the boys wore uniform shorts. Most of the schools we visited, the children wore uniforms.

Gender was not heavily discussed until we met with the students at the collegiate level. A freshman student majoring in English expressed how he felt like one of the few males in the English program. "Generally, women are teachers and with an English degree—you can teach." He talked about having supportive parents, and how he was happy to be studying English even though it was uncommon for males to take on this major at the university.

The freshman student also mentioned that many of the male students study science, math or computers. "I think it is good to be in education, all my friends that are majoring in something else ask me to hook them up with the girls that are in the English program," he says jokingly.

Another interesting observation was that many students on the panel were first-generation college students, meaning that they were the first students in their families to go to college. This same student talked about being a first-generation college student. "I am the first one in my family to go to school. My family is very proud of me."

In another conversation with a student about her career aspirations, an English major said she was really interested in math. I asked her why she didn't major in math, and she said, "It would be hard for me to get a job...they don't usually hire women." She also talked about her math scores, and how that also influenced her decision to major in English.

At another university, we had the opportunity to talk to some of the master's level students, and these conversations also yielded interesting results. When I spoke with one group of female students, I told them I was a doctoral student. I asked them what their postgraduate plans were, and they said to get a job. I asked them if they had plans to get their doctorate, and they replied with a strong, "No, I want to get married one day; no man would marry me if I had a doctorate." They also discussed plans of having a family and how a plan to get a doctorate would eliminate these plans of ever having a family.

The third university we visited had a different vibe than the previous two. While talking with the students, they were nervous about speaking English to native English speakers; however, they spoke very clearly. After breaking up into groups, the university students began asking us questions about our favorite foods and places that we have visited. As an American student observer, we asked the university students about their experience at the school. The students shared they did not know the school was poor in resources. Many of these students stated they did not see the school before attending and if they had, they likely would not have come. Most of these students were first-generation college students and shared that their parents did not push them to attend college; however, being recruited by the school is what made them attend.

Contrary to some beliefs, there were both males and females serving in positions of power at the primary and secondary schools. Even though males held many of the major titles at the university, many of the women served in major roles at the primary and secondary schools. For example, the founder of the primary school was a woman even though the principal was a man.

In all of the urban schools visited, there was a good mix of male and female students. However, not many of the female students were majoring or wanting to go into science professions. Many women wanted to major in English or translation. This was a key component related to the history of what is considered jobs for females versus males, and this also helped frame the question of gender roles in the Asian culture.

Gender norms and expectations were not very apparent in the Chinese K–12 system through our classroom observations. However, a major theme emerged during our conversations with the college students. During the college visits, students repeatedly talked about the nature of the English language program. There were a lot of female majors in this program because it is a pathway that leads to being a translator or teacher. The students described a lot of these roles as "good positions" for women.

LIMITATIONS

We are two African American female doctoral students in the educational leadership program at the University of North Carolina Charlotte collecting information from students, teachers, and administrators with less than three-hour interaction. With the array of information received, a more extended visit in Xian would have added to this research. These results are from our own experiences and reflections in Xian, China. The results of this study are derived from our first educational experience in the country, and much of the culture was new to us. The results below are viewed through these lenses. We analyzed field notes, pictures, written accounts, and audio recordings to document our time in the city.

DISCUSSION

The trends observed and explained by the students in Xian, reflected many of the same problems Americans face in higher education: the lack of female leaders in organizations, the struggles of first-generation college students, quality of education by class structure, and the disproportionate amount of women in the sciences and engineering fields. In a 2013 study conducted at the University of Denver Colorado's Women College, the findings revealed that 75% of public school teachers are female, but 70% of the educational administrators are men. Even though women are earning college degrees at a faster rate than men, they are underrepresented at colleges and universities as tenured faculty and full professors, and in higher positions such as deans and presidents (Lennon, 2013). This aligns with other research conducted on women in leadership positions. There is only a small percentage of women in leadership positions in the business sector, making up less than 5% of CEOs of Standard and Poor's 500 (S&P 500) companies (Warner, 2014). These studies show that there are gaps between the number of women in leadership positions in comparison to men in a variety of sectors globally.

Another theme that emerged from the students who identified as first-generation college students was their lack of information about the college choice process. The students talked about how they wish they had more information about the school before they attended. In the interviews, the students revealed that they had limited resources from an advisor. Their

14 ■ Y. KENNEDY and A. SMITH

parents did not attend college, so they were not sure what to expect. Similarly, in America, first-generation students face similar challenges. In Xian, the issue of college choice emerged. In the United States often, first-generation students have little help with their decision on what college to attend (Saenz, 2007; Vargas, 2004). Students usually apply to schools with limited help from their counselors, and many only apply to a single college. Because the parents are unable to help with the process, students are unsure of how to determine a good fit.

The findings also suggest that there was a huge influence of class and income on student's educational pathways. The tour guide talked about how the free education system was not good, and in order to get a semi-decent education for their children, parents have to pay. In China, the education of the student is heavily influenced by testing and grades, and students are more likely to get better scores on tests if they attend a better school. Similar trends are found in the U.S. educational system (Duncan & Murnane, 2011). Over the last couple of years, educational legislators have moved to testing, and there are significant gaps in the test scores based on race and class. Schools that receive more funding score higher on the end of grade testing exams (Duncan & Murnane, 2011).

The last comparison was the presence of females in the math and sciences. In the United States, women are underrepresented in these STEM fields despite the major growth of women in higher education. This is because many environmental and social barriers present in the field include stereotypes, gender bias, and the climate of science and engineering departments in colleges and universities (Hill, Corbett, & St. Rose, 2010). In elementary, middle, and high school, girls and boys take math and science courses in roughly equal numbers; however, by college graduation men outnumber women in the science and engineering fields. Hill et al. (2010) also found that at the graduate level women's representation declines, and it declines further when you examine the workforce.

CONCLUSIONS AND IMPLICATIONS

As research expands in the area of gender roles of women in Chinese culture, more emphasis on women's contribution to education will be provided, but may not be at a high rate. The philosophy of Confucian is still deeply rooted, and though China has come a long way with providing more equality within the genders through education, the barriers that women experience in furthering their education and pursuing certain careers still exist (Hong, 2010). Even though the Chinese government has made major progress in increasing the representation of women in the workplace, more recent research is needed on how these changes are affecting the societal views of women and how those views impact young girls in education. As research regarding equity of women in Asian countries grows, more information will be gained on the types of positions women occupy, and what job opportunities should be examined to ensure that women have equal opportunities in the workplace and educational system.

Although the individual observations and experiences shared in this study are from within a week, it was noticeable to see improvement of women's involvement through education and the determination to be successful for their families as well as themselves.

REFERENCES

Asian American Satellite TV Station. (1997, September 2). *Discussion on history*. Los Angeles, CA: Author.

Au, K. C. (1993). A study of gender roles as defined in primary school textbooks in Hong Kong. *Occasional Paper Series, 18*. Hong Kong Institute of Asia-Pacific Studies, Hong Kong: The Chinese University of Hong Kong.

Barreto, M. E., Ryan, M. K., & Schmitt, M. T. (2009). *The glass ceiling in the 21st century: Understanding barriers to gender equality*. Washington, DC: American Psychological Association.

Bauer, J., Feng, W., Riley, N. E., & Xiaohua, Z. (1992). Gender inequality in urban China: Education and employment. *Modern China, 18*(3), 333–370.

Brandt, L., & Rawski, T. (Eds.). (2008). *China's great economic transformation*. New York, NY: Cambridge University Press.

Chang, H. (2008). *Autoethnography as a method*. Walnut Creek, CA: Left Coast Press.

Cheung, F. M. (1997). *Engendering Hong Kong society: A gender perspective of women's status*. Hong Kong: Chinese University Press.

Cheung, F. M., Lai, B. L., Au, K. C., & Ngai, S. S. Y. (1997). Gender role identity, stereotypes, and attitudes in Hong Kong. In Cheung, F. M. (Eds.), *Engendering Hong Kong society: A gender perspective of women's status* (pp. 201–236). Hong Kong: The Chinese University Press.

Chuang, S. F. (2007). *The influence of Confucian philosophy on adult learners who come from Confucian-influenced societies*. 2007 AHRD Proceedings, 503–510. Retrieved from https://digitalcommons.lsu.edu/gradschool_dissertations/2631

Conway, M. M. (2001). Women and political participation. *Political science & politics, 34*(2), 231–233.

Davis, E. L. (Eds.). (2009). *Encyclopedia of contemporary Chinese culture*. New York, NY: Routledge.

Duncan, G. J., & Murnane, R. J. (Eds.). (2011). *Whither opportunity? Rising inequality, schools, and children's life chances*. New York, NY: Russell Sage Foundation.

Fincher, L. H. (2016). *Leftover women: The resurgence of gender inequality in China*. London, England: Zed Books.

Glewwe, P., & Kremer, M. (2006). Schools, teachers and education outcomes in developing countries. In E. Hanushek, S. Machin, & L. Woessmann, (Eds.), *Handbook of the economics of education* (pp. 945–1017). New York, NY: Elsevier.

Gustafsson, B., & Li, S. (2003). The ethnic minority–majority income gap in rural China during transition. *Economic Development and Cultural Change, 51*(4), 805–822.

Hannum, E. (1999). Political change and the urban-rural gap in basic education in China, 1949–1990. *Comparative Education Review, 43*(2), 193–211.

Hannum, E. (2002). Educational stratification by ethnicity in China: Enrollment and attainment in the early reform years. *Demography, 39,* (1), 95–117.

Hannum, E., Behrman, J., Wang, M., & Liu, J. (2008). Education in the reform era. In L. Brandt & T. G. Rawski (Eds.), *Great economic transformation* (pp. 215–249). Cambridge, MA: Cambridge University Press.

Hannum, E., Kong, P., & Zhang, Y. (2009). Family sources of educational gender inequality in rural China: A critical assessment. *International journal of educational development, 29*(5), 474–486.

Hill, C., Corbett, C., & St. Rose, A. (2010). *Why so few? Women in science, technology, engineering, and mathematics.* Washington, DC: American Association of University Women.

Ho, S. C. (1983). Women in management: Challenges and barriers. *Young Executive, 4*(5), 3–5

Hong, Y. (2010). Ethnic groups and educational inequalities: An empirical study of the educational attainment of the ethnic minorities in western China. *Chinese Journal of Sociology, 30*(2), 45–73.

Jacobs, J. A. (1996). Gender inequality and higher education. *Annual Review of Sociology, 22*(1), 153–185.

Lei, L., Chen, Y., & Xiong, X. (1993). *History of Chinese female education.* Wuhan, China: Wuhan.

Lennon, T. (2013). *Benchmarking women's leadership in the United States.* Denver: Colorado Women's College at the University of Denver. Retrieved from https://womenscollege.du.edu/media/documents/BenchmarkingWomensLeadership intheUS.pdf

Leung, A. S. M. (2003). Feminism in transition: Chinese culture, ideology and the development of the women's movement in China. *Asia Pacific Journal of Management, 20,* 359–374.

Liu, J. (1998). Education of females in China: Trends and issues. *Journal of Educational Thought, 32*(10), 43–56.

Liu, J., & Carpenter, M. (2005). Trends and issues of women's education in China. *The Clearing House: A Journal of Educational Strategies, Issues and Ideas, 78* (6), 277–281.

Matthews, R., & Nee, V. (2000). Gender inequality and economic growth in rural China. *Social Science Research, 29*(4), 606–632.

National Bureau of Statistics of China. (2010). China Statistical Yearbook. Retrieved from stats.gov.cn/english/statisticaldata/annualdata/

Pettit, B., & Hook, J. L. (2009). *Gendered tradeoffs: Women, family, and workplace inequality in twenty-one countries.* New York, NY: Russell Sage Foundation.

Rofel, L. (1994). Liberation nostalgia and a yearning for modernity. In C. K. Gilmartin, G. Hershatter, L. Rofel, & T. White (Eds.), *Engendering China* (pp. 226-249). Cambridge, MA: Harvard University Press.

Ronai, C. R. (1995). Multiple reflections of child sex abuse: An argument for a layered account. *Journal of Contemporary Ethnography, 23*(4), 395–426.

Saenz, V. B. (2007). *First in my family: A profile of first-generation college students at four-year institutions since 1971.* Los Angeles, CA: Higher Education Research Institute.

Tan, G. (2012). The one-child policy and privatization of education in China. *International Education, 42*(1), 43–53, 107

Tillmann-Healy, L. M. (2003). Friendship as method. *Qualitative inquiry, 9*(5), 729–749.

Tsai, K. S. (1996). Women and state in post-1949 rural China. *Journal of International Affairs 49*(2), 493–524.

Vargas, J. H. (2004). *College knowledge: Addressing information barriers to college.* Boston, MA: College Access Services: The Education Resources Institute.

Wang, J., & Staver, J. R. (1997). An empirical study of gender differences in Chinese students' science achievement. *The Journal of Educational Research, 90*(4), 252–255.

Warner, J. (2014, March 7). *Fact sheet: The women's leadership gap.* Center for American Progress, 7. Retrieved from https://www.americanprogress.org/issues/women/reports/2014/03/07/85457/fact-sheet-the-womens-leadership-gap/

Wei, Y. (1995). *Chinese female education.* Hangzhou, China: Zhejiang Education.

Zeng, J., Pang, X., Zhang, L., Medina, A., & Rozelle, S. (2014). Gender inequality education in China: A meta-regression analysis. *Contemporary Economic Policy, 32*(2). https://doi.org/10.1111/coep.12006

Zhou, X., Moen, P., & Tuma, N. (1998). Educational stratification in urban China: 1949–1994. *Sociology of Education, 71*(3), 199–222.

CHAPTER 2

FACTORS THAT INFLUENCE PARENT INVOLVEMENT IN AN EDUCATIONAL CONTEXT IN THE UNITED STATES, CHINA, AND SOUTH KOREA

Benefits and Barriers

Elizabeth M. Landon and Peter L. Johnson

As English as a second language (ESL) teachers in North Carolina, our perspective on student success is shaped by our experiences both working with Chinese and Korean students who fit the "model minority" build and also a diverse student population that does not always enjoy the same levels of educational and economic achievement. Often times, Chinese Americans and Korean Americans are portrayed as hard-working self-made immigrants who have successfully assimilated to mainstream American culture through individual effort. This model minority label refers to the idea that certain ethnic groups are somehow empowered with characteristics that

---

Educational Practices in China, Korea, and the United States, pages 19–30
Copyright © 2019 by Information Age Publishing
All rights of reproduction in any form reserved.

allow them to exhibit academic and socioeconomic success. During this study abroad experience, we thought about how Chinese and Korean culture influences success and how parents take a central role in passing on their core values and cultural image to their children. This experience gave us the opportunity to examine the nature of parental involvement through school visits, interviews, and observations. Our purpose for this research was to look at specific aspects of parent involvement in China and Korea and to use these findings to influence our work in an ESL context in the United States. Our research was guided by the following question: "What factors influence parent involvement in China and Korea?" Our findings showed that parental involvement in these countries is closely linked with money and pressure. Relating these findings to an ESL context in the United States led us to question further what the implications are for students whose parents do not have the economic or social advantage to provide optimal conditions for their children's educational success.

LITERATURE REVIEW

Defining Parent Involvement

Parent involvement is based on expectations of a child's ability to achieve in an academic context. The term *parent involvement* describes parent engagement in the home (home-based) and in the school (school-based) to advance children's academic development. Epstein (1995) developed a research model which encompasses six primary levels of parent involvement (Ji & Koblinsky, 2009; Lau, Li, & Rao, 2012). The first, parenting, addresses how parents establish discipline and home conditions that support children as students. The second, communication, refers to parent–school and parent–teacher contact to monitor student progress. The third, volunteering, describes parent involvement in school activities in classrooms and other areas of the school. The fourth level addresses home learning such as helping with homework and tutoring. The fifth level refers to parent organizations such as the Parent–Teacher Association (PTA) that are involved in school decisions. The sixth and final level involves community collaboration designed to strengthen school programs and student learning. For the purpose of this study, we focus on home-based involvement in the form of parent-oriented motivation and financial investment.

Benefits

Benefits of parent involvement have been outlined by various studies verifying its importance in children's development (Barnard, 2014; Epstein,

1995). These studies demonstrate that home-based and school-based involvement is associated with positive outcomes such as an increase in valuable resources (e.g., parent volunteers and materials) and increased academic achievement (Lau et al., 2012). Research also shows that a major reason that parent involvement has been considered beneficial is that it emphasizes the value of education to children via parent-oriented motivation (Cheung & Pomerantz, 2012). Children's motivation in school is parent-oriented when it is driven by a concern with meeting parents' expectations and gaining approval. A study by Cheung and Pomerantz (2012) collected data from seventh- and eighth-grade American and Chinese students who reported on how their parents' style of involvement affected their motivation to do well in school. The findings show that when students are not independently motivated, parent-controlled motivation may get them engaged, fostering a value of school. This extrinsic form of motivation helps students develop their intrinsic motivation over time (Cheung & Pomerantz, 2012).

Cultural and Ideological Context

In order to analyze parent involvement in China and Korea in comparison with the United States, we must first consider the context as a major contributing factor. Because the Western and Eastern educational systems reflect philosophical and governmental differences, parent involvement may also look fundamentally different. The educational system of the United States reflects a democratic and free market society with an individualistic approach. Public education is believed to be an equalizer in that students from all backgrounds, ethnicities, and socioeconomic status have the same opportunity to achieve upward social mobility through education. Legislation such as the Civil Rights Act of 1964 was passed to level the playing field by outlawing discrimination based on race, color, religion, sex, or national origin. All children have the right to a free education in U.S. schools. More recent legislation such as the No Child Left Behind Act of 2001 (NCLB) included a mandate that schools have written parent involvement policies to facilitate school–home relationships. Despite this and other legislative attempts to involve parents and level the playing field when it comes to achieving upward social mobility through education, a portion of the population struggles to achieve the level of academic success that would otherwise help them improve their socioeconomic status.

Both China and Korea are similar to the United States in that education is viewed as the key to social and economic mobility. The educational systems in the Eastern tradition, however, are historically based on Confucian, Buddhist, and Taoist teachings which emphasize qualities such as diligence, endurance, respect for elders, hardship, and perseverance in order to serve the country and benefit society. During our first school visit to a kindergarten in Xi'an, the principal went to great lengths to explain how the school curriculum integrates ten cultural topics (including Chinese etiquette, holidays, Chinese tea, calligraphy, etc.) with the five primary curricular aspects of discipline, positive attitude, pursuit of truth, kindness, and appreciation of beauty. He explained that many young people in China are more interested in learning from Western culture instead of Eastern culture. This is why Chinese culture is emphasized in early education programs such as this one. This focus on ethics and self-cultivation for the benefit of the community is also a reflection of communist ideology. Everywhere we went, there was a distinctive quality of respect for elders or filial piety, a key virtue of Chinese culture. This Confucian concept of filial piety underscores the importance of children's devotion to parents by demonstrating respect and obedience. The value of parental control comes from the Chinese notion of *guan* (training) which includes elements of control, discipline, and love (Ji & Koblinsky, 2009). Most of the observations and interviews we experienced during our trip exemplified this culture of respect and diligence, including an overwhelming social respect for teachers. One overt example that struck us was how students stand in front of the teacher at the beginning of class and also stand to address the teacher when answering questions. The classes we observed were also incredibly well-behaved and obedient. It stands to reason that Chinese parents establish discipline and home conditions that support children as students (Epstein's model of parent involvement, Level 1).

METHOD

Positionality

As ESL teachers in North Carolina, our perspective comes from working with a student population whose parental involvement is often limited by socioeconomic status, educational attainment, work demands, and language barriers. At the same time, we both have experience working with very high achieving international students from China and Korea whose parents play an active role in their education. One of us (P. Johnson) spent a year teaching English at a public school in Korea. His experience there revealed how parents maintain control over students' daily routines, enrolling them in after-school and weekend school programs. Students' daily schedules often begin first thing in the morning and end after dark. This tradition runs counter to what he had experienced in Western schools. The other author (E. Landon), has been a private flute teacher for 10 years and has noticed a particular trend among her Chinese and Korean flute students regarding parental oversight. These parents often sit in the lessons to observe, interject comments and orders directed at their children, send follow-up emails and texts to address student progress, and require additional lessons in advance of an audition. These students are often competing for the same number of limited positions in local youth orchestras. The disparity between achievement levels of Chinese and Korean "model minority" students with our ESL students in urban Charlotte schools led us to question the significance of a correlation between student achievement and parental involvement. This study abroad trip to China and Korea presented us with an opportunity to gain an insight into the nature of parental involvement in an Eastern educational setting.

Setting

We visited a total of nine schools, seven in China, and two in Korea. The one kindergarten, two primary schools, three secondary schools, and three postsecondary schools are all located in largely affluent areas of Xi'an and Seoul. Our participants consisted of students, teachers, administrators, and community members who we met throughout our pre-planned school visits and tours.

We had hoped to view a broad range of schools in not only the affluent areas, but in underserved communities as well. One major limitation of this exploratory study is the narrow scope in which we were able to collect data. Another major limitation we can acknowledge from this study is that we did not have the opportunity to interview parents. The relatively short length of the trip and small number of school visits also limited the results of this study. Future research could include interviews with the parents over the course of a year.

Data Source and Analysis

This study utilizes qualitative inquiry to explore how parents are involved in their children's education. On each of our school visits, we conducted semi-structured interviews and observations of students, teachers, administrators, and other community members. These observations and interviews took place during class, private meetings, and casually throughout our tour. The data are comprised of 35 pages of field notes over 8 days.

The pressure to get into an elite university starts early in China and Korea. During our tour of the Xi'an kindergarten, our tour guide Jane explained that parents begin talking to their children in kindergarten about where they want to attend university. We observed a pre-K class with 3 teachers and 15 students from ages 3–5. Outside each classroom was a bulletin board with information for the parents which included the teachers' private phone numbers. Parents always know what is going on at school.

Parents pay additional fees not only for private extracurricular education but also for coveted placements in highly ranked public schools. Jane explained that school rankings depend on university entrance:

> On June 7th and 8th, 1.8 million students do college entrance exams. If you don't pass the exam for university, you shame your parents and your school. If you cheat on the test, you go to jail. Parents think "no university, no future" because then you go to vocational school. Many students get tutor classes after dinner, sometimes 50-plus students per class. (field note entry from 6/20/2016)

In an interview with Annie, a second-year student studying English at a Xi'an University, we learned that her parents sent her to a foreign language boarding school that was the best school for entrance exam scores. She told us that 3,000 out of 20,000 applicants got into her high school where the focus was entirely on passing the university entrance exam. In her words, "My parents provided the best conditions for my study in preparation for the entrance exam."

In another interview with a student at a Xi'an High School, Sarah, a 10th grader, laughed when we asked if her parents are strict. Sarah explained that she only gets 3 hours of free time to play with her friends on the weekends. She spends the rest of her time practicing the piano (in preparation for two private lessons during the week) and doing her homework. She also began working with a private English tutor from Age 3 and now attends a public boarding school, which is highly competitive. The school displays the pictures and test scores of the highest ranking students in the country. Students must pass an entrance exam to get into the school. According to our guide, students with the highest test scores get in for free. Those with lower scores must pay to attend. She explained that the government provides free primary and middle schooling, but most parents opt to pay to have their children sent to "better" schools. Each of the primary and secondary schools we visited in China are public institutions. However, each school comes with a cost, whether it is in the form of tuition or arbitrary enrollment fees. One reason for this is that China's education has "moved from a highly centralized publicly funded system to a more locally controlled self-financed system" (Wang, Ma, & Martin, 2015, p. 5), which has changed what was once a free educational system into one with additional fees and charges.

At a boarding high school in Korea, we had the opportunity to observe a 10th grade English class of 27 students comparing the struggle of migrant Turkish workers in Germany to the struggles of Korean immigrants in the United States in the 1970s. At this time in history, Korean intellectuals who lost their jobs moved to America expecting opportunities based on merit. Despite their ability and diligence, their successes were limited by the language barrier and other challenges in assimilation including discrimination in this "land of opportunity." The teacher asked his students to consider the question: "Do we have a land of opportunity in Korea today?" The response we observed was an emphatic "No." After class, we asked a group of students their opinions on the issue. One student said that you can be very smart, but if you are poor, you won't have the same opportunities as those who have money. The ability of parents to provide educational opportunities for their children to succeed in a highly competitive atmosphere depends on their socioeconomic status. In our interview with the teacher of this class, he remarked that teachers receive upwards of a hundred text messages per day from parents who ultimately evaluate teachers' effectiveness. There is often more pressure on teachers from parents rather than from administrators.

Results

We embarked on this trip with a preconceived notion about "model minority" Chinese and Korean students based on our prior experiences as educators. The data gathered from our interviews and observations yielded what we interpreted as a cultural pattern of parental involvement. Throughout discussions with students, teachers, and our guides in China and Korea, it became clear that parental involvement is often about pressure to perform and monetary investment.

The data pieces revealed examples of pressure: discussion about educational expectations as early as kindergarten, direct lines of contact between parents and teachers, publicly displayed school and student rankings, limited free time outside of studies, and extremely high-stakes testing. The data from interviews and observations also showed how parents pay additional school fees and hired tutors in hopes of seeing a financial return on their investment.

DISCUSSION

Parent-Oriented Motivation: Pressure and Money

Educational research that focuses on Asian American students shows that parents place greater value on education than other ethnic groups including the Anglo American majority (Guo, 2011). In light of previous studies and our observations and interviews during the study abroad trip, the act of placing greater value on education to achieve upward social mobility and higher levels of educational achievement seems to come in two primary forms in both Chinese and Korean culture. The first is parent-oriented motivation (pressure to succeed) as described by the work of Cheung and Pomerantz (2012). On June 7 and 8, millions of students in China take the National College Entrance Exam, known commonly as the gaokao or "high exam." This test has roots in the imperial examinations that started during the Tang Dynasty (Wang et al., 2015). The results of this test determine where students can attend college, what careers they might have, and ultimately, the rest of their lives. According to our guide, parents in China think, "no university, no future" because "students' future is parents' future." In South Korea, students are under an equal amount of pressure to succeed academically. The Korean equivalent of the gaokao is the College Scholastic Ability Test (CSAT) also known as the suneung. Much like the gaokao, it carries the most weight in determining which university a student can enter and also carries dire implications for his or her entire future. It is no surprise that students are bound by their studies in anticipation of these high-stakes tests. They are under an extraordinary amount of pressure to succeed especially when their academic performance is so closely tied to the reputation and socioeconomic level of their parents. Students with the highest scores can go to the highest ranked schools. Many companies and corporations only hire graduates from these top-ranked schools. In the United States, conversely, the Scholastic Aptitude Test (SAT) is used in conjunction with high school GPAs and other factors to determine college readiness.

In response to the narrow definition of success as measured by the gaokao and suneung, parents virtually move mountains to provide the best conditions for their children's study. This brings us to the second form of parent involvement that became a common theme throughout this study: financial investment. In such a competitive environment where a student's performance on high-stakes tests is a reflection of the entire family and can determine their entire future, private tutoring is customary. Korea has one of the largest tutoring industries in the world. According to one report, "The private tutoring market in tutoring-crazed South Korea alone is projected to reach $13.9 billion—roughly 15% of the entire market—by the end of 2012" (Crotty, 2012). The primary beneficial effect is enhanced academic performance, but this can be a heavy financial burden on families. According to the Korean National Statistics office (Statistics Korea, 2011, p. 2), 87.4% of elementary school students, 74.3% of middle school students, and 62.8% of high school students received private tutoring in 2009. The average monthly expenditure per student was approximately 220 U.S. dollars. According to the 2009 Survey of Private Education Expenditure (SPEE), two-thirds of students sought private tutoring at private academic institutes called hagwon. This amounted to 21.626 trillion KRW, or 2% of Korea's GDP (Choi & Choi, 2016).

Barriers

The schools and universities we visited were all in affluent neighborhoods. Just like in the United States, the population found in low socioeconomic areas struggle to achieve the same upward social mobility that more privileged communities enjoy. Our guide in China mentioned a phenomenon she called the "new immigrants" which refers to migrant families from economically less-developed provinces that seek employment opportunities in urban areas. Research shows that "migrant children are viewed as an at-risk, disadvantaged group for potential school failure given their lack of residence status and lower socioeconomic status" (Guo, 2011, p. 123). Accessing education in urban public schools is a challenge for migrant children because of the "potential poor academic performance...which may lead to a decrease in the overall quality of the school" (Guo, 2011, p. 124). The situation is very similar for immigrant parents in the United States who, for reasons such as poverty, lack of educational attainment, and work demands, cannot provide high levels of parental support. The study makes a case for strong correlations between family financial capital and children's school performance.

According to Lau et al. (2012), there is a well-established correlation between socioeconomic status (SES) and parent school-based and home-based involvement. Parents with a higher SES typically have more advanced levels of education, more flexibility in work schedules, and more capital to invest in extracurricular classes and tutoring. Parents with a lower SES may experience financial and social constraints that hinder their ability to become highly involved (Lau et al., 2012). In an ESL setting in the United States, factors such as poverty, educational attainment level of parents, work demands, and language barriers among others limit the extent to which parents can involve themselves in their children's education. In a 2009 study by Ji and Koblinsky, Chinese immigrant parents were interviewed about their academic expectations, knowledge of student progress at school, their perceived involvement, and barriers to involvement. The result showed that 76% of the parents described English skills as a major barrier. Some described how limited English proficiency not only affects their ability to participate in school activities but also to communicate with their children who often begin to lose the mother tongue. An additional 69% reported that they did not participate in school activities because they were too busy working and could not leave their place of employment. However, the study also demonstrates that low-income, less-educated Chinese immigrant parents share the same high expectations for their children's academic achievement as more affluent, better-educated Chinese immigrant parents. Such expectations reflect Confucian philosophy that self-discipline and hard work are the keys to success.

Implications for Student Success

Existing research points to clear benefits of parent involvement in children's education and also various barriers to such involvement (Cheung & Pomerantz, 2012; Gu, 2008; Ji & Koblinsky, 2009). During our study abroad experience in China and South Korea, we began to sense that parental involvement in these cultures manifests itself in the form of extraordinary pressure and financial investment to navigate a highly competitive educational system. Factors that influence parental involvement include not only a cultural belief system based on Confucian principles but also the financial means to negotiate this competitive educational system. We found that, regardless of socioeconomic status, all parents have high expectations of their children to honor the family through hard work, diligence, and respect. These are the qualities that characterize the "model minority" stereotype in an American context.

After seeing the extent to which affluent Chinese and Korean parents involve themselves in ensuring the success of their children in school, the contrast with parental involvement in an ESL context in U.S. schools became painfully clear. Despite the benefits of parental involvement, the immigrant parents of many of our students are limited by various challenges. Even though U.S. school systems are mandated to have a parental involvement plan to engage parents in their children's education (as is supported by research), we cannot always expect high levels of parent involvement within this demographic. The question then is not how to help parents become more involved, because many lack the time, educational level, English skills, and the social and financial resources that would make meaningful involvement a possibility. The question becomes how can we as teachers, administrators, and community members support our students by filling in the gap that parents are unable to fill.

This is not to say that schools should give up on attempting to increase parental involvement of immigrant families. In fact, we propose that schools make an extra effort to support them and to "scaffold" their involvement much like ESL teachers scaffold instruction for their culturally and linguistically diverse student population. Schools should help low-income immigrant parents understand the importance of maintaining high academic expectations and provide them with specific examples of how to foster a home environment that supports learning (such as designating a quiet area and certain times of the day for study, limiting screen time, and monitoring homework completion). Schools should provide on-site English language classes for parents and also pair recent immigrant families with parents who can help them navigate an unfamiliar system. Schools should identify and connect parents with local resources to extend students' extracurricular education. To increase parent–school communication, schools should create a welcoming atmosphere, provide language translation services at meetings, provide printed education notices and materials in the home language, and schedule meetings and activities when parents are less likely to be at work. These efforts will help support parental involvement but still will not close the gap when comparing the capacity of immigrant parental involvement to that of more affluent parents. For this reason, we propose that a mentorship program is needed to support low-income immigrant students at a local level. School administrators, teachers, and counselors often do not have the time, training, or resources to provide extra support (that would typically come from home) to our culturally and linguistically diverse student population. A mentorship program designed to fill the gaps that parents cannot fill might be the key to putting low-income immigrant students on a more equal footing with their peers.

One common theme rang true in the educational philosophies of China, South Korea, and the United States. All three cultures view education as the key to social mobility and economic success. People all share similar wants and needs in life, but a disadvantaged portion of the population struggles to achieve the same levels of success enjoyed by more privileged parts of society. A "land of opportunity" exists for those who can afford it. The most recent legislation in the United States replaced the NCLB (2001) with the Every Student Succeeds Act (2015). This new legislation gives more decision-making power to the states and local school districts. Going forward, states will decide for themselves how to fix failing schools and close the achievement gap. We believe that local government and school districts have an opportunity to supplement limited levels of parent involvement through mentorship programs designed to provide additional support for our low-income immigrant students. This could lead to more equitable outcomes when it comes to our students' educational achievement and future opportunities.

REFERENCES

Barnard, W. M. (2004). Parent involvement in elementary school and educational attainment. *Children and Youth Services Review, 26*(1), 39–62.

Cheung, C. S., & Pomerantz, E. M. (2012). Why does parents' involvement enhance children's achievement? The role of parent-oriented motivation. *Journal of Educational Psychology, 104*(3), 820–832.

Choi, H., & Choi, A. (2016). Regulating private tutoring consumption in Korea: Lessons from another failure. *International Journal of Educational Development, 49*, 144–156.

Crotty, J. M. (2012, October 30). Global private tutoring market will surpass $102.8 billion by 2018. *Forbes*. Retrieved from https://www.forbes.com/sites/

jamesmarshallcrotty/2012/10/30/global-private-tutoring-market-will-surpass
-102-billion-by-2018/#19d13bbb2ee0

Epstein, J. L. (1995). School/family/community partnerships: Caring for the children we share. *Phi Delta Kappan, 76*(9), 701–712.

Gu, W. G. (2008). New horizons and challenges in China's public schools for parent involvement. *Education. 128*(4), 570–578.

Guo, J. (2011). Family and parent correlates of educational achievement: Migrant children in China. *Asian Social Work and Policy Review, 5*(2), 123–137.

Ji, C. S., & Koblinsky, S. A. (2009). Parent involvement in children's education: An exploratory study of urban, Chinese immigrant families. *Urban Education, 44*(6), 687–709.

Lau, E. Y. H., Li, H., & Rao, N. (2012). Exploring parental involvement in early years education in China: Development and validation of the Chinese early parental involvement scale. *International Journal of Early Years Education, 20*(4), 405–421.

Statistics Korea. (2011, April 6). *The 2010 Survey of Private Education Expenditure* [Press Release]. Retrieved from http://kostat.go.kr/portal/eng/pressReleases/11/2/index.board?bmode=download& bSeq=&aScq=273260&ord=1

Wang, C., Ma, W., & Martin, C. L. (2015). Introduction to Chinese and American education: History and current challenges. In C. Wang, W. Ma, & C. L. Martin (Eds), *Chinese Education from the perspectives of American educators* (pp. 1–18). Charlotte, NC: Information Age.

CHAPTER 3

A COMPARISON STUDY ON THE EFFECTS OF PARENTAL INVOLVEMENT, TEACHER ABILITY, AND SOCIOECONOMIC STATUS ON ACADEMIC ACHIEVEMENT IN THE UNITED STATES, CHINA, AND SOUTH KOREA

Kathryn Wagner and Lauren Schmidt

In an increasingly globalized world, an educated populace has never been more important. The educational systems in the United States, China, and South Korea have rendered a number of large-scale and longitudinal research studies, as these three countries have the economic and global success that are appealing to countries around the world looking for educational reform. However, each of these educational systems continues to

Educational Practices in China, Korea, and the United States, pages 31–48
Copyright © 2019 by Information Age Publishing
All rights of reproduction in any form reserved.

struggle with various aspects of education reform, following results from international assessments and research studies that expose disparities between high and low socioeconomic status (SES) students, as well as minority students and English language learners.

The purpose of this research inquiry is to provide a comparison of various facets of the educational systems in the United States, China, and South Korea, following an educational exchange to Xi'an, China and Seoul, South Korea. During the time observing in different K–12 classrooms in Xi'an and Seoul, we documented the educational practices and policies about the systems in each country. As we both teach in high poverty schools, but were observing prestigious, well-funded schools in Asia, our line of inquiry changed from broad comparisons of the educational systems in the United States, China, and South Korea, and to focus on the impact of parental involvement, teacher ability, and SES on student achievement, as we continued our observations. Thus, the following research question guided our inquiry: What is the impact of parents, teachers, and SES in a student's academic achievement in China and South Korea and how do these differ from those in the United States?

In the following chapter, first we present a review of literature on parental involvement, teacher ability, and SES in the three countries. Next, we outline the methods used for this research study, followed by the results of our interviews and observations. Finally, we present a discussion and brief conclusion, including limitations to, and implications of our research and future research.

LITERATURE REVIEW

In the United States, China, and South Korea, students from high and middle SES backgrounds are often afforded more academic opportunities due to the guidance and support of parents who know how to navigate the educational system and schools with highly qualified teachers, as well as sufficient resources to prepare them for higher education. However, minority and non-English speaking students in the United States, and Chinese and Korean with low SES, a majority of whom live in rural communities, are the ones to feel the effects of an imbalanced educational system most (Bryan, 2005; Zhang & Campbell, 2015).

Parental Involvement

United States

A large body of research conducted in the United States has been dedicated to investigating the role that parents have in the academic achievement of their students (Desimone, 1999; Domina, 2005; Fan, Williams, & Wolters, 2012; Jeynes, 2005; Powell-Smith, Stoner, Shinn, & Good, 2000; Rasinski & Stevenson, 2005; Sheldon & Epstein, 2005; Sirvani, 2007). Parental involvement or influence can be defined in a number of ways, but generally refers to parents' behavior and support at home and in the school setting which supports their children's academic achievement (Karbach, Gottschling, Spengler, Hegewald, & Spinath, 2013; Wilder, 2014). Cheung and Pomerantz (2012) presented evidence to support research on parental involvement and its impact on student achievement. Early parental involvement in students' education increases school achievement in a unique and essential way. Additionally, this study revealed that parents' involvement "was predictive of children's parent-oriented motivation in school" (p. 828), and the nature of parental involvement, while different between American and Chinese parents, contributed positively to students' engagement and grades.

Further, because of the vast amount of research supporting early parental involvement in children's education, U.S. policies on the parent–school relationship have developed with the No Child Left Behind initiative. Unfortunately, this "policy has continuously regulated the parent–school relationship through a normalizing perspective based on middle-class values backed by a century of developmental science focusing on family settings exemplifying those values" (Baquedano-López, Alexander, & Hernández, 2013, p. 150). Urban schools in the United States, where a large number of minority students are in attendance, as compared to those in China and South Korea, are generally afflicted with underfunding, unqualified educators, and students who live in high poverty (deMarrais & LeCompte, 1999). In a 2007 study by the U.S. Department of Education, it was found that great disparities exist between the academic achievement of minority students and their White peers (Fan et al., 2012). Despite these findings, Wilder (2014) notes there is "a strong relationship between parental involvement and academic achievement among urban students regardless of their gender or ethnicity" (p. 383).

Jeynes (2005) put forth a solution for closing the gap between minority students and their White peers. "One remedy for this phenomenon has involved an emphasis on including parents in the education of their children to supplement the learning that occurs at school and decrease the achievement gaps observed across ethnicities" (Fan et al., 2012, p. 24). Additionally, in a majority of schools across the United States, parental involvement is low in students' education "because they feel that teaching is better left to the experts or because they do not feel understood" (Froiland, Peterson, & Davison, 2013, p. 4). As will be discussed in following sections, educators do play an important role in education, however, schools serving minority students and English language learners lack the resources to offer teachers support in the education of their students.

China

Likewise, it is well documented that parental involvement and influence can directly correlate with the academic achievement and emotional well-being of a student in China. However, the overarching cultural influences can help dictate what the degree of parental involvement and structure of parental involvement will look like. Cheung and Pomerantz (2011) conducted a comparison study between China and the United States and found that both Confucian teaching and Socratic teaching had an impact on how parents view learning. For instance, in China, where Confucian teaching is highly influential, "learning is viewed by many as more than simply the pursuit of knowledge as in the United States—it is regarded as a moral endeavor" (p. 933). In contrast, as a whole, Americans tend to be more receptive to Socratic influences, where learning is viewed "in a utilitarian light in which knowledge is gained primarily to understand the world, develop one's skills, and accomplish one's goals" (p. 933). Therefore, while in America, where learning is viewed as a means to understanding the world around us, in China it is seen as more of an end all be all with strong moral implications. Naturally, and as a whole, parents want to see their students succeed in school, but when learning is more than a grade and linked with a student's personal success in all aspects of life, it is natural for a parent to become more involved, as is the case in China.

Further, despite the Chinese students' generally less than positive view of themselves, "Chinese children remained more engaged (e.g., spend more time on their schoolwork outside of school and use more self-regulated learning strategies) in school than do their American counterparts during early adolescence" (Pomerantz & Wang, 2009, p. 944). This phenomenon could be related to deCharms' 1968 study which suggested that students know how to do well in school and do so only because they feel compelled to by their parents. Additionally, Butler (2014) found that parents with higher SES are able to provide their students with more resources, contributing to academic achievement. This demonstrates the importance of parental involvement and how parental influence can strongly shape both self-esteem, learning practices, and academic achievement.

South Korea

While researching parental involvement and its influence on academic achievement in South Korea, it is important to note the lack of prior research studies, comparatively to both China and the United States. However, there is still a direct correlation between parental involvement and heightened academic achievement in school-aged children. Zhao and Akiba (2009) noted that parental involvement at the school had a positive effect on both student behavior and achievement in the United States and South Korea. Interestingly, the study showed that school expectations for parental involvement showed a much greater improvement in academic achievement in mathematics in the United States than in their South Korean counterparts. These findings may be due to the lack of research on the relationship between school expectations in South Korea, as researchers from the United States did conduct case studies that "found that parental involvement was one of the factors that explained high student achievement in Eastern Asian countries such as South Korea and Japan" (p. 412).

It is well documented that South Korean culture places a strong emphasis on education and its connection to social status and self-fulfillment, which in turn plays out in a parent's child rearing decisions regarding schooling (Cho, 2007; Zhou & Kim, 2006). Most South Korean parents have a strong role in monitoring homework assignments, teacher requests and assistance, and supervising attendance both in school and during after school classes. These tactics directly impact academic achievement and possibly correlate with South Korea's rank in the Programme for International Student Assessment exam (PISA), above the United States and the Organisation for Economic Co-operation and Development (OECD) average (Darling-Hammond, 2010). Furthermore, South Korean educators "have recognized that increased parental participation is crucial in the process of democratizing its education system and the society" (Zhao & Akiba, 2009, p. 413).

While there is a lack of research on the relationship between parental involvement and academic achievement in South Korea, there is a comprehensive study done on Korean-American adolescents that is relevant. Kim and Rohner (2002) detailed the relationship between grades and parental involvement in 245 Korean-American students in Grades 6 through 12. This study found that these students did achieve better grades when their parents were more involved at the school. Additionally, we noted that "parental involvement, especially parents' expectations, communication, homework checking, and TV viewing rules, made a positive contribution to adolescents' academic success" (Zhao & Akiba, 2009, p. 415). Thus concluding that parental involvement with schoolwork, monitoring homework, volunteering at the school, and maintaining strong attendance almost always results in higher academic achievement in students around the world.

Teacher Ability

United States

Darling-Hammond (2010) examines the link between highly qualified teachers and student achievement. The author posits that a prescription of "easy access and easy firing" (p. 194) does not necessarily equate to knowledgeable and competent teachers in high poverty schools. "Some have argued that the answer to weak teaching in the United States is to eliminate 'barriers' to teaching, such as teacher education and certification requirements, allow anyone into the classroom who wants to teach, and fire those who prove not to be effective" (p. 194). Darling-Hammond (2010) argues that high-achieving countries, such as Finland, Singapore, and South Korea do not approach teaching in this way; rather the process begins with teacher preparation programs at the university level, along with principals and administration that willingly share effective teaching practices with educators.

Further, for students with low SES, who may also be the first in their families to attend college, the relationship with their school counselor and access to highly qualified teachers is of utmost importance when the time for college preparation arrives. Therefore, as Deil-Amen and Tevis (2010) note, "The delivery of college information through counseling and other means should be channeled in structured ways to improve the college choice process, particularly for first-generation minority students for whom the school system plays an even greater role when neither parent has participated in higher education" (p. 168). High poverty schools in the United States, historically serving Black and Latinx students, are frequently underfunded and under-resourced with high student-to-teacher/counselor ratios. Therefore, teachers and school counselors are not fully prepared to help students enroll in higher education (Holland & Farmer-Hinton, 2009).

Deil-Amen and Tevis (2010) found that the students in low performing schools often did not know the content that would be tested on college entrance exams, or that there was structured preparation (i.e., courses and books) for these exams. Once students received their scores, which were lower than the national average, or not high enough for them to gain acceptance into a college of their choice, students were deflected from choosing a postsecondary pathway. Cohen and Brawer (2008) state "for most students in two-year institutions, the choice is not between the community college and a senior residential institution; it is between the community college and nothing" (p. 130).

Further, students at low achieving schools are often led to believe that the coursework they are taking will be sufficient for college entrance (Deil-Amen & Tevis, 2010). In reality, they have been tracked into coursework that would lead them into remedial classes at the college level. Salas, Portes, D'Amico, and Rios-Aguilar (2011) note that such actions begin in early elementary school and are continued over the K–16 experiences of minority students and English language learners. Additionally, low-ability grouping, starting in the elementary and middle school years, prevents students from being able to enroll in and have access to more advanced courses that would prepare them for college classes (Deil-Amen & Turley, 2007).

China

Moreover, when governing bodies assess influences on student achievement, the qualifications of teachers are a natural point of examination. Zhang and Campbell (2015) present several different studies on the impact of teacher qualifications on student achievement. Although there is a large amount of research examining the effects of teacher qualifications in China, there is a gap in the literature that examines teacher related factors and their influence on student achievement. More so, there are studies that have blatant contradictions despite similar test sets. Zhang and Campbell (2015) mention a couple of reviews conducted by Hanushek (1989, 1997) that "concluded that no strong evidence existed to suggest that teacher education and experience had positive effects on student achievement" (p. 493). However, a similar review done by Hedges, Lain, and Greenwald (1994) find that "resource variables that attempt to describe the quality of teachers (education level and experience) show very strong relations with student achievement" (p. 493). This data does raise the question about what research methods could be currently taking place to continue to try to discover the relationship between teacher qualities and student achievement; it would be interesting to see what teacher preparation programs could be improving upon to have more of an impact on student accomplishment. Zhang and Campbell (2015) note, "Researchers have long regarded teacher quality as a driving force and powerful school-related factor responsible for student achievement" (p. 490), however it can be observed that there is a lack of solid evidence to support this claim.

In China, although there have been and continue to be many efforts to establish criteria for appropriate teacher qualifications, there have not been many studies examining the relationship between teacher qualifications and their impact on student achievement. However, as a large developing country with an extremely high population of students and teachers, there is a central focus on what can be done for education reform. Moreover, data examined from the 2003 *Trends in International Math and Science Study* (TIMSS) found that China and 46 other "countries with better math teacher quality produced higher math achievement" (Zhang & Campbell, 2015, p. 494). It should also be noted that other studies, including Rice (2003) and Goldhaber and Brewer (1996, 2000), found that specific bachelor degrees correlated with the specific courses taught did result in higher levels of student achievement than teachers with non-class specific degrees. This also is related to the fact that more studies showed a connection between student achievement and teacher qualifications in upper grade levels rather than elementary schools. In conclusion, Zhang and Campbell (2015), raise several questions about the true influence of teacher qualifications on student achievement, especially since many of the case studies included are contradicting. Moving forward, it is essential to continue to

Student SES

United States

As Bryan (2005) notes, "racial and ethnic minority students in many urban schools often feel powerless in a majority-dominated school culture where language, class, and culture differences are seen as deficits" (p. 219). In an increasingly diverse country, the educational system in the United States continues to marginalize minority students, English language learners, and students who live in poverty. As research has shown, "children who live in poverty experience more absences from school, a lack of attention and con-centration . . . and difficulty with motivation" (Carney & Shields, 2013, p. 1). Thus, one of the greatest indicators of students' academic achievement is parent SES along with parent involvement (Carney & Shields, 2013). The structure of schools in the United States is organized to fail students who do not fall within a high or middle SES. Many stakeholders have offered remedies for the disparities between urban and suburban schools in the United States, but Davies (1996) notes a partnership between family, school, and community empowers the students' family to "gain skills, knowledge, and confidence that help them in rearing their children, in improving their economic condition, and in being good citizens" (p. 221).

China

Throughout various studies, it has become common knowledge that SES can have drastic influences on a student's academic achievement. Zhang and Campbell (2015) find an interesting connection between the qualifications of Chinese teachers and a student's SES. The findings of the study "suggest that in China a disparity was found between high and low SES schools with respect to access to quality teachers. It is believed that such a result actually reflects the current reality in China whereby high SES schools possess high quality education resources including better schools, equipment, and a more qualified teacher workforce" (p. 507). Furthermore, the study finds that there are much more notable differences between the high and low socioeconomic schools than could be observed between the medium and high socioeconomic schools, with both the medium and high SES schools having comparable teacher attributes and degree levels. In examining the test scores between low and high socioeconomic schools in China, the lower level SES group was found to 42 points lower than the high socioeconomic students and schools. This could be tied into the lower access to highly qualified teachers, but studies conclude that a connection can be made between a lack of school resources and the influence of a possibly lower self-esteem that is often seen in students who are aware of the inequality that affects them. As Darling-Hammond (2006) points out, the unequal distribution of resources and highly qualified teachers in China could very well be contributing to the long-lasting achievement gap between majority and minority students as well as high versus low poverty students.

South Korea

Currently, South Korea is well regarded for having excellent scores on international exams, thus rendering many researchers into their education system. One aspect of their education system is in the way they designate school assignment. Byun, Kim, and Park (2012) researched South Korea's high school equalization policy (HSEP) extensively. In 1973, the Ministry of Education in Korea proposed HSEP in response to many of the social and educational problems that were caused by the extreme competition to enter high performing secondary schools in the late 1960s and early 1970s. The drive to be the best and enter the most elite schools was causing serious inequalities between these high performing schools and other schools, in terms of quality of teachers, SES, and academic ability. To counteract this issue, HSEP was proposed. High school equalization policy in practice is a system "that assigns academic high school bound students to schools within their residential area on the basis of a random computerized lottery" (Byun et al., 2012, p. 159). Students are screened for placement from their middle school test scores, and are then allowed to apply to two or three academic high schools within their district which they are randomly assigned to based off of the lottery system. Proponents of the system say that HSEP helps to improve academic achievement for the lower SES students because they are now able to attend a more sociologically integrated school. Critics, on the other hand, are concerned that the "implementation would increase inequality between the haves and the have nots in a sense that it tends to trap lower SES parents and students into their neighborhood schools, which are usually of low quality" (p. 159). Today, the decision to adopt HSEP "is made by the local education district office based on an agreement among the members of the community, a majority of Korean students and parents favor the HSEP" (p. 162).

Byun et al. (2012) present research which "showed significant (unadjusted) differences in reading achievement, student characteristics, and school factors between the HSEP and non-HSEP regions. With respective to reading achievement, on average, students in the regions of HSEP implementation (60.95) outperformed their counterparts in the regions of non-HSEP implementation (53.19)" (p. 169). However, there are still many inequalities in place today due to the sporadic implementation of HSEP, in which HSEP is generally associated with students of high SES, likely from two parent homes with smaller family size. It is also important to recognize that the socioeconomic composition of the school itself has an equal if not even greater impact on student achievement than the individual student's SES. Although, a student's lower SES is often connected to general disadvantages at home and school that impact a student in more ways than one, such as lower self-esteem, which is also closely connected with student achievement.

METHODS

We are both English as a second language (ESL) teachers in a large, urban school district in North Carolina. Additionally, we have experiences traveling, studying, and teaching abroad before settling down to teach in North Carolina. While the district where we teach is represented by students from over 165 different countries who speak 187 different languages, the majority of our own students are Spanish-speaking and of low SES. Lauren Schmidt teaches at a medium-sized high school outside of the city with a current EL population of 81 LEP direct students, representing a wide variety of nations and levels of proficiency. Kathryn Wagner teaches at one of the largest elementary schools in the district with a current EL population of 316 LEP direct students (about 30% of the school's population). Wagner's students also represent a variety of nations and levels of proficiency.

When the opportunity for a cross-cultural exchange to Xi'an, China and Seoul, South Korea was presented, neither of us hesitated to participate. During the 11-day trip (7 days in Xi'an and 4 days in Seoul), we joined a group of participants who were public and private school teachers, professors, master's students, and doctoral students. Our group visited six public and private schools (kindergarten, elementary, middle, and secondary) and three universities in Xi'an and Seoul. During the school visits, there were tours, classroom observations, as well as formal, informal, and panel interviews with administrators, teachers, and students. Each of the schools visited in Xi'an and Seoul were located in bustling, urban centers, and were well-funded schools with adequate resources for the students and teachers. While the schools themselves were different in comparison to each of our schools in terms of funding and allocation of resources, we were able to take field notes—noting commonalities and differences. When we returned, we were able to analyze various aspects of education in the United States, China, and South Korea.

Before we left for the cross-cultural exchange to China and South Korea, each of us had prepared for the school visits by focusing on and reading literature on topics of interests such as academic achievement, college preparation, familial support, and the disparities in school resources. During the visit to a prestigious local university, "Middle China University,"[1] we took part in a question and answer session with four first year English majors. During that panel interview, we realized our research interests overlapped, thus deciding to collaborate. In addition to the student panel interview at "Middle China University," we used interview data from teachers and administrators at "Gioxan Middle School" and teachers and administrators at "Wonsu School of Language" in Seoul, South Korea.

With our research interests focused, we conducted two semi-structured group interviews, two focus groups, observations and field notes, reflective journals from both of us, and photographs. During our time in China and South Korea, our group visited a number of preschools, K–12 schools, and universities. We chose to analyze data from "Middle China University," "Gioxan Middle School," and "Wonsu School of Language" because we were able to set up interviews and focus groups during our visits to each school. Following, we analyzed our data, coding for emerging themes. After analyzing the interviews from the three school visits, we synthesized the data to inform this study.

RESULTS

The United States, China, and South Korea do converge in one goal of education: gaining social status and self-fulfillment. A common theme we found during our time in China and South Korea, and as teachers in the United States, is that students and parents across the world see education as a way to better their economic situations. This was illustrated during the panel interview at "Middle China University":

> **Author 1:** To what extent do parents play a role in your decision and academics?
>
> **Student 1 (male):** For me, my parents were not well educated, so they always told me that education is very important. They stressed that I should study hard. Now is the time to make a difference for your life. Education can lead to a better job and happy family. They encouraged me to do my best.
>
> **Student 2 (female):** Education provides you with more choices to see what you like.

To include context for this conversation, Student 1 took the national exam after high school in order to attend "Middle China University," while Student 2 was able to attend based on a recommendation by the principal of her private high school. These two students come from different SES, yet their thoughts on education were the same. During their cross-cultural exchange, we also noted how many schools relied on parents for volunteering and resources. For example, at "Gioxan Middle School," the school leader informed the group that parents donate books, volunteer their time by offering psychological services, security, and other commitments. In addition, the teachers and administrator at "Wonsu School of Language" note that parents actively participate in the PTA committee, have constant contact with the students and teachers throughout the year, and that the school is open two times per year for parent visits.

Likewise, just as in the United States, schools in China and South Korea experience educational disparities between teacher qualifications and allotment of resources across the country. In our field notes, we noted an abundance of resources, both in terms of learning aids and technology, like 3D printing labs, and parental involvement and volunteering, in the more affluent neighborhoods we visited. We speculated that these types of resources vary across the country depending on the overall wealth of the neighborhood in which the school is placed. In this particular example with the 3D printing lab, the school we are referencing is located in the "high tech zone," which explains the plethora of technological resources. In the United States, disparities lie between urban and suburban schools. Historically, urban schools have faced underfunding and under-qualified teachers, as urban centers tend to see the highest poverty in cities across the United States (Ladson-Billings, 2013).

In contrast, the urban schools in China and South Korea that we visited were beacons of success with an abundance of resources, highly qualified teachers, and exceptional national and international test scores. In these two countries, the life as a farmer in rural communities is difficult, and the only way to escape their low SES is to move to the urban centers and receive a quality education. Through conversations with students in some of the urban universities we visited, the importance of education as a means to success was highly stressed. Many of the students explained their educational pathways and how Chinese students are often sent to boarding schools in the cities to receive a better education that will in turn make them more competitive for admittance to a well-respected university. Additionally, the topic of parents sacrificing financial capital to send students to schools with better test scores, teachers, and technological resources was often mentioned by the students we spoke with, which further accentuates the educational gap we often see with wealth and resource disparities.

DISCUSSION

As the review of literature illustrated, despite variations in educational philosophies and degrees of parental and school involvement between the

United States, China, and South Korea, early parental involvement was found to be the most influential and essential indicator of student academic success. As the first role models in a child's life, parents play an important role in shaping their child's school readiness and willingness to succeed. While Froiland, Peterson, and Davison (2013) found that parents in the United States view education as the responsibility of the teacher and the school, it is still important to note that high parental expectations positively influence academic achievement. Likewise, Chinese and South Korean culture have a greater impact on how parents view their children's educations. As both educational systems aim to produce students who are beneficial assets to their societies, parents play a supportive and guiding role for their children, offering resources and financial support where possible.

While examining the differences in parental involvement across the United States, China, and South Korea, it is important to note the implications of culture and how they affect the methods and level of parental involvement in regards to its particular relationship with academic achievement. For example, in both South Korea and China, the widespread importance of Confucian teachings, "including the beliefs that that education is pivotal to success in life and that learners must both listen to and obey their teachers" (Linse, 2011, p. 473), played a large role in how many Asian parents choose to interact with their children and the schools they attend. The overarching influence of Confucian thought led to a heightened level of priority in regards to education and general respect, leading to highly involved parents and an increased amount of pressure for academic success in their children.

In the United States, as Confucian teachings are not culturally explicit, a larger variation in parental involvement is seen. The way parental involvement in academics presents itself within the United States may be more connected to the parents' SES, region, and level of education. According to Bempechat and Shernoff (2012), "parents are their children's first and primary guides through their schooling experiences, and therefore can serve to greatly buffer or compound risk factors for disengagement and low achievement" (p. 316). The diverse student population across the United States, including native born and immigrants, highlights the research on the impacts of parental involvement. Whether a student is from an impoverished area where graduation rates fluctuate between 50% and 60%, the son or daughter of an immigrant, or native born and raised in an upper middle class White family, the way their parents choose to interact with their education will likely shape and impact their academic success. The largest difference between South Korea, China, and the United States could be summarized as the complete melting pot of cultures, child rearing strategies, and importance placed on education that is seen within the United States.

LIMITATIONS

At various points throughout our research, we found limitations due to our short time spent in South Korea, the lack of diversity in observed schools (namely, private schools with upper class families), and the lack of applicable research in regards to the influences of academic achievement in South Korea. Although our 2016 cultural exchange to China and South Korea only spanned 2 weeks in total, we spent the majority of that time observing schools in China, and only 3 days spent in South Korea. This led to us being able to collect more data from our school visits in China, as opposed to South Korea. Additionally, we could have conducted a thorough comparison on the influences on academic achievement in China, South Korea, and the United States with a more diverse group of schools that represented a variety of SES, parenting styles, and sizes.

Furthermore, as we gathered additional research about the influences of SES, parent involvement and teacher ability on academic achievement after our return to the United States, we noticed a lack of applicable research regarding parent influence and teacher preparation programs in South Korea. This gap in the literature may have presented a limitation within this study, yet it allows for future comparison studies. Additionally, there is not a universal examination that spans across China, South Korea, and the United States that validly compares academic achievement, leading to more subjective interpretations of academic achievement in the three focus countries in this comparison.

CONCLUSION

Through the research and observations presented in this study, the implications of the higher test scores seen in China and South Korea show that the United States may have some "catching up" to do in terms of performance on assessments. Further research on these countries and their educational systems would be productive in analyzing where we can make changes here in the United States. We learned that investing in early childhood education does greatly influence academic success in children, particularly in conjunction with early parental involvement. We are of the opinion that investing more in early childhood education, with a focus on increasing parental involvement, has the potential to improve student achievement in the United States. Additionally, it is impossible to ignore the impact of the Confucian philosophies in China and how those philosophies have positively influenced the academic achievement of Chinese students. By studying countries with Confucian philosophies, we believe the United States could see positive impacts from incorporating culture in the classroom and encouraging our society to honor education.

After this cross-cultural exchange opportunity, we were able to reflect on the similarities and differences between three dominant educational systems around the world. In a comparison of the educational systems in the United States, China, and South Korea, it can be noted that each of the countries can benefit immensely from cross-cultural exchanges of educators and scholars. During their research, as noted in the chapter, we found a gap in the literature on South Korean parental involvement and academic achievement, while there is an abundance of studies from researchers in the United States on this topic. As a country who consistently outperforms both the United States and China on international exams, it would benefit scholars and educators in these and other countries to travel to and study the high performing schools in South Korea. Additionally, exchanges such as this may inform policy makers as they try to reconcile the vast disparities between students of high, middle, and low SES.

NOTE

1. Pseudonyms are used to protect identities.

REFERENCES

Baquedano-López, P., Alexander, R., & Hernández, S. (2013). Equity issues in parental and community involvement in schools: What teacher educators need to know. *Review of Research in Education, 37*(1), 149–182.

Bempechat, J., & Shernoff, D. (2012). Parental influences on achievement motivation and student engagement. In S. Christenson, A. Reschly, & C. Wylie (Eds.), *Handbook of research on student engagement* (pp. 315–342). New York, NY: Springer.

Bryan, J. (2005). Fostering educational resilience and achievement in urban schools through school-family community partnerships. *Partnerships/Community, 22.* Retrieved from http://digitalcommons.unomaha.edu/slcepartnerships/22

Butler, Y. (2014). Parental factors and early English education as a foreign language: A case study in Mainland China. *Research Papers in Education, 29*(4), 410–437.

Byun, S.-Y., Kim, K.-K., & Park, H. (2012). School choice and educational inequality in South Korea. *Journal of School Choice, 6*(2), 158–183.

Carney, I., & Shields, T. (2013, June 11). Worn down and worn out. *Style Weekly.* Retrieved from http://www.styleweekly.com/richmond/worn-down-and-worn -out/Content?oid=1906874

Cheung, C., & Pomerantz, E. (2011). Parents' involvement in children's learning in the United States and China: Implications for children's academic and emotional adjustment. *Child Development, 82*(3), 932–950. https://doi.org/10.1111/j.1467-8624.2011.01582.x

Cheung, C., & Pomerantz, E. (2012). Why does parents' involvement enhance children's achievement? The role of parent-oriented motivation. *Journal of Educational Psychology, 104*(3), 820–832.

Cho, Y. (2007). The diaspora of Korean children: A cross-cultural study of the educational crisis in contemporary South Korea. Graduate Student Theses, Dissertations, & Professional Papers, 1244. Retrieved from https://scholarworks.umt.edu/etd/1244

Cohen, A., & Brawer, F. (2008). *The American community college* (5th ed.). San Francisco, CA: Jossey-Bass.

Darling-Hammond, L. (2006). Securing the right to learn: Policy and practice for powerful teaching and learning. *Educational Researcher, 35*(7), 13–24.

Darling-Hammond, L. (2010). *The flat world and education: How America's commitment to equity will determine our future.* New York, NY: Teachers College Press.

Davies, D. (1996). Partnerships for student success. *New Schools, New Communities, 12,* 14–21.

deCharms, R. C. (1968). *Personal causation.* New York, NY: Academic Press.

Deil-Amen, R., & Tevis, T. (2010). Circumscribed agency: The relevance of standardized college entrance exams for low SES high school students. *The Review of Higher Education, 33*(2), 141–175.

Deil-Amen, R., & Turley, R. L. (2007). A review of the transition to college literature in sociology. *Teachers College Record, 109*(10), 2324–2366.

DeMarrais, K., & LeCompte, M. (1999). *The way schools work: A sociological analysis of education.* New York, NY: Addison-Wesley.

Desimone, L. (1999). Linking parent involvement with student achievement: Do race and income matter? *The Journal of Educational Research, 93*(1), 11–30.

Domina, T. (2005). Leveling the home advantage: Assessing the effectiveness of parental involvement in elementary school. *Sociology of Education, 78*(3), 233–249.

Fan, W., Williams, C., & Wolters, C. (2012). Parental involvement in predicting school motivation: Similar and differential effects across ethnic groups. *The Journal of Educational Research, 105*(1), 21–35.

Froiland, J., Peterson, A., & Davison, M. (2013). The long-term effects of early parent involvement and parent expectation in the USA. *School Psychology International, 34,* 33–50.

Goldhaber, D., & Brewer, D. (1996, January). *Why don't schools and teachers seem to matter? Assessing the impact of unobservables on educational productivity.* Revised version of a paper presented at Meetings of the Econometric Society, San Francisco, CA.

Goldhaber, D., & Brewer, D. (2000). Does teacher certification matter? High school teacher certification status and student achievement. *Educational Evaluation and Policy Analysis, 22*(2), 129–145.

Hanushek, E. (1989). The impact of differential expenditures on school performance. *Educational Researcher, 18*(4), 45–65.

Hanushek, E. (1997). Assessing the effects of school resources on student performance: An update. *Educational Evaluation and Policy Analysis, 19*(2), 141–164.

Hedges, L., Lain, R., & Greenwald, R. (1994). Does money matter? A meta-analysis of studies of the effects of differential school inputs on student outcomes. *Educational Researcher, 23*(3), 5–14.

Holland, N., & Farmer-Hinton, R. (2009). Leave no schools behind: The importance of a college culture in urban public high schools. *High School Journal, 92*(3), 24–43.

Jeynes, W. (2005). A meta-analysis of the relation of parental involvement to urban elementary school student academic achievement. *Urban education, 40*(3), 237–269.

Karbach, J., Gottschling, J., Spengler, M., Hegewald, K., & Spinath, F. (2013). Parental involvement and general cognitive ability as predictors of domain-specific academic achievement in early adolescence. *Learning and Instruction, 23*, 43–51.

Kim, K., & Rohner, R. (2002). Parental warmth, control, and involvement in schooling predicting academic achievement among Korean American adolescents. *Journal of Cross-Cultural Psychology, 33*(2), 127–140.

Ladson-Billings, G. (2013). Lack of achievement or loss of opportunity? In P. L. Carter & K. G. Welner (Eds.), *Closing the Opportunity Gap: What America Must do to Give Every Child an Even Chance* (pp. 11–22). New York, NY: Oxford University Press.

Linse, C. (2011). Korean parental beliefs about ELT from the perspective of teachers. *Tesol Journal, 2*(4), 473–491.

Pomerantz, E., & Wang, Q. (2009). The role of parental control in children's development in Western and East Asian countries. *Current Directions in Psychological Science, 18*(5), 285–289.

Powell-Smith, K., Stoner, G., Shinn, M., & Good, R., III (2000). Parent tutoring in reading using literature and curriculum materials: Impact on student reading achievement. *School Psychology Review, 29*(1), 5–27.

Pultorak, E., & Markle, G. (2008). Snapshots of Chinese classrooms illustrate disparities. *Phi Delta Kappan, 90*(1), 45–49.

Rasinski, T., & Stevenson, B. (2005). The effects of fast start reading: A fluency-based home involvement reading program. *Reading Psychology, 26*(2), 109–125.

Rice, J. K. (2003). *Teacher quality: Understanding the effectiveness of teacher attributes.* Washington, DC: Economic Policy Institute.

Salas, S., Portes, P., D'Amico, M., & Rios-Aguilar, C. (2011). Generación 1.5: A cultural historical agenda for research at the 2-year college. *Community College Review, 39*(2), 121–135.

Sheldon, S., & Epstein, J. (2005). Involvement counts: Family and community partnerships and mathematics achievement. *The Journal of Educational Research, 98*(4), 196–207.

Sirvani, H. (2007). The effect of teacher communication with parents on students' mathematics achievement. *American Secondary Education, 31*–46.

Wilder, S. (2014). Effects of parental involvement on academic achievement: A meta-synthesis. *Educational Review, 66*(3), 377–397.

Zhang, D., & Campbell, T. (2015). An examination of the impact of teacher quality and "Opportunity Gap" on student science achievement in China. *International Journal of Science and Mathematics Education, 13*(3), 489–513.

Zhao, H., & Akiba, M. (2009). School expectations for parental involvement and student mathematics achievement: A comparative study of middle schools in the US and South Korea. *Compare: A Journal of Comparative and International Education, 39*(3), 411–428.

Zhou, M., & Kim, S. (2006). Community forces, social capital, and educational achievement: The case of supplementary education in the Chinese and Korean immigrant communities. *Harvard Educational Review, 76*(1), 1–29.

CHAPTER 4

EDUCATION AND THE ECONOMY

An Examination Into the Effectiveness of Education in China, the United States, and South Korea

Taylor Allen and Michelle Chen

*Education is an economic issue. Education is the economic issue of our time...
Education is an economic issue when we know beyond a shadow of a doubt that countries that out-educate us today, they will out-compete us tomorrow... The single most
important thing we can do is to make sure we've got a world-class education system
for everybody. That is a prerequisite for prosperity. It is an obligation
that we have for the next generation.*

—President Obama (2010)

There has never been a more educated generation with such confusing prospects. You need a college degree to be marketable, but it won't guarantee a job. Education is our most valuable asset. The public demands more accountability of teachers, while design, implementation, and assessment is moved further from the classroom. Professional educators are leaving the field as salaries stagnate or decrease (Allegretto & Mishel, 2016). If we are

---

Educational Practices in China, Korea, and the United States, pages 49–70
Copyright © 2019 by Information Age Publishing
All rights of reproduction in any form reserved.

going to guarantee a quality education for the next generation, we need to be sure of our commitment to it. And that requires a decision about what it has to accomplish. Education is a progressive field; information is added and updated as it is discovered and disseminated; think of the changes in biology classes after Watson and Crick published their paper about DNA, or in physics after Einstein published his paper on relativity. If educators continued teaching the way they had before, their students would not be prepared for the fields they hoped to enter.

Obviously, President Obama is not the only person who sees a link between the economy and education. Education and the economy are often headline issues, and the 2016 U.S. presidential election again brought both into the sphere of public debate. Recall that President Trump built a campaign platform around the loss of manufacturing jobs and the desire to retain U.S. business (Trump, 2016). But in fact both parties promised educational reforms that promise to train U.S. workers for more competitive future jobs. But we were left wondering how one might tailor education for that purpose. We found Hanushek and Woessmann's (2010) literature review to be particularly helpful, because it creates three primary categories for describing the intersection between education and the economy. His categories are increasing human capital (Mankiw, Romer, & Weil, 1990), increasing innovation capacity to develop new technologies (Lucas, 1988; Romer, 1990), and transferring knowledge to understand new processes and technology (Benhabib & Spiegel, 1994; Nelson & Phelps, 1966). Our interest ultimately lies with the second category regarding economic innovation. But in order to pursue our topic of economic innovation, it is first necessary to look at how educational achievements are assessed.

Traditionally, a composite score from standardized tests is created and then split into three main categories: math, science, and literacy (Desilver, 2015; NCES, 2015b). Most news reports and comparative studies are based on these numbers. Millennials will recall the very famous opening scene to the Aaron Sorkin (2012) television program, *Newsroom*, in which an irreverent journalist Will McAvoy (portrayed by Jeff Daniels) responds to the question "What makes America the greatest country in the world?" with:

> There's absolutely no evidence to support the statement that we're the greatest country in the world. We're 7th in literacy, 27th in math, 22nd in science, 49th in life expectancy, 178th in infant mortality, 3rd in median household income, number 4 in labor force and number 4 in exports. We lead the world in only three categories: number of incarcerated citizens per capita, number of adults who believe angels are real and defense spending, where we spend more than the next 26 countries combined, 25 of whom are allies. (Episode 1)

Now, we included the quote, not because we agree and not because the numbers are entirely accurate, but because we have grown up in a culture

Education and the Economy ▪ **51**

where more young people access news from comedy programs like this, or *The Daily Show,* or on Twitter rather than traditional news organizations like CBS. In fact, even back in 2004, Pew Research Center (2004) reported that the number of people under 30 who regularly learned something about politics from comedy news increased to 29%. But as recently as 2015, American Press Institute (2015) found that social networking platforms are the primary platform for people 18–34 to get news. It cited Youtube, Twitter (a favorite of Congress and President Trump), Instagram, and Facebook as the main sources, but also included web-communities like Reddit as a way to engage in discussions. But it cautioned that it is easy to passively consume media that is exposed to you on one of those platforms; however, they also suggested that millennials are particularly savvy at recognizing they are in a "filter bubble" and they want to look for corroborating sources.

In 2016, with data from the Pew Research Institute, Nina Godlewski amended the list to include the entertainment platforms Snapchat and Buzzfeed as *the* key news sources. So, as strange as it is, we find that it is relevant to point out that speeches on programs like *Newsroom* or a presidential tweet or a snap-story can deeply affect the opinions of people who are about to pay heavily for the same education that our pop culture is denigrating. But is it really failing? Is it enough to look at standardized test scores alone?

So getting back to those numbers that cause so much concern, it is true that Desilver (2015) and the NCES (2015b) all show U.S. educational composite scores outside the Top 20. The Pew Research Study (Desilver, 2015) reports that more and more Americans have a negative perception of American math and science scores as we continue a downward trend compared against other developed nations; this is despite the fact that our scores are actually improving compared to ourselves. This is why Hanushek and Woessman (2010) make a great case for looking at metrics beyond test scores that help illustrate the quality of the education system. If we look back at the U.S. economy in the 1980s and 1990s, most readers will recall that it was actually quite strong. And there has only been a marked increase in the science and engineering economic sector over the last 20 years. Baby Boomers remember that President Clinton oversaw one of the most significant economic growths in recent memory; unemployment was down, GDP grew by 3.8% real growth, inflation was stable, and median income grew (Matthews, 2012). Granted there were persistent problems during the Clinton administration regarding extreme poverty and income inequality, but overall it was a relatively stable era. So if we focus our attention on the 1990s, when our math scores were significantly lower (NCES, 2016), we see some conflicting results in the economy.

Well-invested readers may fondly recall that a decade after releasing the Microsoft Office suite in 1988, Bill Gates announced a partnership with Steve Jobs to release an Apple friendly version in 1997 for the upcoming iMac, which helped Apple find its way out of a decade long slump and well on its way to being a modern colossus (Guglielmo, 2012). A month later a couple of unknown programmers named Larry and Sergei founded a company called Google in September 1998 (Alphabet Inc., 2017). Meanwhile, a small online sales company called Amazon.com was getting on its feet after Jeff Bezos started it in 1994 (Brandt, 2011). Three of the most profitable tech companies in history emerged when math and science scores were near their lowest. Sure, some of them were founded by men who eschewed higher education, but they were supported by engineers and scientists who *did* attend traditional institutions; and ostensibly, they were institutions who had quickly adapted to respond to the increasing profitability of computer-based jobs. Shouldn't that always be the goal of education; to support emerging changes in the economy and culture?

Facts and figures are always helpful in determining efficacy, but as we've noticed, the data we collect might not always tell the whole story and it is usually a failure in the methodology. Hanushek and Woessman (2010) mentioned that the most traditional metric for measuring educational proficiency is: years of formal education. Traditionally, scholars looked at how many years students are in school and believe it or not there is actually a strong link between countries with longer educational systems and their economic development. But, he is quick to caution readers that even though students go to school in Zambia, Jamaica, or Lesotho for the same amount of time as students in Spain, Singapore, and Taiwan one cannot reasonably expect the former countries to be as successful as the later countries because the quality of education is significantly different in the latter countries.

Therefore, to address the weakness of this single metric, Hanushek and Woessman's (2010) most recent work takes more data into account, including: standardized test scores, a comprehensive metric for economic development as defined by openness to global trade, security of intellectual property rights, fertility, and geography. While the model for years of schooling does show a statistically significant relationship between education and the economy, when it is compared to a much stronger model which includes more economic factors the relationship is no longer statistically significant. Reliable data from China can be hard to find, but anecdotally and logically it makes sense that more prosperous countries will have more international trading partners to either buy or sell goods and will therefore also have more prosperous companies looking to benefit from that relationship. When we look at China, widely considered to be our largest international rival now and in the future, we do not see the prosperity that should have emerged from a country with such a fertile population and abundant with so many natural resources. Why isn't China exporting products people want to buy—cars, electronics, and so forth? Why are China's biggest companies banks and not creative companies?

Our fear in comparing and contrasting the United States, China, and Korea was that ethnocentrism and personal experiences would contaminate our research, but our second discussion seeks to examine the reality of American education, which *has* been very successful, but is poised for changes that could be detrimental (Ravitch, 2010). We will shift our focus to the effectiveness of each system of education to address the bigger question of how it can support growth in the future. As educators and students we have a vested interest in learning and teaching best practices that will support student growth, the acquisition of skills for learning, and the two most important elements: creativity and expression.

Thus, we use data from one study abroad trip to China and Korea to explore the following two discussions that guide this chapter. The first discussion focuses on the current state of Chinese education traced from the Great Leap Forward and it includes strengths and weaknesses identified through research and observations. The second discussion tackles a bigger issue. Which education system will best support future growth? We approached it by asking ourselves a few questions: Is the United States truly going backwards as newscasters and politicians warn? Is China on the right track as they begin to move towards a more holistic system? Where does Korea fit on that spectrum? How should we define educational and economic success?

LITERATURE REVIEW

The prerequisite for understanding Chinese education is understanding the rigor and emphasis applied to their testing programs. They are extremely high stakes and have often been criticized for deterring creativity and expression. Contrast this with American best practices in public education and teaching English as a second/foreign language (TESL/TEFL), which indicate that group cooperation leads to better understanding and expression (Ellis, 1991; Lazonick, 2003; Long, 1985; Long, 1996; NEA, 2015). However, our informal observations and interviews in Xi'an indicate there may be a change in Chinese thinking regarding best practices in assessment. This comes as the United States is pivoting to *more* standardized testing (Preus, 2007). In order to illustrate the significance of this change in thinking, we examine the history of Chinese education from its Soviet roots to its modern involvement in global engineering and banking. We also spend time defining funding in China, which has long been a hindrance to equal access between rural and urban students, with the purpose of demonstrating the value of education in the Chinese economy.

An Examination of Chinese Education

In order to discuss the reforms and progress that China has achieved in pursuit of their goals for education, it is pertinent to discuss their history and why they have established the goals that they have. In context, China's population has long been a concern, hence the implementation of the one-child policy in 1979 (CIA, 2017). Even in light of this measure to control population, China's population is still more than four times that of the United States (The World Bank, 2015d). Given the vast numbers, the task of creating successful programs and implementing reform or policy change is a considerable undertaking. With the history of the current education system, it is evident that China desires change in their structure, but this change will take time to come to fruition.

Several significant changes occurred with China's education system following World War II. In design and structure, Chinese education came to rely on Soviet models and became primarily content and teacher focused. Several years later, during the Great Leap Forward and a massive growth in industrialization, childcare became a critical component of education design (Lee, 1992). These changes necessitated rapid school development but resulted in a disorganized design of the programs (Fees, Hoover, & Zheng, 2014). Funding for public schools was not well defined and schools began to decline because of the rising costs of maintenance (Chinese Ministry of Education, 2015). This created space for private schools to grow, yet the funding and organization was still not well established. This period was described as an industrialization of education because of its rapid growth and having the characteristics of high fees and intense competition (Yang, 2006). In 1990, major education reform began in China (Preus, 2007). That turned the nation towards its current direction of development, a hybrid of Confucian ideals and relationship-based learning (Fees et al., 2014).

China has a long-established history of testing to elevate social and political position. The curriculum and teaching style was heavily influenced by Confucianism, Communism, and Western curricular ideals (Fees et al., 2014). This is evidenced by teacher-centered classes. The test that was once used to determine positions for high ranking officials was applied to the primary and secondary school systems. And tests were included to determine progression from primary to secondary schools and from secondary schools to college. These are high stakes for students. A high score determines if a student can attend a secondary school that is known for high secondary test scores. These schools are known to prepare students to achieve high test scores that will improve their chances of gaining entrance to a prestigious and well-known college. Attendance at these colleges will improve job opportunities and the chance to achieve financial success.

This current structure of education in China places a high value on taking tests in order to determine a person's qualifications. Though the "Gao Kao" is the better known test that high school students prepare 3 years for in order to enter college, students also take tests at the end of middle school to determine where they will attend high school. In China, primary school is Grade 1–6, middle school is 7–9, and high school consists of Grades 10–12 (China Education Center Ltd., 2016). Grades 1–9 are compulsory (Yang, 2006). For each level, pressure increases steadily as each grade becomes more and more significant in influencing future opportunities. The classes are primarily teacher focused and lecture heavy, with an emphasis on personal achievement (Fees et al., 2014). The structure of the test is also one that has received media attention for the high amount of stress placed on the students in preparing to take the test. Students feel pressure from parents, society, instructors, and from themselves. This results in internal and external stress that often manifests physically and is a topic of concern in the public eye (Yang, 2006).

While the pressure is universal for students all over China, the funding structure for schools is much less uniform and has been subject to much criticism. Though China's GDP has grown, the percentage allocated for education has not followed suit (Yang, 2006). In education, the funding structure is determined by the affiliation of the school. If the school is government affiliated and public in nature, the school receives funds from the government based on staffing requirements set by the national government. Privately owned schools receive some governmental support and neighborhood schools receive funds as designated by the local civil administration (Zeng, 2008). This diversity in funding methods creates inequality in the access to resources, which results in disparity in quality of education. This causes dissatisfaction within the public sphere. People feel that high test scores can be bought and this causes division (Yang, 2006).

One pronounced discrepancy is the funding structure between urban and rural schools and this is reflective of wide gaps in socioeconomic status across China. While there is a wide range of quality between schools within one city, the disparity is even greater when compared with schools in rural areas. Often the counties are responsible for funding the schools and are excluded from governmental funding (Zeng, 2008). This considerable challenge of supplying funding results in underfunded and understaffed schools (Pultorak & Markle, 2008; Yang, 2006). Frequently, teachers are less qualified but are the only ones available. In addition, students are required to pay fees, which is a significant financial burden for agricultural families. If a family is able to produce the funds to pay the fees to support their child through compulsory education and high school and their student gains entrance to college, the financial strain only increases. Through Yang's calculations, it would take the wages of four farmers to support one college student, a feat not achievable for most families in rural areas (2006). In order to address this substantial gap in education and socioeconomic status, reform at a governmental level will be critical.

With this testing system effective nationwide, the high stakes increase competition because of the high population. Implementing change to this system requires a massive overhaul that would be far reaching in influence. Thus, any change will take time to demonstrate evidence of reform. In deciding direction for reform, many feel that more care should be given to clarifying funding policies and increasing attention paid to public service areas. While change has been implemented to reduce and create exemptions for school fees (Yang, 2006), there are still many concerns that more permanent positive changes need to occur. One concern is that the government has been too preoccupied with economic growth and now that China has grown financially, the government should turn its attention to public services such as health care, social development, and education (Yang, 2006). This change will necessitate structural changes in policy in order to be effective. Zeng suggests that the government should have a more interactive and standardized role in school funding but also incorporate community involvement and ownership (2008). Regulations and funding policies will need to be clearly defined and equitably distributed to address the disparity between rural and urban schools.

In addition to change in funding policy, reform in the actual practices and goals of education have been initiated, with several overarching goals in mind. In determining direction of Chinese education, decentralization has been a guiding element (Preus, 2007). This has also influenced China's desire to have a "quality-oriented" system, moving away from standardized and high-stakes testing. Schools have also been encouraged to consider the individuality of the student as they teach as opposed to teaching to the group (Fees et al., 2014). Increasingly, schools are also incorporating explicit instruction of Chinese culture and customs. While these changes are all well intentioned, execution of these new initiatives in a system that has for so long relied on testing scores to determine success is complicated and not without struggle.

China has been progressing in the direction of decentralizing curriculum and standards. Where these were previously mandated by the government and standard across the entire nation, now there is development in shifting that responsibility to the local governments (Preus, 2007). Within specific guidelines, schools now have some choice in textbook choice and design. This is in accord with China's desire to create what they have termed a "quality-oriented" system. This considers the growth of the entire person and not only their intellectual capacity (Fees et al., 2014). This also includes a distancing from a test based system. The tradition of test based education has been credited not only with creating passive students who desire only to learn for tests, but also creates many other negative pressures from society and within the student. The testing system is also credited with stifling creativity, a quality that is seen as contributing to success (Preus, 2007). In an effort to nurture creativity, philosophical approaches to pedagogy have been undergoing changes to give more value to developing the individual.

While interviewing teachers at a university affiliated school, the teachers attested to the changes that they were witnessing in approach to education and curriculum. They found that there is more focus on the student as an individual and that the process of education is becoming much more open and inclusive to the community. Where the classroom was once seen as a collective group, now the teachers are encouraged to develop the entire person and be mindful of the interests, needs, and talents of each individual student. Teachers are not just providing academic instruction to the students, but are also concerned with physical and mental development. In addition, the atmosphere of the classroom has become much more familiar. The classrooms are meant to make students feel at home with more student work displayed. Further, classrooms are no longer limited by the four walls, but are extending to other areas. This also incorporates family and community involvement. Where classrooms were previously closed to parents, involvement is now not only encouraged but expected. Where applicable, students have opportunities to learn outside the classroom, making learning much more experientially based (Fees et al., 2014).

Learning is also intentionally incorporating elements of Chinese culture. During the Cultural Revolution, many customs and historical practices were designated as detrimental and harmful to forward progress. In trying to eradicate this history, identity and culture were harmed, and with a renewed effort to teach these traditions, China is moving towards reestablishing national identity and pride. It has become important to teach the values and customs of China to its youth, and the governmental initiative has been supported by a public desire to revive and teach traditional Chinese culture (Yang, 2006).

These goals for the entirety of Chinese education are not without their challenges. The greatest challenge is implementing this change across such a massive population with a diversity of systems already in operation. Debate within the academic community also contributes to the challenge of finding agreement in how policies should be formed and mandated. From a teacher's perspective, considering the individual is a beneficial and good approach to education, but the challenge is the lack of resources. With large classes, differentiation is challenging with so much diversity and a high student to teacher ratio. This diversity is also present from student backgrounds and upbringing (Fees et al., 2014).

While the longstanding tradition of testing has been difficult to separate from, the disorganization of existing structures has also presented its own challenges. In order to provide a more equitable education regardless of location, the method by which schools are funded and structured will need to be organized in some fashion (Zeng, 2008). Creating consistency in how government is involved with and provides funding to schools will help to normalize how they are staffed and provided with resources. This change will mean better resources for underfunded schools and better capability to hire qualified staff.

The environment in China is currently receptive to change, both in political and public spheres. In academic discussions, the attitude is positive towards implementing policy and several suggestions for reform are promising. To encourage involvement and personal responsibility for education, one suggestion is to maintain current funding and policy establishments with gradual transfer of responsibility to communities. Long term, this model would require clarity and uniformity in how funding is allocated but could be successful in closing existing gaps in education (Zeng, 2008). Others call for a holistic shift in policy perspective. Moving from a purely economic focused establishment to one that is also concerned with many public needs such as healthcare and social progress would naturally include development in education. This would also necessitate clear balance for government involvement and designate balance in distribution of authority. Making these areas clear would allow local contributions and involvement, empowering local responsibility regarding education. This would require not just effort and dedication on the part of the government, but would require public commitment to ensure lasting change (Yang, 2006). However the government decides to direct change in Chinese education, it is clear that detailed planning will be an essential component of a successful initiative. In planning, it will also be critical to consider the role and influence of Chinese culture and how it informs pedagogy and curriculum so that policies will be successful and promote positive growth in China.

Relationships Between Education, Innovation, and Success

China is moving towards more holistic education. The United States is playing tug-of-war in conference rooms across the nation debating the best assessment practices, but institutionally is leaning towards increased standardized testing to ensure accountability and quality (Preus, 2007). Anecdotally, Korea splits the difference with high test scores and creative kids, and they use a variety of assessments. A natural question arises from our observations: Which system is most effective? It is important to note that neither of us, and hopefully none of our readers, believe that one system will work everywhere in the world, but there has to be a benchmark for assessing education in the culture and location it serves.

Education and the Economy ▪ **59**

In this discussion, we are evaluating two metrics to assess the effectiveness of education in preparing students to operate in a global economy. The first is employment based on educational attainment versus unemployment. And the second is innovation coming out of industry. China falls behind the United States in unemployed or underemployed educated young people by at least 50%. Korea's unemployment rate is less than half the United States.

The traditional metric Hanushek and Woessmann (2010) mentioned to link education with the economy is years in school. Table 4.1 shows that students in the United States attend school 3 years longer than students in China and Korea, which would rightly suggest that the United States should outpace those countries in the economic sector.

However, it is impossible to compare China and the United States directly, because as Table 4.2 demonstrates, China is in its own category in terms of raw labor force with almost 2.4 times more people in the labor

TABLE 4.1 Duration of Compulsory Education (2014)	
Country	Years
China	9
Korea	9
United States	12

Note: Adapted from "World Bank. (2015a). *World Databank.* [Duration of Compulsory Education, 2014; China, Korea, United States]." Retrieved from http://data.worldbank.org/indicator/SE.COM.DURS?locations=CN-US-KR

TABLE 4.2 Total Labor Force and Unemployment Rates of China, Korea and United States			
Year	China	Korea	United States
1990	637.30	19.20	128.20
2000	637.30	22.70	147.30
2006	767.10	24.30	154.70
2007	772.10	24.50	155.90
2008	776.10	24.60	157.70
2009	779.90	24.60	157.90
2010	781.10	24.90	157.60
2011	790.20	25.40	157.90
2012	795.90	25.80	159.30
2013	801.80	26.10	159.80
2014	806.50	27.40	161.10

Note: Adapted from "World Bank. (2015c). World Databank. [Labor Force, total; China, Korea, United States]. " Retrieved from http://data.worldbank.org/indicator/SL.TLF.TOTL.IN?locations=CN-US-KR

force than there are total population living in the entire United States. And interestingly, over 62% of their population is considered capable of or willing to work. The same can be said of how many students they are educating; it is on a scale entirely its own. Korea's labor force is relatively small on a global scale, but the percentage of people considered to be part of the labor force—52%—is average across the globe. The United States is relatively low (47%) after many people dropped out of the labor force following the recession in 2008.

Despite their large labor force, China has had relatively low and stable unemployment rate over the past decade and a half (Figure 4.1), however China's GDP per capita suggests that not every employed worker works in a lucrative job, and China's income inequality further casts doubt on their low employment numbers. Korea is consistently closer to full employment than either of the other two countries and their GDP per capita is at least above the poverty line in the United States. In addition, they have relatively equal income distribution compared to the other two countries (The World Bank, 2015b).

The real picture of education and its influence on economic opportunity emerges in Table 4.3. We have isolated levels of unemployment based on educational attainment. The tagline in the news, from our parents, from our peers, from our government, and from our future employers is that a college degree is fast becoming a prerequisite to employment and it

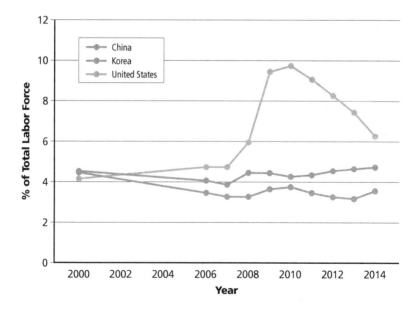

Figure 4.1 Unemployment rates in China, Korea, and United States from 2000 to 2014. Adapted from World Bank. (2015e).

Education and the Economy ▪ **61**

TABLE 4.3 Unemployment Rates, by Highest Level of Education in 2011		
Country	High School	University
China	8.2%	16.4%
United States	21.6%	8.7%
Korea	—	3.0%

Note: Data is a compilation from three separate sources: *Wall Street Journal*, National Center for Education Statistics (NCES, 2015a), and Country Note. Please see references for detailed information.

actually turns out to be true; we found that U.S. citizens with a bachelor's degree are more than twice as likely to be employed than a high school graduate—although both groups are still underemployed compared to the country as a whole. The fact that a college degree is becoming necessary is reflective of the evolving nature of our economy; jobs in the United States are more specialized and require more specialized training. Manufacturing jobs—historically performed by high school graduates—are going abroad to places like China where people without a college degree are able to secure those manufacturing jobs and are willing to do them for low pay. A college educated student in China, with a job, is more likely to enjoy a more prosperous life, but their chances of finding a job suitable for their skill level is statistically worse. This is a reflection of the challenge China has in creating a new, creative economic sector to support the increased amount of college students they are turning out. Anecdotally, Korea has an extremely well organized educational system that strongly supports its economy. They are very strong in math and science which is reflected by their top companies, Samsung and Hyundai. However, both of those companies are creative, which was supported by the high levels of group work and collaborative learning we witnessed in the classrooms. Educated students in Korea have a 97% chance of finding gainful employment upon graduation.

It is impossible to predict what the global economy will look like in 20 years, although many try. In such a climate of uncertainty, schools can only hope to instill their pupils with useful skills and knowledge to adapt to future opportunities. One could argue that creativity and expression are the most important skills a student can acquire in school, and it is reflected in the output of creative companies. In a brief survey of the top Fortune 500 companies we were able to demonstrate the diversity of U.S. and Korean companies in addition to the large quantity which we believe is representative of the strong relationship between education and the jobs students want after graduation.

Figure 4.2 illustrates the predominance of American businesses around the world with nearly 600 of the top 2,000 companies making over US$1

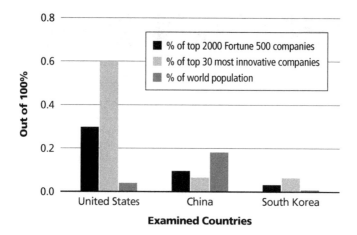

Figure 4.2 Comparison of innovation and population.

billion per year (Forbes, 2016). In the top 10, China has the top 3 in addition to number 6 which are all banking companies, while the United States has five in the top 10 including the creative company, Apple. Japan slots in with number 10, Toyota. One has to look to number 18 to find Samsung Electronics, Korea's top company (also a creative company).

Perhaps it is surprising the difference between the total number of large companies compared to the percentage of world population. Or perhaps it is surprising that most of China's top companies are banks and investment holdings companies. The United States and Korea have a wide variety of companies throughout key industries. Perhaps it is not so surprising.

Innovation and creativity will always be important skills, especially as many developed economies are moving away from manufacturing to creative-based economies. For some time, manufacturing has moved away from the United States to places like Taiwan, China, and Malaysia. Education and preparation is put into sharp relief when they are analyzed using an innovation metric. Forbes (2015) developed and published a measurement which they use to calculate a company's "innovation premium." They "[measure] how much the company's current valuation exceeds the value implicit in its current business." If markets are operating relatively efficiently (questionable in China), there is an excess of investment in companies, beyond what their current operating level is, based on investors' confidence in the company to produce future products (Dyer & Gregersen, 2015). Therefore, investors are very likely to put a larger percentage of investment money into a company like Tesla (#1 most innovative company) than a competitor like Ford. The same can be said of online companies like Amazon.com (#8), Baidu (#11), and Netflix (#27) compared to their brick-and-mortar competitors (Forbes, 2015).

Education and the Economy • **63**

METHODS

Positionality

As researchers, it is easy to see the influence of education in our own families. We've been friends since we started our master's degree a few years ago, but we might not have arrived if it weren't for the commitment to education in our families.

Taylor

Eighty years ago, my American co-author's great grandparents were lucky to have a primary or secondary education. Only one person in my family had a college education before the Depression; the others owned or worked in a dry-goods store. My great grandmother got her first job working in a Rosie-the-Riveter stamping plant in the late 1930s to support the war effort. But gradually, my grandparents' generation started to see a growing emphasis on national education; in fact, my maternal grandfather became the first person in my family to go to college; he took his degree and secured a good job as an automotive engineer for General Motors until he retired 45 years later. My paternal grandfather (whose own father had a college degree) received a medical degree with the Navy during the Korean War. Today it is significant, but perhaps not surprising, that all of my parents and stepparents, and all of my aunts and uncles have college degrees or higher. All of my cousins and siblings are currently attending college. As I told Michelle while working on this project, it is clear that the education they received adequately prepared for the jobs they wanted and the environment they lived in. And clearly, the success they had from investing in education has continued through the generations of which I am the fortunate beneficiary.

Michelle

I grew up and was educated outside of the United States, so my experience is a direct representation of global development. Travel is easier and more accessible than ever. And communication is easier and faster than ever. My father is American and my mother is Singaporean Chinese and they met in Taiwan. I grew up in China and was educated at international schools until I came to America for college. My parents still live in Asia. My American grandparents started but did not complete college. They survived by selling potato sacks during the Depression. But my aunt and uncles are all college educated now. On my mother's side, my grandfather had an elementary education but my grandmother did not go to school at all. She taught herself to read a little and was only able to write her name. My mother is the youngest of six siblings, and with her uneducated mother's support, was the first in her family to go to college. Both of my parents are educators now. My mother was educated in a traditional Chinese fashion and she disliked the rote memorization approach to learning. When she returned to the workforce after having giving birth to my brother, she went back to school to earn her Master's degree and now loves teaching. Without the progress made in global travel and opportunities to live and work internationally, my parents would never have met. My brothers and I, along with Taylor and his brothers are evidence of the value and influence of education throughout the generations. Our families have provided us with access to education and opportunity, and they have modelled success and intellectual fulfillment.

We both agree that an education from the 1920s would not be suitable for someone in the job market today. Education has changed, and the economy is more specialized. Jobs exist now that no one in the 1920s, 1930s, 1940s, 1950s, 1960s, 1970s, 1980s, 1990s, or even the 2000s could have ever imagined. How do we educate for those types of jobs? How do we educate for an unknown future? We would suggest that looking around the world might be a good place to start.

As I've gotten to know my co-author over the years, it has come to my attention how interconnected the world is. We have both benefited from a commitment to education, but we have to consider whether we believe the United States is still successful in education or not. As students and educators, we have a vested interest in making sure we're pointed in the right direction. We took notice, because there is growing concern surrounding the United States' poor educational performance when measured globally. Most metrics are focused on math, science, and literacy scores and they often do not favor the United States. In all three categories, we fall significantly below other developed countries like the United Kingdom, Germany, Australia, Canada, Japan, Korea, Singapore, and most Chinese regions including the mainland and Hong Kong (NCES, 2015b). As education students with a shared interest in assessment it strikes us as odd that each of these categories are measured with one tool: standardized test scores. Despite our scores, the United States remains a world leader in almost every industry and continues to shape global economics. We don't think that happens without success in the classroom—but it begs the question of how we should define success in the future.

So, after our most recent trip to China and Korea, we were left with questions. We were trying our best to reconcile what we had heard about China and Korea through newscasts, research, and pop culture with what we saw and heard on the ground. Our interviews and observations in addition to further research and public data helped us formulate open-ended discussions about the relationship between education, the economy, and the three countries we studied.

We were fortunate to have been able to travel to China in 2016 with a group of researchers, in-service teachers, and graduate students. The similarities in content areas among the participants made for interesting observations and discussions in our downtime, but we were both grateful that each type of participant on the trip brought a different lens to our experiences. The in-service teachers were looking at classroom management and lesson design. The researchers were looking at school structure and administration. And the grad students were looking at methodology. But we were particularly grateful that both of us had prior experience in Chinese schools (as a student and as a teacher). This gave us a very useful lens for looking at the bigger picture of educational outcomes.

Because this was not a formal study, our data collection was based on: professional in-service teacher experience; classroom observations in the United States, Korea, and China;and quantified research about educational outcomes on the economy. We were very fortunate to have so much time in foreign classrooms, because our observations really helped shape our focus within this research segment. Additionally, we had access to many informed persons in the education profession ranging from our own faculty leaders, to professors in China, and teachers of all grade-levels in China and Korea. While these interviews were largely left out of our final product, they helped shape our early thinking towards a practical and actionable research question.

DISCUSSION

Assessing China is an exercise in juggling massive, mind-boggling numbers. It is hard to find reliable data. It is hard to find historical data. And without a native grasp of the language, research is always second hand, so we ended up with more questions than conclusions. The biggest question we are left with is, "What did we expect?" Previous experience in China has always created a strange separation between the fear and caution of China portrayed in the news and the reality on the ground. Walking through slums in Beijing, Shanghai, Xi'an, Qingdao, and China's other leading cities—let alone the rural areas and over half of China's population—is a reminder that prosperity is not shared and most people are working hard to survive. Our guide in Xi'an confessed that the future looks bleak for most people; the Chinese dream involves going to college and getting a good government job, but without admission to college there is very little to look forward to. She has never felt the optimism for opportunity that most Americans believe exist; upward mobility is not achieved through hard work. She and others we talked to always chuckled when we told them about how the American media portray China as a powerhouse. They don't feel as powerful as China apparently is.

That said, how influential did we expect China to be? Racking our brain before departing from San Francisco we couldn't come up with a single major Chinese creative company. We thought of Baidu and Alibaba, and we thought of ICBC banks which we saw frequently in the mainland. But we could not come up with a creative company other than Roewe Motors, which had recently been belittled as a sub-par car company on popular motoring TV shows. For such a large country, and *smart* country, where are all the creative people? Where are all the products?

We were left with two conclusions, both highly theoretical and worthy of debate. First, standardized testing does not promote creativity—admittedly not a groundbreaking conclusion. It is often debated in the United States as well. China, due to the sheer volume of students, must rely on a more pragmatic sorting system than the United States or Korea. Companies and colleges need to find highly qualified students and there might be tens of thousands of people applying for the same position. Therefore, a rigid hierarchy of rankings is helpful from an efficiency standpoint. The original Gao Kao was intended to find the brightest students and give them an opportunity to serve their government, and looking back at Chinese history it was successful. The modern Gao Kao is stressful and successful students tend to be the ones with money to pay for specialized tutoring—perhaps this system is not as successful as it once was.

So, what did we expect to see in the Chinese schools? Well frankly, we did not expect to see imminent educational changes in China, but the fault is our own because China has shown an incredible capacity to adapt and make sweeping social changes on a scale most countries will never reach. What we observed is a system that is frustrated with standardized testing. We saw a system that has raised its college acceptance rates from 10%–15% 30 years ago to closer to 70% now, at least according to a professor at Jiaotong University. We saw preschools and preparatory schools that emphasized liberal arts education. We saw language schools with collaborative activities rather than lectures. We heard people say that they were proud to be Chinese, proud to be living in China, and were hopeful for the future. We saw an intentional effort to teach these perspectives. We saw a concerted effort to decentralize education and allow schools and teachers to make better assessments. We saw college students who were there not because their Gao Kao scores were high, but because their teachers saw an aptitude for something other than math and science and thought they deserved to continue their education. We saw more and more emphasis on providing education in the rural education or helping farmers move to the cities where services are more accessible. We saw China ready to leap forward again. That is not what we expected.

Turning our gaze on the United States, I was proud that all the best companies I could think of are American. Americans have the coolest gadgets, a comfortable way of life, opportunity, and freedom. There can't be anything wrong with the American system, right? Perhaps not, unless it changes in the wrong direction. Isn't it significant that China, in an attempt to become more creative, is moving away from standardized testing? Isn't it significant that we saw collaboration and creativity in Korea rather than standardized testing? Isn't it significant that assessments are getting further and further away from the teachers in American classrooms? What do we expect will happen when assessment is outsourced from the classroom and all the curriculum decisions are made outside the community, outside the district, outside the state?

IMPLICATIONS

Our second conclusion is more debatable and harder to portray. Why are the United States and Korea—and frankly a lot of other nations—more creative than China? Is it the American education system? Kids in the United States go to school longer, so maybe they *are* better prepared. Or is it something more abstract? Risking self-aggrandizement and eye-rolling patriotism, the United States has a key ingredient China does not: freedom. Freedom to create, freedom to compete, freedom to work in your own interest to profit. The United States and Korea have laws protecting companies and intellectual property, which is paramount in a competitive global economy (Lazonick, 2003; Sakhapov & Absalyamova, 2013). It gives companies an incentive to create something that solves a problem and then profit from their hard work. China has state sponsored companies to backwards-engineer products and produce them in large quantities. They don't profit from their efforts. Even though Korea is a small country, their two main industries are highly competitive which has pushed them to excel. Would Samsung be as competitive without LG? Would Hyundai be as competitive without Daewoo? Would Microsoft be what it is without Steve Jobs and Apple pushing them? Would Google be what it is without Yahoo? We submit to you, no!

Competition and the freedom to profit drives the economy. China has changed a lot and will continue to evolve, but perhaps not as far as it would if it had more competition and less censorship and control. Should China become a free market, capitalist democracy? No. But fewer restrictions would promote the competition and innovation that its students are currently being prepared for. What do we expect from China in the future? Who knows. What do we expect from education in the United States? Who knows; we can only seek to move forward and prepare our students for a creative world. Does that involve competing with other nations over algebra scores on the SAT, or does it mean encouraging students to collaborate and learn beyond the scope of the test they have to take? Does it mean encouraging teachers to continue seeking professional development in order to be masters of their curriculum and enthusiastic practitioners of up-to-date methodology? Does it mean school systems and state legislatures giving their highly qualified teachers the flexibility to use alternative assessments and authentic, holistic data to design lessons? Yes, it means all of these things! Moving backwards is not an option for education!

REFERENCES

Allegretto, S., & Mishel, L. (2016). *The teacher pay gap is wider than ever.* Retrieved from http://www.epi.org/publication/the-teacher-pay-gap-is-wider-than-ever-teachers-pay-continues-to-fall-further-behind-pay-of-comparable-workers/

Alphabet Inc. (2017). *Our history in depth.* Retrieved from https://about.google/intl/en_us/our-story/

American Press Institute. (2015). *How millennials get news: Inside the habits of America's first digital generation.* Retrieved from https://www.americanpressinstitute.org/publications/reports/survey-research/millennials-news/

Benhabib, J., & Spiegel, M. M. (1994). The role of human capital in economic development: Evidence from aggregate cross-country data. *Journal of Monetary Economics 34*(2), 143–174.

Brandt, R. L. (2011). Birth of a salesman. *The Wall Street Journal.* Retrieved from https://www.wsj.com/articles/SB10001424052970203914304576627102996831200

China Education Center Ltd. (2016). *Primary and secondary education.* Retrieved from http://www.chinaeducenter.com/en/cedu/psedu.php

Chinese Ministry of Education. (2015). 教育部 国家统计局 财政部关于2014年全国教育经费执行情况统计公告 [Implementation of the 2014 national education finance statistical bulletin]. Retrieved from http://www.moe.gov.cn/srcsite/A05/s3040/201510/t20151013_213129.html

CIA World Factbook (2017). *East and Southeast Asia: China.* Retrieved from https://www.cia.gov/library/publications/the-world-factbook/geos/ch.html

Desilver, D. (2015). U.S. students improving—slowly—in math and science, but still lagging internationally. *Pew Research Center.* Retrieved from https://www.pewresearch.org/fact-tank/2017/02/15/u-s-students-internationally-math-science/

Dyer, J., & Gregerson, H. (2015). How we rank the world's most innovative companies 2015. *Forbes.* Retrieved from http://www.forbes.com/sites/innovatorsdna/2015/08/19/how-we-rank-the-worlds-most-innovative-companies-2015/#55b83ec34524

Ellis, R. (1991, April). The interaction hypothesis: A critical evaluation. *Eric Education.* Paper presented at Regional Language Center Seminar. Singapore.

Fees, B. S., Hoover, L., & Zheng, F. (2014). Chinese kindergarten teachers' perceived changes in their teaching philosophies and practices: A case study in a university-affiliated program. *International Journal of Early Childhood, 46*(2), 231–252.

Forbes. (2015). *The world's most innovative companies* [2015 Ranking]. Retrieved from https://www.forbes.com/innovative-companies/#75fbd7271d65

Forbes. (2016). *The world's biggest public companies* [2016 Ranking]. Retrieved from http://www.forbes.com/global2000/list/#tab:overall

Godlewski, N. (2016). Teens are getting almost all of their news from Snapchat and Twitter these days. *Business Insider.* Retrieved from http://www.business insider.com/how-do-teens-get-news-2016-6

Guglielmo, C. (2012). A Steve Jobs moment that mattered: Macworld, August 1997. *Forbes Tech.* Retrieved from http://www.forbes.com/sites/connieguglielmo/2012/10/07/a-steve-jobs-moment-that-mattered-macworld-august-1997/#1ff9ab033ff5

Hanushek, E. A., & Woessmann, A. L. (2010). Education and Economic Growth. In D. J. Brewer & P. J. McEwan (Eds.), *International Encyclopedia of Education* (2nd ed., pp. 245–252). Oxford, England: Pergamon.

Lazonick, W. (2003). The theory of the market economy and the social foundations of innovative enterprise. *Economic and Industrial Democracy, 24*(1), 9–44.

Lee, L. C. (1992). Day care in the People's Republic of China. In M. E. Lamb, K. J. Sternberg, C.-P. Hwang, & A. G. Broberg (Eds.), *Child care in context: Cross-cultural perspectives,* (pp. 355–392). Hillsdale, NJ: Erlbaum.

Long, M. (1985). Input and Second Language Acquisition Theory. In S. M. Gass & C. G. Madden (Eds.), *Input in second language acquisition* (pp. 377–393). Rowley, MA: Newbury House.

Long, M. (1996). The role of the linguistic environment in second language acquisition. In W. C. Ritchie & T. K. Bhatia (Eds.), *Handbook of second language acquisition* (pp. 413–468.). San Diego, CA: Academic Press.

Lucas, R. E. (1988). On the mechanics of economic development. *Journal of Monetary Economics 22,* 3–42.

Mankiw, N. G., Romer, D., & Weil, D. (1992). A contribution to the empirics of economic growth. *Quarterly Journal of Economics 107*(2), 407–437

Matthews, D. (2012). The Clinton economy, in charts. *The Washington Post.* Retrieved from https://www.washingtonpost.com/news/wonk/wp/2012/09/05/the-clinton-economy-in-charts/

National Center for Education Statistics. (2015a). *Digest of education statistics.* [Unemployment rates of persons 16 to 64 years old, by age group and highest level of educational attainment: Selected years, 1975 through 2015]. Retrieved from http://nces.ed.gov/programs/digest/d15/tables/dt15_501.80.asp

National Center for Education Statistics. (2015b). *Program for international student assessment (2015 data set).* Retrieved from https://nces.ed.gov/surveys/pisa/pisa2015/index.asp

National Center for Education Statistics. (2016). *Mathematics performance* (2015 data set). Retrieved from https://nces.ed.gov/programs/coe/indicator_cnc.asp

National Education Association. (2015). *Research spotlight on cooperative learning.* Retrieved from http://www.nea.org/tools/16870.htm

Nelson, R. R., & Phelps, E. (1966). Investment in humans, technology diffusion and economic growth. *American Economic Review 56*(2), 69–75.

Obama, B. H. (2010). *Remarks on higher education and the economy.* Austin: University of Texas. Retrieved from https://www.whitehouse.gov/the-press-office/2010/08/09/remarks-president-higher-education-and-economy-university-texas-austin

Pew Research Center (2004). *Cable and Internet loom large in fragmented political news universe: Perceptions of partisan bias seen as growing, especially by democrats.* Retreived from https://www.people-press.org/2004/01/11/cable-and-internet-loom-large-in-fragmented-political-news-universe

Preus, B. (2007). Educational trends in China and the United States: Proverbial pendulum or potential to balance. *Phi Delta Kappan, 89*(2), 115–118.

Pultorak, E. G., & Markle, G. C. (2008). Snapshots of Chinese classrooms illustrate disparities: A visit to China highlights the poverty, isolation, and diversity that challenge one of the world's largest educational systems. *Phi Delta Kappan, 90*(1), 45–49.

Ravitch, D. (2010). *The death and life of the great american school system: How testing and choice are undermining education* (3rd ed.). New York, NY: Basic Books.

Romer, P. (1990). Endogenous technological change. *Journal of Political Economy 99*(5, pt. II), S71–S102.

Sakhapov, R. L., & Absalyamova, S. G. (2013). Integration of universities and businesses as the condition of formation of the innovative economy. 16th International Conference on *Interactive Collaborative Learning* (pp. 189–191). Kazan National Research Technological University, Kazan, Russian Federation.

Sorkin, A. (2012). The newsroom script episode 1. *Goodreads.* Retrieved from https://www.goodreads.com/work/quotes/23633463-the-newsroom-script-episode-1

The World Bank. (2015a). Compulsory education, duration (years). Retrieved from http://data.worldbank.org/indicator/SE.COM.DURS?locations=CN-US-KR

The World Bank. (2015b). GINI index (World Bank Estimate). Retrieved from http://data.worldbank.org/indicator/SI.POV.GINI?locations=CN-US-KR

The World Bank. (2015c). Labor Force, total. Retrieved from http://data.worldbank.org/indicator/SL.TLF.TOTL.IN?locations=CN-US-KR

The World Bank. (2015d). Population, total. Retrieved from http://data.worldbank.org/indicator/SP.POP.TOTL?locations=CN-US

The World Bank. (2016e). Unemployment, total (% of total labor force; modeled ILO estimate). Retrieved from http://data.worldbank.org/indicator/SL.UEM.TOTL.ZS?locations=CN-US-KR

Trump, D. J. (2016, June). *Declaring American economic independence.* Speech delivered in Monessen, PA. Full text available at https://www.politico.com/story/2016/06/full-transcript-trump-job-plan-speech-224891

Yang, D. (2006). Pursuing harmony and fairness in education. *Chinese Education & Society, 39*(6), 3–44.

Zeng, X. (2008). A design of an appropriate early childhood education funding system in China. *Chinese Education & Society. 41*(2), 8–19.

PART II
TEACHING AND LEARNING

CHAPTER 5

COMPARATIVE ANALYSIS OF INSTRUCTIONAL TEXTS AND THE CROSS-CULTURAL DIALOGUE BETWEEN TEACHERS

Scenes From a Chinese and an American Classroom

Laurie Dymes

Selected instructional texts are utilized differently in educational settings based on the curriculum and institutional goals. For some, this may incorporate learning processes, while for others, there may be a cultural component more heavily embedded within the learning objectives. This chapter examines two textbooks, *Standard Textbook for Compulsory Education* (Institute of Curriculum Development, 2015) and *Realms of Gold* (Marshall & Hirsch, 2000). The goal was to find the similarities and differences in the practices of the Chinese and American classrooms in which textbooks are

Educational Practices in China, Korea, and the United States, pages 73–87
Copyright © 2019 by Information Age Publishing
All rights of reproduction in any form reserved.

used. Based on the interpretations of the two textbooks, I was interested in determining what cultural traits could be extracted from the selected texts to provide insight into the values of the two cultures. Furthermore, this chapter explores the benefits to the field of education to initiate network opportunities that allow educators from across oceans to collaborate and learn from one another.

LITERATURE REVIEW

The Role of School as a Social Institution

Schools serve many intellectual and social functions. As a social institution, schools are expected to teach particular knowledge and skills necessary for individual participation in the larger society. Throughout history, the goals of schools "are bound to universalistic intellectual or social functions associated with the dominant society" (Barnhardt, 1981, p. 1). These principles are often reflected in the cultural traditions of the people.

Based on current educational philosophies, the goals of the school expand to include learning objectives such as knowledge, attitudes, and skills that are appropriate for the cultural context in which they serve. All children around the globe have similar learning needs, and it is the responsibility of the schools to help children meet those needs in a way that makes learning personal and socially significant (Tyler, 1949, p. 54).

In a 21st century world, there continues to be a much larger interface for students to experience cultures in a global context, making the transmission of worldviews, principles, customs, and educational practices more easily accessible. This accessibility helps to continuously redefine the manner in which one views intercultural and cross-cultural experiences. According to Bai, Eppert, Scott, Tait, and Nguyen (2015), intercultural refers to "an in-between relationship open to cultural identity transformation" (p. 636). This relationship is based on mutual acceptance and reciprocity between the two cultures. Cross-cultural refers more to "cultures moving across geographies and being compared and contrasted for their differences and commonality" (Bai et al., 2015, p. 636). Both cultural approaches are applicable for the scope of this chapter.

It is the continued role and responsibility of all educators to examine the cultural exchanges accessible to students. Through the planning of appropriate instructional materials, worldviews and values can be represented to introduce mutually healthy cultural relationships. These implicit teachable moments extend beyond the factual knowledge and move in to include exploration of humanity. To further support classroom efforts, philosophers of education, as cultural ambassadors, would benefit from creating intercultural networks with others in similar positions. Bai et al. (2015) suggests that relationships such as these allow students to challenge the underpinnings of beliefs and values by examining past and present cultural exchanges. With newfound knowledge and expertise, philosophers of education provide insight and possibilities to help guide curriculum development that would be most meaningful to global education and students alike.

Curriculum Philosophies

It is expected that the philosophers of education worldwide act as leaders, modifying practices to eliminate damaging pedagogies and practices that are monocentric and moving towards an encompassing educational philosophy of diverse learning goals. This philosophy creates a continued exploration of knowledge by examining cross-cultural and intercultural practices and integrating new practices into existing curriculum.

According to Barnhardt (1981), curriculum refers to selection and organization of subject matter to fit the learning needs of students. Furthermore, curriculum development is complex with much consideration needed for the philosophy and rationale that support it: the development of thinking frameworks, alignment of curriculum and assessment models, assurance that the needs of all students are met, and selection of instruction materials to support each level of this process ("K–12 Standards, Curriculum and Instruction," 2018).

Educators, paving the path, find it essential that the curriculum honors and promotes diverse histories, cultures, and traditions (Bai et al., 2015; Panikkar, 1992). A current examination of the philosophy of education in North America might cast one of insularity and singularity, as America tends to focus on the individual. The United States, although overseen by the Department of Education, has variances within its system because the responsibilities and authority of education are placed at the regional and local level (Stephens, Warren, & Harner, 2015). Together with the local systems, the United States Department of Education's mission is "to promote student achievement and preparation for global competitiveness by fostering educational excellence and ensuring equal access" (U.S. Department of Education, 2011). Eppert (2013) called this a separationist ethos, as it stresses differences in individuals and reveres the self before community. As discussed by Bai et al. (2015), this is characteristic of hegemonic cultures. Contrary, in Chinese culture, there is a heavy emphasis on the community embedded within the education philosophy instead. The Education Law of 1995 guides the educational practices in the People's Republic of China. The education system stands "for promoting among learners' patriotism, collectivism and socialism as well as ideals, ethics, discipline, legality, national defence, and ethnic unity" (International Bureau of Education, 2012, p. 2). The Ministry of Education promotes a singular systematic approach through a centralized education.

The education systems in China and the United States have similarities and differences. It is important to note that it is beyond the scope of this chapter to articulate all areas of comparison, but there are a few items that are helpful to provide context. For example, the sheer volume of students is noteworthy for both countries. The school-aged population (Ages 5–29) is 1.3 billion in China, while the United States has 106.2 million school-aged children. Of the students in the age range of 15–19, the Chinese participation rate in education is 34%, while the United States has a participation rate of 80% (Stephens et al., 2015). It is also beneficial to understand the educational levels and whether the level is compulsory in each country, as it aids the understanding of the competitiveness of postsecondary and tertiary levels.

China and the United States both offer non-compulsory "preprimary" level (preschool, prekindergarten, and/or nursery school) beginning at Age 3. Most of these are private institutions. Both countries offer "primary" (elementary or grade school) as compulsory for 6 years followed by "lower secondary" (middle school, junior high, common junior middle school) for 3 years. The "upper secondary" (high school, senior high school, common senior middle school [gaozhong]; secondary vocational education [zhongzhuan]) varies across countries. In China, this is not a compulsory level. There are entrance examinations to enter this level of education and a required exit exam, "general ability test," that reflects nine subjects such as physics and biology, as well as an assessment in moral and political development. In the United States, the beginning years to this level are compulsory up to the age of 17. There are not generally entrance or exit examinations that are standardized, but students who plan on attending college take the Scholastic Aptitude Test (SAT) or American College Testing (ACT), determining a portion of their college entrance applications. Students from both countries have varying cultural capital in accessing and navigating the system in preparation for higher education. Many rely on the professionals and their professional judgments within the system for guidance.

Educational philosophy governs the belief system and structure for which questions, goals, and objectives are aligned. Everything that is created on behalf of that system afterwards should be in direct alignment with the end result. Within school structures, there are cultural principles ingrained into said philosophies that support and sustain the practices and belief structure of the community. Tyler (1949) outlines four fundamental questions, which he felt should be considered when developing any curriculum and plan of instruction that are still worthy of consideration today: (a) "What educational purposes should the school seek to attain?"; (b) "What educational experiences can be provided that are likely to attain these purposes?"; (c) "How can these educational experiences be effectively organized?"; and (d) "How can we determine whether these purposes are being attained?" Specifically, the focus of this chapter is to examine the second fundamental question posed by Tyler (1949).

CONTEXT OF THIS STUDY

As part of a study abroad experience through my university, we visited Xi'an, China and Seoul, South Korea for just over two weeks. The purpose of the study abroad program was to introduce the participants to the "educational policies and practices through a comparison with American educational system" (syllabus, personal communication, 2016). While visiting, we had the opportunity to visit many educational institutions, ranging from kindergarten, elementary, middle, high, and college classes. Throughout our visit, there were planned excursions to immerse us in the culture and history of the two large cities, which helped us to better understand the context of the education systems. As a language arts teacher, I was fascinated by the historical literacy practices that spanned centuries. I knew early on in the visit that I wanted to learn more about how literacy practices were impacted by cultural beliefs and how these cultural beliefs were embedded into the canons of the school and the system at large.

Instructional Texts to Support Philosophies

My research question began with a small textbook that was being used in a seventh-grade classroom in Xi'an, China. During the observation of a middle school Chinese-language classroom, the students were feverously combing over a passage. It was a similar method my students back in the states use as they analyze text. They seek to understand the implicit meaning and derive a connection to their own experiences. The comparable experience of this classroom to that of my own English language arts classroom was not lost on me. Immediately, I was interested in the stories that were deemed worthy and selected by the Ministry of Education to create this anthology that is used to instruct most Chinese seventh-graders in the whole of the Shaanxi Province. Also, I sought to determine what part of Chinese culture was implied through the use of selected texts. Comparatively, what did this imply about the stories selected by the textbook companies that I use with my middle grade students in the states? Finally, how do these instructional texts align with the schools' goals?

Chinese Curriculum

A native Chinese teacher, April (all names are pseudonyms), who has taught middle grades for 10 years at Xi'an Middle School No. 1 (all school names are pseudonyms), had recognized my interest in the school's textbook. After lunch, we had an informal conversation. April had informed me that all Grade 7 students in the Shaanxi Province use the same textbook for their second semester. In fact, upon further conversation with April, the textbook is being used across the whole of China. It is a new textbook; every few years, a new one is published with some changes to the text selections. We further discussed Chinese educational practices and how there is much to offer and learn from the exchange between Chinese and American educators. It was during this conversation that April had shared with me the tenets of Chinese culture that are embedded into the curriculum throughout the students' experience from preschool to graduation. Since my visit to her school, we have continued our discussion through a social media platform that has allowed us to maintain our collegiality and friendship.

These same tenets were then reaffirmed through a speech by a principal from Xi'an Preschool No. 1. The principal detailed that these equivalent principles are used within all content areas with his own students: (a) Chinese etiquette, (b) festivals and holidays, (c) aesthetics (e.g., define beauty), (d) Chinese children's development (child's responsibility to the community), (e) Chinese festivals, (f) styles and trends (historical and contemporary), (g) patriotism/love of culture and love of family, (h) Chinese tea, (i) calligraphy, and (j) the Chinese dragon, of which all Chinese believe they are the descendants. The ten aspects are introduced as spiral curriculum to students at a young age. It is considered a spiral curriculum because the children are exposed, year after year, in increasing complexity until at the highest level of education they can acquire the deepest understanding of each tenet (Harden & Stamper, 1999). In addition, it is also important to note that, according to the two aforementioned educators, the Chinese also include "the five aspects of Ren (people)" into the curriculum: discipline, positive attitude, pursue truths, be kind (to others, plants, and animals), and an appreciation of beauty.

American Curriculum

Prior to the advent of science and the Industrial Revolution, the body of knowledge that was considered academically noteworthy was small, so there were little competing academic philosophies about selecting the most significant pieces from America's cultural heritage to showcase in schools. By the late 1800s a desire for educational standardization had been felt in

Comparative Analysis of Instructional Texts and the Cross-Cultural Dialogue ▪ **79**

the United States. The Committee of Ten was a group of educators, who pushed for a standardization of American curriculum, especially at the high school level. The general format of eight elementary grades followed by 4 more years of more rigorous instruction comes from the model of The Committee of Ten. The recommendation report outlined important knowledge within each subject area to guide curricular agendas (Tyack & Tobin, 1994). Today, the United States is culturally and ethnically diverse and the driving forces behind most agendas spin around the concept of multiculturalism, especially in the education system.

The canons currently in use in secondary education are typically selected by interest groups or critics who judge texts based on their own agendas or critical perspectives. At the middle school level, there are three strong guiding forces that create canons: Newbery Medal Winners, Printz Award winners, and the textbook and testing companies. The Newbery Medal books tend to favor historical fiction, featuring White and abled protagonists. Some of the common themes that have emerged from Printz Award titles center around issues that are deemed relevant to young adults such as "teenage angst leading to self-actualization," relationships, and diversity that reflects the vast readership (Cart, 2010). The textbook and testing companies also have their own agendas. Thein and Beach (2013) state these entities, "hold significant sway in shaping context and instruction to make context choices for financial reasons and based on teacher familiarity with certain texts" (p. 11).

With a diverse student population, the American education system steers away from a set of ingrained principles in which the content is taught. Rather, much of the instructional texts that are employed in the school systems incorporate learning processes that emphasize the metacognition skills, rather than the cultural principles: such as "analysis, inference, classification, synthesis, integration, and evaluation" (Barnhardt, 1981, p. 9). An importance of themes is placed on literary works in the higher elementary to secondary grades, but this is used as a means of analysis, and not necessarily a tie to cultural components. Still, while cultural literacy is heavily engrained into the text selections of the Chinese anthology, it was of interest to identify what, if any, cultural themes could be excavated from the selected text for similar aged students in the United States.

Many regions and local administrations utilize their autonomy in textbook selections. Truly, any textbook could have been used for a comparison as the Western sample, as there is not one that is mandated for all pupils. For the purpose of this chapter, *Realms of Gold, Volume 2* (Marshall & Hirsch, 2000) was selected because it has a reputation of an anthology that has collected poems, stories, essays, speeches, and autobiographical excerpts, including "classic works" of each genre. Furthermore, its anthological format and challenging text permitted a comparable side-by-side evaluation of the two textbooks.

80 ▪ L. DYMES

METHOD

The Chinese middle school in which the textbook is used was founded in 1922 as a private school and became a public school in 1950. There are 77 teachers and 14 staff members at the site. In comparison, the American middle school in which its textbook is used is a charter school that was established in 1998. It has two campuses that serve a rural North Carolina community in K–12 education. There are 126 teachers and 23 staff members, whose responsibilities range from instructional support to administrative assistant. The instructional texts are used in Shaanxi Province, China and a rural school system in North Carolina, United States. First, the educational objectives become the criteria by which materials are selected. Then, these objectives become the guide to which all program elements are based. If we are to study an educational program systematically and intelligently, we must first be aware of the cultural objectives embedded within the social structures that have guided the objectives (Tyler, 1949). Each selection of the two textbooks were read and analyzed, looking for literary themes in which to code and relate.

To determine if the cultural tenets prevalent in the Chinese education system were embedded in the adopted anthology, I had the opportunity to sit with a professor from the University of North Carolina, Charlotte. This professor is a native Chinese speaker and had agreed to go through the anthology with me at great length. The professor had understood that my research interests were to identify connections to the selected texts and the Chinese cultural values that I had learned about from our time in China. After numbering each selection (1 through 30) from the anthology for identification purposes, the professor aided me translating the titles and content of each of the selections from the textbook. Some of the titles that I was familiar with such as *Ugly Duckling* (3) and *Real Hero* (24) left little to be analyzed, but texts that originated in Asia such as *The Last Lesson* (7) and the tale about mimicking sounds in nature/storytelling (20) required supplemental reading for interpretation. Once the premise of each selection was identified and validated by the professor, the above ten tenets were cross-referenced to these ideas, looking for selections that aligned with the ten cultural principles. Upon examination, each fiction, nonfiction, and poetry piece contained in the anthology could be identifiable as one of the ten tenets shared by the Chinese teacher and principal; however, three of the tenets were not visible in the selections at all. Instead, these three tenets were more applicable to real-world experiences (see Table 5.1). Interestingly, throughout many of our school visits, these cultural aspects were highly visible through fine arts, and the principles were extracted from the textbook for analysis.

Comparative Analysis of Instructional Texts and the Cross-Cultural Dialogue ▪ **81**

TABLE 5.1 Emerging Chinese Tenets Within Text

Ten Chinese Curriculum Tenets	Chapters Aligning With Principles[a]
Chinese etiquette and character	*Ren* (11)—Hero, who helped developed nuclear weapons
	Biography of Chinese author with strong character traits (12)
	Great Tragedy (renamed by editor) "What is a success/what is a failure?" (21)
	In the Middle of the Desert (French) "How to account after rescue measures fail" (22)
	Reaching top of Himalaya Mountain—Teamwork and persistence (23)
	Cat—three emotional experiences (happy, sad, angry) (26)
	Tibetan Goat—reverence (27)
	Tiger—Personification (28)
	Horse—Brave, handsome, free (29)
	Wolf—Cunning (30)
Festivals and Holidays	Essay narrative (16)
	Cultural drums (17)
	Indian Dance—(beauty) (19)
Aesthetics	*Ugly Duckling* (3) "taste (beauty)/value"
	Beethoven "taste (beauty)/appreciation" (13)
	Bamboo—nonfiction/description (18)
Chinese children development	"Children, go outside of the classroom and learn beauty from the world" (1)
	"Don't only teach classic knowledge, learn from nature, too" (1)
	Understanding parental expectations (2)
	"You inherit talents but those are not important to determine success. Hard work = success" (5)
Styles and trends	Mimicking sounds in nature/storytelling (20)
Patriotism/ love of culture and love of family	*The Last Lesson* (7)
	Japanese Invasion WWII (9)
	Patriotism (10)
	"Real Hero" Ronald Reagan's speech after Challenger explosion (24)

Note: Data for emerging tenets from Translations provided by Dr. Chuang Wang, University of North Carolina, Charlotte (2016) and Standard textbook for compulsory education: Chinese (Seventh Grade—B)] (2015). Beijing, China: People's Education Press.

[a] The selection number beside each title indicates the passage number as it corresponds to the anthology's Table of Contents.

Similarly, I read through the texts that were supplied in *Realms of Gold* (Marshall & Hirsch, 2000) and applied a thematic analysis to each. I used the same strategy that I teach middle school students when identifying theme. First, I summarized the plot, using one cogent sentence, and identified the subject of the work. Then I looked for an insight that was implied about the subject. This is usually centered around the protagonist and what the intended lesson was about the subject. The theme can usually be derived by understanding what the protagonist was meant to learn and how it was learned. After I completed this thematic analysis for each text, I began to seek common themes within the anthology to better understand why these particular texts may have been chosen as a canon for middle school students.

RESULTS

As shown in Table 5.1, the tenets were visible throughout the anthology. The exceptions, Chinese tea, calligraphy, and Chinese dragons, were not evident in the text; however, after consulting with a university professor, who is well versed in Chinese text, it was determined that there are a variety of texts available addressing such topics that may have been selected to use in other volumes, especially text incorporating Chinese tea.

The top ten most frequent emerging themes are shown in Table 5.2. These themes were extracted using a thematic analysis as described above.

DISCUSSIONS

Textbook Analysis

Literature can be seen as a means of personal exploration of belief systems, thought processes, and intellectual awakening. Adolescent readers are "preoccupied with seeking equilibrium in their perceptions of who they are and what they are becoming" (Broughton, 2002, p. 5) and what better way than to expose students to the written works of people from around the world. Middle school students are on the cusp of an age where what they learn empowers their development (DaLie, 2001). In a cultural context, opportunities to explore various literature permits the individual to have experiences that are beyond their immediate ability of participation whether that is physically or mentally. Most literacy educators recognize and appreciate the dynamic effect literature can play in students' lives. The experiences permitted through literature extend beyond the boundaries of a middle school student's reality, and it gives the individual a safe place in which to participate throughout the pages. In this sense, another purpose of literature is to develop and nurture reading interest and habits.

These points are especially poignant as we examine the relatedness between the instructional texts used in Eastern and Western literacy teaching for middle grades. Through the analysis of the two textbook anthologies,

Comparative Analysis of Instructional Texts and the Cross-Cultural Dialogue ▪ **83**

TABLE 5.2 Frequent Emerging Themes from Middle School Textbook

Themes	Corresponding Analysis with selection numbers
Character Development	Ability to remain optimistic despite despair (6b)
	Helen Keller (internal strength) (40)
	Desire for acceptance (27)
	Desire for affection (28)
	Desire for humanity (29)
Greed	The speaker knows he should not indulge in the taste but cannot resist (11b)
	Consequences of being blinded by selfishness (24)
Growing Up	Orphaned—understanding gap between reality and ideals (1)
	"Days gone by"—sung around the world (2)
	Separation from parents for own identity (30)
	Self-awareness (31)
Life and Death	Completely at ease about death (3)
	Opposite ends of spectrum—love vs. hate (5)
	The reality of death and how one deals with the aftermath (10)
	Death as a consequence of war (17)
	It will not be in vain (23)
Love	The speaker does not give up on love even after death (8)
	Love is shown through selfless acts (26)
Multiculturalism	*The Negro Speaks of Rivers*—Global perspective (6a)
	Limitations of American Dream (6c)
Patriotism	Translation: *It is sweet and proper to die for one's country* (7)
	Six different perspectives (33, 34, 35, 36, 37, 38)
Perseverance	A neglected, once-useful wheelbarrow stands out in the rain (11a)
	Benjamin Franklin is at the forefront of the beginning of a new country (39)
Religion	A celebration of natural creation (16)
	God and forces controlling one's life (14)
Symbolism	Death of an elephant = death of the innocent (32)
	Jar = civilization (21)

Note: Data for emerging themes from thematic analysis. Text selections from Marshall & Hirsch (2000).

[a] The selection number beside each title indicates the passage number as it corresponds to the anthology's Table of Contents.

both textbooks included an array of regional and cross-cultural authors, who continue to bring salient points to the eyes of adolescents through their teachings. It was merely by an extension of a friendly hand and chance encounter that I was able to receive a copy of the middle grades textbooks

84 ▪ L. DYMES

to analyze. Furthermore, again by chance, that I found a comparable anthology that is used locally for this chapter's intent.

Learning From One Another

Educators fulfill an important role in and outside of the classroom as cultural workers. As Bai et al. (2015) explains:

> Throughout history, philosophers, also known in different cultures as wise elders, or sages, have been leaders of people. As leaders, their vocation was to identify weaknesses and sicknesses in the culture that were compromising mutual flourishing, and point to practices of thinking, perceiving, feeling, acting, and interacting that would promise better flourishing. In other words, philosophers have long been cultural workers. (p. 638)

"We can learn from each other"; these were the parting words from my new friend, April, who teaches in China. For some, it is a once-in-a-lifetime opportunity to find someone worlds apart, who is willing to be the counterpart in a cultural exchange in education. It suggests a promise that both individuals will find commonality in the goals of education to create successful cultural exchanges that better their own practice and experiences of their students. Drawing from the work of Armstrong (1993), Clark (1997), Dussell (2000), Hobson (2004), and Smith (2008), the occidental and oriental geographies have shared a cultural and intellectual exchange for centuries, and that the belief Western philosophy is directly derived from Greek influence has been disputed by scholars, who have shown the considerable influence between the East and West. Mall (2000) further emphasizes "that wisdom is no one's possession, and that cultures have always borrowed from and been influenced by one another" (p. 5). There is plenty that educators can learn from borrowing and influencing one another's practices cross-culturally. Opening an intercultural dialogue makes one's own cultural structure more transparent. This allows an individual to critically examine the components of the educational system more clearly, highlighting areas of strengths and prospective change. The dialogue carries a fresh perspective to a social structure that one may have accepted by default through years of exposure. Likewise, the exchange reciprocates the clarity. These exchanges are welcomed as found in the collaboration with my Chinese middle school peer teacher. Since my visit, we have maintained contact through social media, as we have celebrated one another's academic achievements and collaborated on various teaching practices from the East and West. Together, potential for curricular development and creative revisions in the education system are possible (Bai & Romanycia, 2013; King, 1999).

Additionally, the work of Paul Freire (1970) examines the roles of students and teachers in education. As teachers acquire and access this cross-cultural dialogue, they can see themselves as both the teacher and the student in this mutual relationship with other global educators. Freire also emphasized the necessity of dialogue in critical pedagogy. Bai and Romanycia (2013) described the essence of humanity in intercultural exchanges, as a recommitment to faith in humanity and restoration of hope. In summary, cross-cultural and intercultural approaches can be equally beneficial to Chinese and American literacy teachers with an open dialogue. The overall benefit of philosophy of education is that it has the potential of changing the perception of cultural learning objectives and methods beyond instructional texts.

CONCLUSION

"[The emphasis of school's goals] is inevitably bound to a specific cultural definition of appropriate knowledge and skills" for the individual to be a productive member of society (Barnhardt, 1981, p. 2). School, as a social institution, serves a function to developing citizenship. This can look vastly different depending on the cultural community or country, but it serves the same function to its society. "Broadly speaking, culture is composed of worldviews, values, habits and practices. Different cultures mean different sets of these contents. In other words, different cultures have different ways of conceptualizing, interpreting, configuring, and negotiating reality" (Bai et al., 2015, p. 638). I am proposing that the diverse texts within a given textbook anthology allow for school personnel to address and support the cultural heritage through educational goals, while simultaneously providing a platform to open intercultural dialogue between international educators about educational philosophy.

The *New World Encyclopedia* defines eclecticism (n.d.) as "a conceptual approach that does not hold rigidly to a single paradigm or set of assumptions, but instead draws upon multiple theories, styles, or ideas to gain complementary insights into a subject, or applies different theories in particular cases." This encompasses the sentiments of intercultural and cross-cultural practices to develop literacy skills world-wide and offers hope for those within the two educational systems to work together and learn from one another. It is through my study abroad experience, cultural exchange, new Chinese friends, and my analysis of middle grades texts between these two countries that my realization is how similar our two worlds are. While the Chinese anthology did indeed adhere to the ten tenets in Chinese cultural education, if I were to take a different approach to coding the Chinese text, it would not surprise me to find it could be done by the Western practices of literary themes.

Literature, no matter its language, has a common speech that is voiced to the hearts and minds of those it captures. A curriculum design that is built around processes to create objectives that students will potentially encounter in their everyday, global lives fosters a meaningful learning environment that enhances cultural attributes of the students. Purposeful text selection provides a platform for middle-grade students to explore rich topics of diversity. Students examine threads of culture by analyzing counter-narratives that differ from those they are accustomed (Ketter & Buter, 2004). Capturing the diversity of the world through texts provides a platform for the 21st century learner to combine those experiences to create a worldview that will contribute to the goal of cultural eclecticism and discovering how we can all learn from one another.

REFERENCES

Armstrong, K. (1993). *A history of God: The 4000-year quest of Judaism Christianity, and Islam.* New York, NY: Gramercy.

Bai, H., & Romanycia, S. (2013). Learning from hermit crabs, mycelia and banyan: Education, ethics and ecology. In M. Brody, J. Dillon, R. B. Stevenson, & A. E. J. Wals (Eds.), *International handbook on research in environmental education* (pp. 101–107). London, England: Routledge.

Bai, H., Eppert, C., Scott, C., Tait, S., & Nguyen, T. (2015). Towards intercultural philosophy of education. *Studies in Philosophy and Education, 34*(6), 635–649.

Barnhardt, R. (1981). *Culture, community and the curriculum.* Fairbanks, AK: Center for Cross Cultural Studies. Retrieved from http://ankn.uaf.edu/Curriculum/Articles/RayBarnhardt/CCC.html

Broughton, M. A. (2002). The performance and construction of subjectivities of early adolescent girls in book club discussion groups. *Journal of Literary Research, 34*(1), 1–38.

Cart, M. (2010). A new literature for a new millenium? The first decade of the Printz Award. *Young Adult Library Services, 8*(3), 28–31.

Clarke, J. J. (1997). *Oriental enlightenment: The encounter between Asian and Western thought.* New York, NY: Routledge.

DaLie, S. O. (2001). Students becoming real readers: Literature circles in high school English classes. In B. O. Ericson (Ed.), *Teaching reading in high school english classes* (pp. 84–100). Urbana, IL: National Council of Teachers of English.

Dussell, E. (2000). Europe, modernity and eurocentrism. *Nepantia: Views from the South, 1*(3), 465–477.

Eclecticism. (n.d.). In *New world online encyclopedia.* Retrieved from http://www.new worldencyclopedia.org/entry/Eclecticism

Eppert, C. (2013). *Perennial wisdom, intercultural dialogue, and elemental life education: Histories of east-west contemplative journeys to personal and social transformation.* Unpublished manuscript.

Freire, P. (1970). *Pedagogy of the oppressed.* New York, NY: Continuum.

Hobson, J. M. (2004). *The eastern origins of western civilization.* Cambridge, England: Cambridge University Press.

Harden, R. M., & Stamper, N. (1999). What is a spiral curriculum? *Medical Teacher, 21*(2), 141–143.

Institute of Curriculum Development. (2015). 义务教育课程标准实验教材书：语文（七年级下册）[Standard textbook for compulsory education: Chinese (Seventh Grade–B)]. Beijing, China: People's Education Press.

International Bureau of Education. (2012). World data on education. *People's Republic of China.* (7th ed., 2010/11). Geneva, Switzerland: Author. Retrieved from http://www.ibe.unesco.org/fileadmin/user_upload/Publications/WDE/2010/pdf-versions/China.pdf

K–12 Standards, Curriculum and Instruction (2018). Retrieved from http://www.dpi.state.nc.us/curriculum/

Ketter, J., & Buter, D. (2004). Transcending spaces: Exploring identity in a rural American middle school. *The English Journal, 93*(6), 47–53.

King, R. (1999). *Indian philosophy: An introduction to Hindu and Buddhist thought.* Washington, DC: Georgetown University Press.

Mall, R. A. (2000). *Intercultural philosophy.* Lanham, MD: Rowman & Littlefield.

Marshall, M. J., & Hirsch, E. D., Jr. (Eds.). (2000). *Realms of Gold.* Charlottesville, VA: Core Knowledge Foundation.

Panikkar, R. (1992). A nonary of priorities. In J. Ogilyvy (Ed.), *Revisioning philosophy* (pp. 235–236). New York, NY: State University of New York Press.

Smith, D. G. (2008). The farthest west is but the farthest east: The long way of oriental/occidental engagement. In C. Eppert & H. Wang (Eds.), *Cross-cultural studies in curriculum: Eastern thought educational insights* (pp. 1–33). New York, NY: Taylor and Francis.

Stephens, M., Warren, L. K., & Harner, A. L. (2015). Comparative indicators of education in the United States and other G-20 countries: 2015. *U.S. Department of Education, National Center for Education Statistics.* Washington, DC: U.S. Government Printing Office.

Thein, A. H., & Beach, R. (2013). Critiquing and constructing canons in middle grade English language arts classroom. *Voices from the Middle, 21*(1), 10–14.

Tyack, D., & Tobin, W. (1994). The "grammar" of schooling: Why has it been so hard to change? *American Educational Research Association, 31*(3), 453–479.

Tyler, R. W. (1949). *Basic principles of curriculum and instruction.* Chicago, IL: The University of Chicago Press.

U.S. Department of Education. (2011). *About ED Mission.* Washington, DC: Author. Retrieved from https://www2.ed.gov/about/overview/mission/mission.html

CHAPTER 6

COMPARISONS OF TEACHING ENGLISH AS A SECOND LANGUAGE IN THE UNITED STATES AND CHINA

Kelsey Alvarez and Jessie Lay

It is very apparent that our world is becoming more diverse no matter what country you are living in. In today's society being bilingual is a valuable quality to have. Although English may not be as widely spoken in all countries, this is a great foundational language to have for small communication. Whether you live in the United States learning English as a second language (ESL), or you are someone in China learning English to become bilingual, there are several research-based teaching methods that will help with language acquisition. In the United States these teaching methods are being used widely across many classrooms of all ages (Echevarría, 2012). Some of the most successful and commonly used methods in the classroom are the sheltered instruction observation protocol, total physical response, and Ex-cELL. Students learning English in China who are being taught with these same methods show a higher intelligence and understanding of

Educational Practices in China, Korea, and the United States, pages 89–99
Copyright © 2019 by Information Age Publishing
All rights of reproduction in any form reserved.

the language, especially at young ages, rather than students with only one language. It is important to note that with these methods being used "it is the structure it provides for teacher–student interaction that is the key to future development and exploitation, as learners take the original task in unforeseen directions" (Bygate, Skehan, & Swain, 2013, p. 6). For these research methods to show success in learners, teachers should focus their instruction on the interactions students have with the language; the way the target language is being received and the output produced from students. The research we conducted focuses on a few of the most successful methods used in the United States as well as being used in China. Our research has shown that these methods used in both countries can attribute to the successful rates of second language acquisition.

REVIEW OF THE LITERATURE

The Sheltered Instruction Observation Protocol Model

The sheltered instruction observation protocol (SIOP) is a researched-based model of sheltered instruction (SI) developed by Jana Echevarría, MaryEllen Vogt, and Deborah J. Short. "Sheltered instruction is an approach for teaching content to English learners (EL) in strategic ways that makes the subject matter concepts comprehensible while promoting the students' English language development" (Echevarría, Vogt, & Short, 2010, p. 6). The SIOP model was developed through a 7 year (1996–2003) research study conducted for the Center for Research on Education, Diversity, and Excellence (CREDE) called "The Effects of Sheltered Instruction on the Achievement of Limited English Proficient Students." The SIOP model was first published in 2000.

The SIOP model focuses on enhancing English language acquisition through meaningful use and interaction while incorporating the four domains—listening, speaking, reading, and writing. It consists of eight components that include lesson preparation, building background, comprehensible input, strategies, interaction, practice and application, lesson delivery, and last but not least, review and assessment. The SIOP model includes language objectives in every content lesson, as well as content objectives. It also allows for practice and application of the language objectives and emphasizes key content vocabulary.

Teachers using the SIOP model "make the content comprehensible through techniques such as the use of visual aids, modeling, demonstrations, graphic organizers, vocabulary previews, adapted texts, cooperative learning, peer tutoring, and native language support" and by making connections between student experiences, prior knowledge, and the content

(Echevarría et al., 2010, p. 19). SIOP lessons also include a high level of student engagement and interaction with not only the teacher, but also with other students. The SIOP model also allows for the use of supplementary materials that not only enhance student learning but can also help teachers provide information to students with different proficiency levels (Echevarría et al., 2010, p. 20). These materials can include but are not limited to the use of books, graphs, models, and other visuals. The SIOP model also offers students multiple ways to demonstrate their knowledge of the content.

The SIOP model is widely accepted in the academic community in the United States. Research conducted by Echevarría, Short, and Powers (2006) showed that English language learners in sheltered classes with teachers trained in implementing the SIOP model improved their writing and outperformed students in the control classes. The SIOP model was a focus of the Center for Research on the Educational Achievement and Teaching of English Language Learners (CREATE) science study done by Echevarría, Richards-Tutor, Canges, and Francis in 2011. The results of this study showed that students in a classroom taught by teachers who had received professional development on the SIOP model outperformed those who were not taught by SIOP trained teachers (Echevarría & Short, 2011). A study by Echevarría, Richards-Tutor, Chin, and Ratleff (2011) also showed that the higher level of SIOP implementation, the better the students performed.

There have also been many successful stories in schools with implementing the SIOP model. In Jana Echevarría's 2012 brief for CREATE, she mentioned two successful implementations of the program. The first is at Pasadena Memorial High School in Pasadena, Texas. The results of implementing the SIOP model showed a steady increase in the percentage of English language learners who passed the Texas Assessment of Knowledge and Skills (TAKS) in all content areas since the method was introduced to the school in 2008–2009 (Echevarría, 2012). In 2011–2012, the school was the highest ranked high school in the district, with 65% of their limited English proficient population making progress (Echevarría, 2012). Another success story, mentioned in Echevarría's brief, comes from Tiffany Park Elementary in Renton, Washington. After implementing the SIOP model, Tiffany Park Elementary showed an overall increase in math, science, reading, and math scores in 2010–2011 assessments, as well as showed a surpass of the overall average scores for the state for their English language learners (Echevarría, 2012).

The EXC-ELL Program

The ExC-ELL program is a researched-based instruction for literacy and language development, which was developed by Margarita Calderón.

ExC-ELL stands for Expediting Comprehension for English Language Learners. Calderón's program gives English language learners (ELLs) a balance of ESL and sheltered instruction with a depth of vocabulary and reading and writing in content domains. ExC-ELL has ten instructional components that include pre-teaching of vocabulary, teacher modeling, students practicing skills with peers, students practicing skills independently, students orally summarizing content using new vocabulary, teacher–student discussions, cooperative learning, students writing with new vocabulary and content, formative and summative assessments, professional development, and on-site coaching of each teacher after analysis of student assessments (Calderón, 2011). Calderón's program is based on research focusing on the importance of vocabulary in the academic success of English learners and other students, as well as explicit vocabulary instruction. The program is also based on research showing the benefits of cooperative learning approached in a mixed ability group setting.

Calderón's program puts a focus on teaching vocabulary before, during, and after students read since comprehension depends on knowing between 90% and 95% of the words in the text and in order to know a word, a student must have 12 opportunities to produce the word (Calderón, 2011). The ExC-ELL method categorizes words into three tiers: Tier 1 being simple words, Tier 2 being process words, idioms, polysemous words, specific words, transition words, and so on, and Tier 3 being content words and key vocabulary. Words that have been selected from the text are then pre-taught using seven steps. These steps include: (a) teacher says the word; (b) student repeats the word three times; (c) teacher states the word in context from the text; (d) teacher provides a dictionary definition; (e) teacher provides a student-friendly definition; (f) students engage in activities to develop word knowledge; and (g) teacher highlights grammar, spelling, polysemy, pronunciation, and so on (Calderón, 2011). After pre-teaching the vocabulary, the teacher models a reading comprehension skill in a think-aloud and then students practice the skill with their peers, as well as partner read, discuss content and vocabulary, and summarize (Calderón, 2011).

Finally the ExC-ELL program uses a variety of games, visuals, and cooperative learning strategies that are used after these steps to teach words after reading or to anchor knowledge. These strategies include, but are not limited to: jigsaw, corners, numbered heads, turn to your partner, exit ticket, roundtable, partner, and team products. Finally students write related to the text. Like the SIOP model, ExC-ELL uses the four domains, listening, reading, writing, and speaking to teach language across content areas.

Total Physical Response Method

Total physical response (TPR) is a language teaching method that was developed by James Asher, a professor at San Jose State University. It uses the coordination of a target language and physical movement. This teaching method is described as an experience that helps students of all ages to understand the target language with very few exposures. The first and most important experience in TPR involves the physical action that the student uses to interact with the language (Asher, 2009). For example, when students hear "stand up" they would say the word, and complete the action. Asher (2009) states, "With translation, students use repetition to associate a connection between their native language and the target language (p. 1)."

The use of TPR teaches students a physical and verbal model command where the students will respond with that specified command as modeled. This allows students to "develop receptive language before expressive language emerges" (Asher, 1995, p. 1). The development of the language using this approach allows for speech production to be a result of student comprehension and language acquisition, which is great for second language learners. According to Asher (1995), "If you are teaching students who are in the initial stage of language acquisition, you should definitely use TPR because the sounds and patterns of the new language can be internalized rapidly through language–body conversation (p. 2)." Using this method also shows long-term retention, which is motivation to teachers and learners to see growth in language acquisition skills according to the study. Students enjoy using TPR because it brings more excitement to their learning, while showing results in their language, which is the best way to encourage students to learn a second language. Asher (1995) states that TPR is "aptitude-free. This means that the approach is effective for everyone in the normal curve ability, not just those with high academic ability" (p. 1). This is especially important when teaching a second language to learners because the students come in with different amounts of prior knowledge of the English language. So no matter the wide range of learners in a classroom, TPR will target all learners to help them learn the target language.

METHODS

The information in this chapter reflects qualitative research in both the United States and in China. Data collected were obtained from observations. In the United States, we took on the role as participants, actually teaching using the teaching methods described in the literature review. In China, we took on the role as the observers. Interactions with participants involved asking questions to clarify. Data was collected daily in journal writings while artifacts include pictures, notes from the presentations, and informal conversations. In order to analyze the data, connections and comparisons were made based off of what we do in our classroom to support our ELLs and what teachers in China do based off of the methods we observed in all classrooms.

RESULTS

Sheltered Instruction Observation Protocol

There is not a day that goes by that you will not see SIOP being used in our classrooms! Each subject lesson that is being planned incorporates some aspect of the SIOP method into the activity or direct instruction. This includes an independent quick write followed by students sharing their writing with a buddy to something more elaborate where students complete a gallery walk sharing, reading, and listening to other classmates' ideas on a topic. Every component of SIOP is easily adaptable into all content areas and creates great student engagement that highly benefits ELLs. Sheltered instruction observation protocol is one of the most successful teaching strategies that teachers can incorporate into each lesson they teach. The engagement level and work ethic of students rise because of how active students are when using these strategies. Students love to talk to their friends, and this is exactly how they are able to do this during class. The academic content becomes very difficult in the upper grade levels, but using SIOP has helped to make the content comprehensible for all learners. In every lesson we are sure to include many visuals to make connections, build background knowledge for students, model expectations clearly, and at times are able to support students by connecting through their native language. When we clearly model our expectations for students they have a better understanding of the expectations and have seen or heard it which makes the content much easier to understand. Students rely on our visuals provided because it allows them to build their background knowledge based on their native language.

Sheltered instruction observation protocol components were easy to see in the lessons in all of the schools that we visited while in Xi'an, China. Specifically at a visited middle school, SIOP was heavily used in the teacher's lesson and it was very evident that students understood the concept being taught based on informal observations made throughout the lesson. This teaching strategy relies heavily on modeling, building background, making content comprehensible and using as much interaction as possible. The lesson we observed taught students how to change verbs from present tense to past tense. The teacher in this classroom always modeled her expectation before she had students practice with their partner by changing a verb in a sentence from past to present. She also visually showed students how to do this by having a sentence stem such as "go to the zoo" under the picture and changed it to past tense by writing the word "went" in red, followed by "to the zoo." This clearly gave the students a model of what they were to do and how to do it. What was especially great about this lesson was that the teacher was able to pull from the students' background by using pictures from field trips they had actually taken this school year. This created more engagement in the students, and it helped them to think about what they had already done in their native language, before translating it into English.

In many classrooms in the United States, changing the tense of words would have been a very difficult concept (even for native English speakers), however the students in the classrooms observed in China were easily able to complete this lesson. The reason for this is the use of SIOP strategies that helped to break down changing from present to past tense and allowed for multiple opportunities to do so. Providing students with many examples, visuals to go along with the sentences and giving sentence stems for each trip they took, helped to scaffold for students in order to make the content comprehensible. Prior to calling on students to come write the past tense phrase on the board, Mrs. Wang allowed students to interact with one another by sharing with a partner and then coming to the board. By doing this, she allowed her students many opportunities to share their ideas and then practice with their partner before having to go in front of the whole class.

Through this lesson, it shows how successful SIOP is, when used correctly in the classroom. The students enjoyed the lesson and appeared to understand how to change from present tense to past tense. Sheltered instruction observation protocol can be used in any classroom level for any content areas and continue to show successful results that were seen in this classroom at the middle school level. Using SIOP daily can help students grow in their language acquisition through the use of visuals, models, and the many other strategies suggested by the SIOP model.

EXC-ELL

ExC-ELLis an up and coming strategy that is being used in the United States in many classrooms that have several ELLs (Calderón, 2011). The many components of ExC-ELL provide a wide variety of strategies to use each day for any content area, making it very easy to incorporate into all lessons. In our classrooms we have seen a high growth rate in our ELLs, especially with vocabulary and learning the academic language in content areas. This strategy is so successful in our classrooms because of the many opportunities students are provided to use the four domains of reading, writing, listening, and speaking within the lessons. The more a student has the opportunity to produce the language in the four domains, the faster language acquisition may occur. We also use ExC-ELL's seven step vocabulary program and cooperative learning strategies every day in our classrooms to see success and growth in our ELLs.

Cooperative learning strategies are a major component of the ExC-ELL instructional strategies. While in China, there were many classrooms using these strategies that help to expedite the reading process in students who are ELLs. There is an unbelievably talented first year English teacher, Mrs. Zhang, teaching middle school levels who used partner pair work in her lesson very well. Just as described in the use of SIOP strategies, the students were learning about taking a trip and changing the verb from present tense to past tense. Mrs. Zhang would put up a picture and have the students turn to a partner to change the sentence to past tense, as she would walk around the room to listen before she called on a student to change the sentence to make it past tense. This is a great cooperative learning strategy to use because it allows students to confirm their thoughts and ideas with someone else before sharing out loud. If a student is unsure, this gives an opportunity for them to hear from a partner and it also allows students who know the answer to help their partner understand. Both partners in this situation are enhancing their language acquisition by orally sharing and at times teaching each other the concepts being learned. This gives students the opportunity to feel more confident and willing to speak during class because they had a partner help them or confirm their ideas.

The continued use of ExC-ELL in this classroom will show great growth in language acquisition in the students. Not only will their language skills continue to grow, but their comprehension of their academics will be greater. Students in this classroom were able to reach the lesson objectives with the help of partner and team productions, which are just two of the many strategies suggested in the ExC-ELL strategy. We strongly encourage the teachers to continue to use these strategies as well as to further look into the many other strategies suggested to ensure further success in the students.

TOTAL PHYSICAL RESPONSE

In the United States, TPR is used in ESL classrooms daily. This is very useful for teaching students basic expressions in English like, "Can I go to the nurse?" To use TPR, the teacher may act out having a stomachache so that the student can understand what it means to go to the nurse and why they may go to the nurse. The student is expected to act this out with the teacher so they are able to remember the expression and meaning. Using TPR in upper grades can be useful for beginners because they are often embarrassed to practice their oral language skills. Total physical response allows them to not always have to speak out loud if they are feeling uncomfortable or in their silent period. In our classrooms, we use TPR because it makes learning fun! When students begin to enter middle school and high school, it becomes more difficult to motivate students to want to learn, and to do well in school. Using TPR in the classroom is a way to engage students and allow them to be creative and active with their learning. It is important for ESL teachers to use a wide variety of reading, writing, listening, and speaking in their classrooms. There are teachers who struggle to incorporate listening and speaking, but using TPR can easily fix this. Students must listen to the command that is modeled by the teacher, and then repeat the command and act out as they respond.

This is an excellent way to allow students to get out of their seats and act out commands, expressions, and vocabulary terms. We have observed that when students are able to get up, be energetic and creative with their learning, they retain more information and are excited to learn. Our ESL students have had the most success in content areas where they are encouraged to use their body language and be active while learning the academic content. This ensures that students are engaged in their learning, while being able to produce the target language in a fun and memorable method.

While in China, TPR was used in almost every classroom we had the opportunity to visit. At these schools, students were able to hold very advanced conversations with adults, although they expressed their concerns of being poor speakers of English. While visiting a high school English class, students were presented a lesson that was focused on body language, and what better way to teach this than using TPR? At this high school, students were very engaged in their learning and were advanced in their English speaking skills. Mr. Zhao did a great job of incorporating a generous amount of TPR as well as modeling expectations before sending students off to practice on their own. Mr. Zhao would model, the students would repeat or respond to his model, and then he asked students to complete the task in small groups. To teach what body language is, he first showed a video so that students were able to see an example. This was followed by the use of TPR, and call and response. Mr. Zhao asked the students to show him what it looks like to be angry, sad, confused, and so forth. The use of TPR here allows students to hear the expression and then acting out the expression leads to the understanding of the meaning, which helps with expressive language acquisition.

In this lesson students used a great amount of listening and speaking skills, which led to a greater understanding of the importance of body language. Students were then shown pictures of their classmates, and were asked to call out the expression they may have been experiencing. The next component to the lesson was acting out a scenario that involved confusion and anger. By having students act out and talk during the scene, they were using TPR to show their expressions. The final challenge of the lesson was to act out the scene only using gestures to show their emotions. The students in this classroom did an amazing job with this activity and had a very high engagement level. Students were excited to get out of their seats, listen to their classmates, and simply enjoy the lesson. Total physical response allows for a low affective filter while learning a second language, which ultimately results in a better rate of language acquisition. The use of TPR in this high school classroom shows the school's effort to improve students' English learning skills at a growing rate.

CONCLUSION

From the research provided, students learning English in China are exposed to a variety of successful teaching methods that are also used within classrooms in the United States. One strategy that was not seen in our observations was explicit vocabulary instruction, which is a large component to both the SIOP method and the ExC-ELL method. Since comprehension depends highly on understanding and having many exposures to vocabulary words, it is recommended for teachers in China to pre-teach vocabulary extensively to enhance the experience of their ELLs. A great method to use to pre-teach vocabulary would be Calderón's seven-step vocabulary method which gives students those opportunities. With this being said, it is possible that teachers in China explicitly teach vocabulary, it was just not observed in lessons we viewed. In conclusion, students learning English in China who are being taught with highly successful methods, such as the SIOP model, the ExC-ELL program, and the TPR method, show a high intelligence and understanding of the language, especially at such young ages. These methods being used in both countries can attribute to the successful rates of second language acquisition.

REFERENCES

Asher, J. (1995). TPR and education. *Ideas for Excellence, 3*(4). Retrieved from http://www.tpr-world.com/mm5/TPRarticles/ideas_excellence.pdf

Asher, J. (2009). The total physical response (TPR): Review of the evidence. Los Gatos, CA: Sky Oaks Productions. Retrieved from http://www.tpr-world.com/mm5/TPRarticles/TPR_review_evidence.pdf

Bygate, M., Skehan, P., & Swain, M. (2013). *Researching pedagogic tasks: Second language learning, teaching, and testing*. London, England: Routledge.

Calderón, M. (2011). *Teaching reading & comprehension to English learners, K–5.* Bloomington, IN: Solution Tree Press.

Echevarría, J. (2012). Effective practices for increasing the achievement of English learners (Research Report). Retrieved from CREATE Brief website: http://www.cal.org/create/publications/briefs/index.html

Echevarría, J., Richards-Tutor, C., Canges, R., & Francis, D. (2011). Using the SIOP Model to promote the acquisition of language and science concepts with English learners. *Bilingual Research Journal, 34* (3), 334–351.Echevarría, J., Short, D., & Powers, K. (2006). School reform and standards-based education: An instructional model for English language learners. *Journal of Educational Research, 99* (4), 195–211.

Echevarría, J., Richards-Tutor, C., Chinn, V., & Ratleff, P. (2011). Did they get it? The role of fidelity in teaching English learners. *Journal of Adolescent and Adult Literacy, 54*(6) 425–434.

Echevarría, J., & Short, D. (2011). *The SIOP® Model: A professional development framework for comprehensive schoolwide intervention.* Washington, DC: Center for Research on the Educational Achievement and Teaching of English Language Learners. Retrieved from http://siop.pearson.com/downloads/SIOP%20Framework%20PP5.pdf

Echevarría, J., Vogt, M., & Short, D. (2010). *Making content comprehensible for elementary English learners: The SIOP model.* Boston, MA: Allyn & Bacon.

CHAPTER 7

ENGLISH AS A FOREIGN LANGUAGE AND FOREIGN LANGUAGE EDUCATION IN THE UNITED STATES, CHINA, AND SOUTH KOREA

Jennifer James

Despite its status as an economic powerhouse that dominates the global markets, the United States seems to lag far behind in the foreign language instruction of its citizens (Devlin, 2015). With the exception of immersion magnet schools, where children are exposed to a foreign language at an early age and taught content in a foreign language, many students in American schools are not exposed to a second language until late middle or early high school. Because English is the world's lingua franca, the acquisition of a second language is not viewed as being as crucial to success in the United States as it is in South Korea and China. As such, second language courses are often considered electives and are viewed as an afterthought in English speaking countries, such as the United States and Britain (Devlin, 2015).

Educational Practices in China, Korea, and the United States, pages 101–115
Copyright © 2019 by Information Age Publishing
All rights of reproduction in any form reserved.

Additionally, most of the foreign language courses in American classrooms are taught in English, with grammar drills and functional competence emphasized over interactive, communicative proficiency.

This late introduction to foreign languages, and the low priority that second language learning has with many American students, has caused American schools to be at a disadvantage regarding multilingualism (Devlin, 2015). As former Secretary of Education Arne Duncan remarked at the 2010 Foreign Language Summit, American foreign language students lag behind many of their global counterparts because there is little emphasis placed on languages other than English during their school careers. American schools do not place a high priority on foreign language education or on creating bilingual citizens, and as a result, American students do not find second language acquisition to be particularly important (Friedman, 2015).

The structural approach views language as a "system of structurally related elements for the coding of meaning," and sees the mastery of phonological units, grammatical and lexical items as the primary purpose of language learning (Richards & Rodgers, 2014, p. 23). The grammar-translation method, audiolingual method, total physical response (TPR), and the silent way are all examples of language teaching methods which fall into the structural approach. The structural approach was favored by Japanese English as a foreign language (EFL) educators in the early eighteenth century. It was also heavily influential in China from 1902 to 1922 (Keqiang, 1986).

The functional approach is the notion that language is a "vehicle for the expression of functional meaning" (Richards & Rodgers, 2014, p. 24). Adherents to this approach believe that language pedagogy should be "semantically, interactionally, and structurally based" in order for maximum efficiency (Ahmed, 2013, p. 92). Methods of language pedagogy which are based on the functional approach include directed practice, the oral approach, and the situational language approach. In South Korea, the functional approach was the preferred method of teaching EFL at the beginning of the 21st century (Chung & Choi, 2016).

The last approach to second language pedagogy is the interactive approach, which emphasizes the acquisition of language over explicit language teaching through the focus on communication and interaction (Ortega, 2009). Well-known examples of interactive methods include the direct or natural method, the series method, communicative language teaching, language immersion, community language learning, and Suggestopedia. The interactive approach is currently preferred by both the Chinese and South Korean ministries of education, though the reality is that the desired interactions are not always easily achievable in classrooms today (Choi, 1999).

Each pedagogical approach can have benefits and disadvantages, while each distinct location can have factors that might make one approach more or less practical than another. By researching the functional, structural, and

English as a Foreign Language and Foreign Language Education ■ **103**

interactive approaches and their effectiveness in China and South Korea, this chapter explores how different ideas about foreign language learning in the international community might be adapted to potentially create new learning opportunities for American educators and their students.

LITERATURE REVIEW

English Foreign Language Learning in China

English language learning in China has a rich history that can be traced back to the seeds of globalization that were planted there over a century ago. In the late 1800s, the self-strengthening, or "Westernization" movement, was initiated during the Qing dynasty. This movement saw government officials and educational institutions encourage the adoption of cultural and commercial practices from the West. With this shifting cultural emphasis came a demand for the acquisition of Western languages. In 1862, Tongwen Guan became the first government-funded, Western language institute, signifying an important shift from China's avoidance of outside influence to a willingness to embrace Western methodology and practices (Keqiang, 1986).

English language learning in China continued to grow, and in some cases regress, in the years that followed the Westernization movement. From 1902 to 1922, China embraced the structural approach popular with Japanese EFL instructors, with much attention being "paid to reading and translation" and very little emphasis placed on "spoken English" (Keqiang, 1986, p. 153). This is in direct contrast to the British model that immediately followed and encouraged students to listen, speak, and communicate in English in order to acquire interactional and conversational proficiency.

In 1949, the People's Republic of China was founded, and this political revolution brought with it great changes in the way that English was taught. From 1953 to 1956, English acquisition was discouraged and Chinese citizens were instead encouraged to learn Russian. Further setbacks occurred from 1966 to 1969 when universities were forced to close their doors and Chinese children were expected to become workers in factories and in farms instead of furthering their education.

It was not until the Cultural Revolution came to an end in 1977 that the field of Teaching English as a Foreign Language, or TEFL, began to truly flourish in China and make great strides towards becoming the modern industry that it is today. Initially, EFL teachers favored a functional-notional approach, one which emphasized grammar translations and drills over peer interaction and conversational proficiency. This method continued well into the 1980s, with students practicing grammar drills and scripted pieces of conversation, but without students being given sufficient opportunities to develop the receptive and productive oral elements of the language (Keqiang, 1986).

Despite the limitations that students of English taught with a functional approach faced, it took several years for bigger cities and more highly developed areas in China to begin to favor interactive approaches to English language learning instead of previously instituted methodologies. In the 1990s, the State Education Development Commission "introduced a functional syllabus, in which the communicative teaching aim was set" (Xu, 2010, p. 160). Through this reform, communicative proficiency is highly valued, with teachers hoping that students can both develop and produce "written and spoken English appropriately" (Keqiang, 1986, p. 159). The "passive learning styles" of the past were replaced with opportunities for students to become "active and problem-solving" participants in their own learning (Cui & Zhu, 2014, p. 3). Additionally, students are encouraged to communicate with their peers and with their teachers instead of relying heavily upon the grammar translation and rote-memorization drills of outdated textbooks. American media, moreover, has been embraced as a motivational tool, both inside and outside of the classroom, to help students develop a deeper understanding of the culture where the target language is spoken (Keqiang, 1986, p. 155).

Although the goals of the Chinese Ministry of Education have seemingly advocated for an interactive approach to be used in classrooms across the country, the reality is that the interactive approach to English language learning is not so easily implemented in all Chinese classrooms today. Several problems, such as lack of adequate teacher training, limited materials in rural towns and areas with smaller populations, and large class sizes with upwards of 50 students, have all proven to be prohibitive barriers that are challenging to overcome in Chinese EFL classrooms (Keqiang, 1986). It is perhaps because of these limitations that the observations we conducted in EFL classrooms in Xi'an led me to believe that Chinese TEFL educators perhaps still favor a more functional-notional approach to English language learning than officials in the Chinese Ministry of Education might have hoped for.

English Foreign Language Learning in South Korea

Like China, South Korea has undergone a series of changes in its TEFL practices, goals, and policies. The first installment of EFL as a nationwide initiative began in 1953 after Japan had been forced to relinquish its hold on the country after World War II. The northern part of the peninsula aligned itself with China and the Soviet Union, while the southern part

English as a Foreign Language and Foreign Language Education ▪ **105**

of the peninsula became closely tied with the United States. With this allegiance came an employment of policies considered "in vogue in the U.S. at that time, such as contrastive analysis and behaviorism, which was the basis for the Audio-lingual method" (Chung & Choi, 2016, p. 287).

This structural approach to English language learning was replaced by the Ministry of Education under President Park Jung-hee in favor of interactive methods that placed more focus on communicative competency. After President Park's assassination in 1979 and the ascension of Chun Du-hwan to the presidency, several important milestones in EFL pedagogy occurred; "English was allowed to be taught as an extracurricular activity in primary schools for the first time," the "hours of weekly English teaching" in middle schools were increased and students in secondary schools were provided with "student-centered topics" within their English content and the opportunity to increase their competency in four modalities as opposed to just one (Chung & Choi, 2016, p. 288).

The first democratically elected president, Roh Tae-woo, sought to eliminate authoritarian elements from the education systems of South Korea in an effort to emphasize democracy and student individuality instead (Choi, 2006). In this vein, interactive teaching techniques, especially those which sought to increase listening and speaking competence, were once again emphasized (Chung & Choi, 2016).

In the 1990s and early 2000s, South Korea's efforts to become a modern, globalized nation were amplified. It was during this time that the educational frameworks were put into place that gave rise to the TEFL practices and techniques observed in South Korean classrooms today. While communication had been favored during "discourse" activities in the past, EFL became geared almost exclusively towards "cultivating the communicative competence of students through methods suggested under the communicative approach" (Chung & Choi, 2016, p. 288). Fluency and comprehension were "emphasized over accuracy," and a "functional syllabus, as opposed to a structural, grammatical syllabus" was adopted in textbooks (Chung & Choi, 2016, p. 289).

At present, the "MOE's [Ministry of Education's] long promoted goal of developing students' communicative competence is still active in the current discourse of English education policies" (Chung & Choi, 2016, p. 9). A communicative approach is used to teach English to children of all ages, from primary to secondary schools, while grammatical-functional textbooks are still utilized, "acknowledging the recently reclaimed role of grammatical knowledge in language learning" (Chung & Choi, 2016, p. 288). Multimedia is used both inside and outside of classrooms, and English immersion is promoted through EPIK (English Program in Korea) and English villages (Chung & Choi, 2016).

106 ▪ J. JAMES

While there are limitations on the extent to which the policies set forth by the Ministry of Education can be implemented in all classrooms, such as class size, inadequate teacher training, and the grammatical requirements of College Scholastic Ability Test (CSAT), EFL educators in South Korea indeed appeared during our observations there to be utilizing a combination of interactive and functional approaches, with great emphasis placed on student communicative proficiency.

METHODS

Participants

Using convenience sampling, I conducted interviews with students and teachers during my 10 days of school visits in Xi'an, China and Seoul, South Korea. I interviewed one teacher at a Chinese Pre-K, two teachers at a Chinese secondary school, one teacher from a Chinese university, one teacher from a South Korean magnet school, and one teacher from a South Korean primary school. For all interviews, I used semi-structured interview questions. Ten students from a Chinese middle school and three students from a South Korean primary school were also interviewed. I asked specific questions regarding student motivation (i.e., "Are you excited to be learning English?") in order to measure student interest in English language learning. The ease with which students understood my questions and the linguistic complexity of the responses that the students produced were further used to measure their communicative proficiency in English.

Setting

Interviews in Xi'an, China were conducted at two public schools, Alistair No. 3 Middle School[1] and No. 2 Crossroads High School. Interviews in Seoul, South Korea were conducted at one public primary school, Shonback Elementary School, and one private boarding school, the Global Language Academy. Names of schools, students, and teachers have been changed to protect confidentiality.

Data Collection and Analysis

Informal observations were conducted to give me a general idea of student proficiency in the target language. Observations focused on both student performance during scripted classroom activities and organic conversations that students and teachers participated in with me.

This provided me with insight into what school administrators wanted me to believe students were capable of in comparison with what students were actually capable of understanding in a non-scripted context. Information acquired from teacher and student interviews was combined with research collected from relevant literature to create a descriptive picture of language learning goals and realities in China and South Korea.

RESULTS

After 10 days of school visits, classroom observations, and interviews with teachers and students, several themes emerged. These include scripted lessons that lacked authenticity, pressure that students and teachers felt to perform for outsiders, the utilization of drills focusing on memorization and repetition, and opportunities to negotiate for meaning.

Scripted Lessons

Conducting authentic EFL classroom observations in Xi'an, China was a bit of a challenge because, as one English teacher candidly admitted, much of what we saw was heavily scripted. At first glance, many of the students seemed to have a higher than actual level of

English proficiency because most of their interactions were pre-rehearsed and were not as spontaneous as they were made to appear. There were several examples of this occurrence. At Alistair No. 3 Middle School, for instance, the children in the seventh-grade classroom put on a play for us in English. Their teacher gave them directions in English, and the students' vocabulary and grammar were excellent. Once we sat down to talk with the students, however, they were hardly able to comprehend basic sentences in English. Several minutes into our conversation, I noticed that almost all of the children were struggling to understand me. Because of this, I modified my speech to what I normally use when speaking with my newcomer students in the United States. I was surprised that these students who appeared to be using such advanced English vocabulary were actually at a much lower level of English language proficiency than what I would have expected based on my observations of their classroom interactions with their peers and their teachers.

108 ▪ J. JAMES

Performing for Outsiders

This was not the first time that my perception of students' proficiency was inaccurate due to the scripted nature of the lessons which I observed. After viewing a lesson in an English class at the No. 2 Crossroads High School, I was sure that the students were highly capable at communicating in their second language. I had just seen the teacher deliver a lesson entirely in English, with students volunteering to answer intermediate to advanced questions without the use of their first language. Additionally, the students worked in groups to act out plays in English that dealt with the topic which the teacher had described. The plays that the students created were entertaining and clever, indicating that they had apparently understood the concepts of the lesson which had been taught.

Immediately after the conclusion of the lesson, the students were broken up into groups for us to interact with. It was at this point that I realized that there was a disconnect between the lesson which I had observed and the true abilities of these pupils to interact and produce output in the target language. Some students were perfectly capable of responding to questions such as, "What is your favorite color?" or "Do you like playing sports?" Others, however, struggled to comprehend and answer these questions, often relying on their peers for direct translations and support.

As this was not the first time that this phenomenon had occurred, I was quite curious about the gap between the lessons I had observed and the English proficiency of the students in the class. This curiosity led me to ask the teacher, David, about what strategies were really used to teach English in his classroom.

"I knew you were coming from the United States, so we have been practicing this lesson for quite some time," David told me, adding that "most of the English classes here are taught in Chinese."

This was made further evident during our second classroom visit at the No. 2 Crossroads High School. The first year teacher we observed in this course was forced to follow her actual lesson plan rather than create an artificial lesson for our observations because she did not know about our visit to the school until the previous day. In her classroom, the use of the students' first language during L2 instruction was much more obvious. There were signs in Chinese, many of the things that the teacher wrote on the board were in Chinese, and the students also utilized Chinese when they communicated with their peers. The interactions that I had with these students were much more in line with their actual English proficiency levels based on what I had observed of them in class. I was not expecting these children to have a high level of English proficiency because the observations that I had done in their classroom were much more genuine. There are definitive benefits to the use of a student's first language during second language instruction, however, a focus on acquiring the target language must still be

English as a Foreign Language and Foreign Language Education ■ **109**

evident (Cook, 2001). It was obvious that this instructor was using Chinese to help her students acquire English, though the amount of English actually produced in her classroom was very limited.

Drills, Memorization, Repetition

One common theme I noticed in Chinese schools with regards to English language pedagogy was a focus on grammar drills, memorization, repetition, and writing. "To a certain degree, communication skills in English such as listening and speaking are not given enough attention" with many Chinese students unable to communicate in basic English even after years of L2 instruction (Lin, 2002, p. 8). Additionally, because of the emphasis on reading in China's

English classes, "Grammar is mainly taught in Chinese. Classes are relatively large (more than 20 students) so students seldom have a chance to speak" (Lin, 2002, p. 8). Students are exposed to a wide array of English words, phrases, and grammatical patterns, but the scripted, teacher-led nature of these classes did not give them sufficient time to practice producing output in the target language, or to develop their conversational proficiency (Yu, 2010).

The methods of L2 instruction most commonly observed in the English classes in China were the audiolingual method, the grammar translation method, and the situational language approach. These pedagogical practices are indicative of a mostly functional approach to language learning, with the primary goal for English classes being the student mastery of individual components of the language. Research has shown that the communicative approach to language learning allows learners to achieve a "greater degree of self-direction in his or her learning and exponentially increases the variety of opportunities available for developing communicative competence" (Oxford, Lavine, & Crookall, 1989, p. 37). Research has similarly shown that

> if language as interaction, and all it implies, is not taken into account, materials will continue to fall short of developing a learner's communicative competence. While both the functional aspect of language and the formal features of language are necessary considerations in determining what to teach, they are not sufficient. (Berns, 1983, p. 20)

While the repeated grammar drills and scripted exercises that we observed taking place in Xi'an classrooms have no doubt given EFL students in China exposure to grammatical and lexical structure in English, it appears that students' overall communicative abilities and comprehension outside of scripted texts or lessons is not quite at the level that it could be had an interactive, communicative been approach been successfully incorporated (Oxford et al., 1989).

Creating Meaning and Interaction

Despite the fact that we visited a smaller number of schools in South Korea than we did in China, I felt that we were able to get a much more realistic idea of pedagogical styles and typical classroom interactions because the lessons we observed did not appear to be scripted. In the classroom that we sat in on at Shonback Elementary School, for instance, the teacher spoke to the students solely in Korean and seemed unable to speak much English. The proficiency levels of the students varied. Some students were able to read, write, translate, and have conversations in English. Though the course we observed was focused on social studies, English was still incorporated into instruction. Students worked in groups to translate posters from Korean to English, with students at higher English proficiency levels helping those at lower proficiency levels to complete their portion of the project.

This interaction created many opportunities for negotiation for meaning (NfM). Negotiation for meaning occurs when learners attempt to "overcome comprehension difficulties so that incomprehensible or partly comprehensible input becomes comprehensible through negotiating meaning" (Foster & Ohta, 2005, p. 405). As language learners negotiate meaning, working together to understand and be understood, they are producing modified output, which is crucial for their second language acquisition (Foster & Ohta, 2005). These "attempts of a language learner" to "achieve some sort of desired understanding" in the target language are enormously important during the language acquisition process (Bailey, 2010, p. 17).

Student use of NfM was further evidenced during observations conducted at a language immersion school called the Global Language Academy (GLA). While this boarding school was similar to a language immersion magnet school in the United States and not representative of all public high schools in South Korea, the foreign language learning that took place at GLA was truly remarkable. Students had access to language labs, computer rooms, model United Nations-style debate areas, and their own individual study offices that they could use to immerse themselves in the foreign language they had chosen to study.

The immersive methods utilized at this school, as witnessed during a course discussing Korean culture which was taught entirely in English, were highly effective. The students with whom we spoke were not only highly communicative in their second language, they appeared to have mastered academic terminology, as well. Students had no trouble communicating with us during interviews, nor did they struggle to understand the rigorous texts which they needed to read and provide written commentary on in class.

English learning has been of particular importance in South Korea, especially since the expansion of the American military in the region during and after the Korean War. Individuals who could communicate in both

English and Korean were highly sought after, and increased trade with the United States and the Western world in general made the acquisition of English "highly desirable" (Collins, 2005, p. 421).

While many South Koreans want to learn English, there are certain limitations to teaching English in Korean schools. Class sizes are often too large to yield sufficient opportunities for interaction, and many teachers focus more on grammar translation than "communicative competence" (Choi, 1999, p. 65). Despite this fact, there is a push for communicative language teaching (CLT) and other interactive methods in South Korean classrooms, and these techniques have been implemented with growing success since the beginning of the 21st century (Butler, 2005). The increased leanings towards communicative and interactive language teaching in South Korea were evident in Korean classrooms, even ones in which the acquisition of the English language was not the primary goal. The early age at which Korean students are exposed to English, and the ample opportunities for interaction in the target language that they have been provided with, have resulted in a student body with the potential for high levels of English proficiency.

DISCUSSION

The differences in pedagogical methods between the two countries and the United States were striking, and it can be reasonably implied that American educators place far less emphasis on second language proficiency than their peers in South Korea and China. While there are many different strategies used by American foreign language teachers in their respective classrooms, there are several common elements to foreign language teaching in the United States that I have been able to observe. Functional and structural views on foreign language acquisition are effective at teaching students grammatical competency, and teaching methods which fall into these categories are also good ways to expose students to a large amount of vocabulary. Where these methods fall short, however, is in giving students the opportunity to practice and develop communicative competency (Evtyugina, Simonova, & Fedorenko, 2016).

Interactive methods of language teaching and language immersion, on the other hand, can be an effective means of developing communicative proficiency in a second language (Rivers, 1986). Studies have shown that students who learn a second language through interactive methods and immersion appear to be not only highly effective communicators, but proficient in foreign language grammaticality and literacy, as well (Evtyugina et al., 2016). It is therefore advisable that foreign language educators in the United States begin to take advantage of interactive approaches and early exposure to foreign languages so that American students can develop higher interest and proficiency levels in a second language.

CONCLUSION

Implications for U.S. Educators

Interviews of Chinese and South Korean teachers and students revealed several key aspects of foreign language learning in these countries that are not as prevalent in the United States. Students in both of these nations, for instance, were exposed to foreign languages much earlier than their American counterparts. Additionally, proficiency in a foreign language (in most cases, English) is desirable if not mandatory for the majority of the students interviewed. Furthermore, teachers in China and South Korea attempted to incorporate communicative methods of language teaching in their classrooms, even before students had attained high levels of conversational proficiency.

Contrary to attitudes regarding foreign language learning observed abroad, foreign language learning in American schools is, more often than not, seen as being much less important than core subjects such as English language arts and mathematics. As such, students themselves do not see foreign language learning as a necessity (Friedman, 2015). Many American high schools, for instance, require students to successfully complete only 2 consecutive years of a foreign language course. Much of the second language acquired during these required courses, however, has the potential to be gradually forgotten due to students' lack of motivation to continue using or learning their second language (Bardovi-Harlig & Stringer, 2010).

Even the most enthusiastic American foreign language learners might have difficulty acquiring a second language due to the lack of immersive practices in their foreign language classrooms. Foreign language teachers in the United States will often conduct the bulk of their teaching in English, with a focus on grammatical drills and memorization of vocabulary in the target language, but negligible emphasis on communicative competence (Simon, 1980). This further reduces the incentive to seriously study a foreign language, as it makes it challenging for students to acquire the conversational proficiency that might actually be useful to them in real world contexts. The minimal focus on conversational proficiency in favor of rote grammatical learning also results in students who may be unable to carry out a conversation in another language, despite scoring very well on standardized proficiency tests. While the United States might be able to provide students with the opportunity to achieve high scores on foreign language

English as a Foreign Language and Foreign Language Education ▪ **113**

assessments, the opportunity for students to attain true bilingualism will be limited if these trends in foreign language learning continue (Simon, 1980).

American educators should therefore aim to expose students to foreign languages in primary school, as they do in South Korea and China, in order to generate student interest in foreign languages and cultures at an earlier age. Educators should also place an increased emphasis on producing students who can communicate in a foreign language. This will create opportunities for graduates of American high schools to utilize their foreign languages in real-world contexts, thus seeing the value of what they have learned outside of the classroom. By working to positively influence student attitudes about foreign language learning, and by providing them with the tools and supports that they need to become conversationally proficient in another language, the United States can begin to move towards communicative approaches to language teaching that have been successfully implemented in China and South Korea.

Limitations

Due to the short-term nature of the study abroad trip during which observations and interviews were conducted, it is difficult to gain in-depth knowledge of what truly occurs in Chinese and South Korean foreign language classrooms on a daily basis. Further limitations were that researchers were able to directly interact with a small number of students (< 50) in only two cities (Xi'an, China and Seoul, South Korea). In order to strengthen many of the arguments made in this chapter, it would be beneficial to carry out additional studies in which more students and educators in a variety of schools across China and South Korea could be observed over a longer period of time.

NOTE

1. All names of schools and individuals interviewed have been changed to maintain anonymity.

REFERENCES

Ahmed, M. (2013). The functional approach to second language instruction. *World Journal of English Language, 3*(1), 92–105.

Bailey, K. (2010). Coat hangers, cowboys, and communication strategies. In D. Nunan & J. Choi (Eds.), *Language, culture and identity: A microethnographic approach* (pp. 14–22). New York, NY: Routledge.

Bardovi-Harlig, K., & Stringer, D. (2010). Variables in second language attrition: Advancing the state of the art. *Studies in Second Language Acquisition, 32*(1), 1–45. https://doi.org/10.1017/S0272263109990246

Berns, M. S. (1983). Functional approaches to language and language teaching: Another look. *TESL Talk, 15*(2), 44–64.

Butler, Y. G. (2005). Comparative perspectives towards communicative activities among elementary school teachers in South Korea, Japan and Taiwan. *Language Teaching Research, 9*(4), 423–446.

Choi, S. (1999). *Teaching English as a foreign language in Korean middle schools: Exploration of communicative language teaching through teacher's beliefs and self-reported classroom teaching practices* (Doctoral Dissertation), Ohio State University. Retrieved from http://rave.ohiolink.edu/etdc/view?acc_num=osu1220381940

Choi, Y. H. (2006). Impact of politico-economic situations on English language education in Korea. *English Teaching, 61*, 3–26.

Chung, J., & Choi, T. (2016). English education policies in South Korea: Planned and enacted. In R. Kirkpatrick (Ed.), *English language education policy in Asia* (pp. 281–299). Cham, Switzerland: Springer.

Cui, Y., & Zhu, Y. (2014). Curriculum reforms in China: History and the present day. *Open Edition Journals*. Retrieved from https://journals.openedition.org/ries/3846?lang=en

Collins, S. G. (2005). 'Who's this Tong-il?': English, culture and ambivalence in South Korea. *Changing English, 12*(3), 417–429.

Cook, V. (2001). Using the first language in the classroom. *Canadian Modern Language Review, 57*(3), 402–423.

Devlin, K. (2015). Learning a foreign language a "must" in Europe, not so much in America. *Pew Research*. Retrieved from http://www.pewresearch.org/fact-tank/2015/07/13/learning-a-foreign-language-a-must-in-europe-not-so-in-america/

Evtyugina, A., Simonova, M., & Fedorenko, R. (2016). Teaching conversational language skills to foreign students: Blended learning and interactive approaches. *International Electronic Journal of Mathematics Education, 11*(8), 2925–2936.

Foster, P., & Ohta, A. S. (2005). Negotiation for meaning and peer assistance in second language classrooms. *Applied Linguistics, 26*, 402–430.

Friedman, A. (2015). America's lacking language skills. *The Atlantic*. Retrieved from http://www.theatlantic.com/education/archive/2015/05/filling-americas-language-education-potholes/392876/

Keqiang, W. (1986). Teaching English as a foreign language in China. *TESL Canada Journal, 3*(Special Issue), 153–160.

Lin, L. (2002). English education in present-day China. *ABD, 32* (2), 8–9.

Ortega, L. (2009) *Understanding second language acquisition*. London, England: Hodder Education.

Oxford, R. L., Lavine, R. Z., & Crookall, D. (1989). Language learning strategies, the communicative approach, and their classroom implications. *Foreign Language Annals, 22*(1), 29–39.

Richards, J. C., & Rodgers, T. S. (2014). *Approaches and methods in language teaching: A description and analysis* (3rd ed.). Cambridge, England: Cambridge University Press.

Rivers, W. M. (1986). Comprehension and production in interactive language teaching. *The Modern Language Journal, 70,* 1–7. https://doi.org/10.1111/j.1540-4781.1986.tb05234.x

Simon, P. (1980). *The tongue-tied American : Confronting the foreign language crisis.* New York, NY: Continuum.

Xu, Y. (2010). Theories analyzing communicative approach in China's EFL classes. *English Language Teaching, 3*(1), 159–161.

Yu, B. (2010). Learning Chinese abroad: The role of language attitudes and motivation in the adaptation of international students in China. *Journal of Multilingual and Multicultural Development, 31*(3), 301–321.

CHAPTER 8

STUDENT FITNESS ABROAD

A Comparative Analysis
of Physical Education in the
United States, China, and South Korea

Jessica Kapota, Hongjun Qiu, and Gwitaek Park

Discussion of education usually centers on the students' academic growth, their mind, and how to teach it. This chapter discusses instead the students' physical body, and how schools value and approach education incorporating it. The purpose of this study is to compare the United States, China, and South Korea by examining their physical education (PE) in both planning and execution, and the cultural attitudes towards supporting these programs. Physical education approaches student learning holistically by focusing beyond the learner and citizen towards a healthy body. Each author has a unique perspective of a countries' system of PE, and through collaboration have discovered similarities and differences.

This discussion is an overview of how PE has developed and where it stands, according to both the experiences of the authors and researchers in the field. First will be a brief summary of how each country's public education system approaches PE, based on the history and development of those cultures, as

Educational Practices in China, Korea, and the United States, pages 117–130
Copyright © 2019 by Information Age Publishing
All rights of reproduction in any form reserved.

117

written in the current literature. These sections will only give an overview of the institutionalized practices and theories supporting them. Then a comparative analysis will highlight where the practices differ and are similar, and what issues affect the response to each. Methods include observation and personal experience to confirm what the literature has discussed. Only public school, preschool to high school ages, will be examined.

LITERATURE REVIEW

The United States

Physical education in the United States typically takes the form of a separate class or activity during the students' daily schedule. Depending on the age of the student, this can vary greatly in time and structure. Recess is a common unstructured playtime provided to younger students, decreasing in time up until Grade 6, after which it is eliminated. From that point physical activity (PA) comes in the form of a structured course during the subjects of the day. In high school, this becomes optional to a degree, though as students age they participate more in recreational physical activities.

There is a heavy emphasis on after school sports teams in American childhood culture, especially upon reaching eighth grade and after. Students join as both social engagement and extracurricular for college applications. Athletics even dictate the time that school starts each day: Despite research showing that later start times improve student performance, many high schools begin before 8:00 a.m., partly to reserve afternoon daylight hours for sports practice (Ripley, 2013). Participation extends to the community through parent participation, pep rallies, and the involvement of other groups like bands and student committees. While PE as a course may be lax, there is money and time spent extensively on these associated but exclusive programs.

The rise of child obesity in the United States is a growing concern for both health care providers and educators (Edwards & Cheely, 2016; Perlman & Pearson, 2012). Nutrition is a developmental asset that advances positive youth development and positive student outcomes. In addition, they highlight interdisciplinary measures available to school mental health professionals that advance good nutritional practices (Edwards & Cheeley, 2016). This correlates with a growing schedule of physical activity both in and outside of school hours. Multiple methods for incorporating physical activity into lessons and the classroom are advisable, thus increasing the amount outside of a designated PE hour (Perlman & Pearson, 2012). This however brings to bear the question of assessment of student physical activity. Some assessment suggested includes: teacher observation, self-monitoring, self-reporting, and activity monitors.

Technology has an increasing role in the obesity epidemic, but can also be used to combat it. Smartphones and computer games are sedentary activities and decrease the average amount of physical activity (Cummiskey, 2011). But new apps developed for tracking, promoting, and educating about physical activity and nutrition are being promoted by schools to their students. There are apps that teach yoga, dance, and tennis; measure heart rate; and track step counts. Teachers may incorporate the use of smartphones by introducing such apps in class and allowing students to use them to track their progress, share results, plan projects, search databases, motivate improvement, form collaborations, and submit homework. There is still resistance against using phones in class due to their distraction, but perhaps controlled use would be possible for this case or a particular lesson about the use of these apps. It also assumes all children have access to such technology, which while rising, is not the case. This is particularly true the younger the children are, in which case the use of apps may be beyond them regardless.

Sleep is researched in adolescents and has been shown to be associated with a wide variety of adverse outcomes, from poor mental and physical health, to behavioral problems and lower academic grades (Wheaton, Chapman, & Croft, 2016). Research shows that school times should be pushed later to accommodate the average lack of sleep experienced by most high school students. Most studies reviewed provide evidence that delaying the school start time increases weeknight sleep duration among adolescents, primarily by delaying rise times and increasing sleep duration even with relatively small delays in start times of half an hour or so. Unfortunately, delayed start times can inconvenience working parents, hence the lack of community support for them. Chinese high school students may also have sleep deficits due to the academic load required and correlating study time.

Family and community involvement in the United States for implementation of new policies varies greatly. Although there are several evidence-based recommendations directed at improving nutrition and physical activity standards in schools, these guidelines have not been uniformly adopted throughout the United States (Kehm, Davey, & Nanney, 2015). Family and community involvement were associated with schools more frequently utilizing healthy eating strategies and offering students healthier food options. Further, involvement was associated with greater support for PE staff and more intramural sports opportunities for students. Unfortunately, involvement is low and research has not yet solved how to increase it.

China

Chinese education stems from a tradition in Confucianism, which has three core values of perfect self: responsibility to society, learning virtues, and emphasis on action (Wang, Ma, & Martin, 2015). Responsibility to society is especially important to education since it is the student's duty to grow into an excellent citizen through learning and knowledge. This dedication to learning ensures students take their studies seriously, as do parents and the community. It is because of this overarching involvement in education that policies and practices are implemented and encouraged within and outside of school settings. Physical education is a purposeful, planned, and organized educational process through physical activity and other auxiliary means. It is compulsory for students from primary school to sophomore year of college and an elective course thereafter. Currently, primary school students and junior high school students take three PE classes a week at 45 minutes per class, dropping to two a week in senior high. In addition to those classes, there are morning exercises (running, 10–15 minutes) and classroom maintenance exercise (25 minutes) every day. The course focuses on track and field in primary school and adds other team based sports, such as basketball and volleyball, in middle and high school.

China has a centralized federal government which finds advantage in uniform order and consistent standards to maintain the overall interests of the organization and implement policies. The government established standards and practices of PE with national guidelines for its educators, and mandated satisfactory completion in PE as a requirement for advancement to the next grade in 1992 for public schools (Liang, Walls, & Lu, 2005). Seven mandates were established in 1995, establishing PE as a regular part of academics that needs resources and assessment:

1. PE is a regular part of school education.
2. PE classes are listed as an academic course that is regularly assessed and sufficient to meet the needs of special students.
3. Time must be allocated for students to participate in physical activities every day for the purpose of meeting national fitness standards.
4. A variety of after-school physical activity programs, training, and sports competitions are provided; annually, a school-wide physical activity and sport meet is conducted.
5. Physical educators need to be qualified according to national regulations and should have benefits related to the job specifications.
6. Physical activity fields, facilities, and equipment must be used for physical activities only.
7. Student physical examinations must be given, and administrative supervision for the improvement of students' fitness must be provided.

In 2011, based on the implementation of the aforementioned mandates, four standards were published in a second edition for both elementary and secondary schools. They specified what physical activity participation included, mastery of knowledge and skill, and developing physical and mental health (Ding, Li, & Wu, 2014). This marked a distinct shift in a focus on sports for PE to developing health and fitness. This is a more health-first focus, and formed a basis for a new program around fitness development and education. The basic concepts of PE in China are to promote student health by following the guiding principle of "health first." Physical education fosters students' consciousness of lifelong physical training by stimulating their interest in sports, which help build interpersonal skills. They also ensure every student benefits by taking a student-oriented approach and tailoring the programs to meet the different needs of students. Enhancing physical fitness and health knowledge has many benefits to the student beyond public education. It cultivates interest in sport hobbies and helps form habits of regular exercise. It promotes psychological health, team building, sportsmanship, and a positive and optimistic attitude of life.

Most PE teachers have a bachelor's degree in physical education and thus are qualified and competent in teaching, with the exception of those in remote areas where the need for educated teachers is higher than the availability. Assessment is conducted each semester for PE classes in primary schools, mainly focusing on track and field. The main form of sports competition is an annual track and field meet in primary and secondary schools. Yet, the evaluation system is very simple due to the little academic value attached to primary students' sports performance. Some schools give students a score directly without conducting any true assessment. This changes in junior high when students are preparing for senior high entrance exams, where PE accounts for a total of 50 points (about 1/10 of the students' total score). This results in more standardized assessment of PE for older students.

Once in senior high, the value of PE once again drops as students' academic pressure increases and opportunity decreases. There are few competitions between classes and grades. One of the biggest problems facing schools at present is the shortage of sports funds, insufficient field space, and outdated sports equipment. Most schools do not have indoor gymnasiums, so PE is cancelled for rainy days or bad weather. Many schools fail to give their sports facilities appropriate maintenance, thus making them old and dilapidated. The situation is especially serious in rural schools. Students' enthusiasm for PE diminishes with the clear lack or structure and support. Physical education pedagogy becomes limited to simpler activities like running. Physical education teachers in middle schools mainly train students in running, some sports, and simple physical exercises. With "play safe" as the guideline, challenging or confrontational sports such as gymnastics, football, and so forth are excluded from PE, and have no base to grow in senior grades.. Student personality and interests are not taken into account so they feel that PE is simplistic and boring, thus removing motivation to explore sports in other contexts. The context of PE is to build up a sound ideological and moral foundation, shape an ideal personality, and develop strong interpersonal communication skills and team spirit. At present, most schools and parents view the purpose of PE as limited to exercise and improving physical function. Sports are only a viable second career choice or interest if a child is poor in other academic subjects.

Physical education as a whole is often ignored academically, regardless of mandates otherwise. Schools are more concerned with pursuing higher enrollment, challenging learning activities, frequent examinations, and preparation for good secondary and post-secondary schools. A school is often judged based on its enrollment rate and the examination results of science subjects, thus the teaching quality of such subjects are generally the primary concern of the general population and school administrators. This is especially true in rural schools. These schools focus on getting a high enrollment rate and give little attention to PE classes. These priorities make PE classes secondary, thus suppressing the PE teachers' enthusiasm and motivation. Exercise time is replaced by tutoring sessions or other supplementary learning activities. It also affects the schedule and time given to different subjects, which adversely affects the normal teaching order and reduces students' time for exercise. This seriously affects the health development of younger generations. According to the 2010, "China Youth Physical Health Development Report" data show that the health quality of Chinese adolescents is overall still in a downward trend. The report showed rising obesity, lower heart and lung function becoming more common, and even poor vision health.

Obesity is a growing concern in China among children and encouraging attention toward PE. New models involving both the school and parents are showing success in attitude, behavior, and lifestyle (Qian, Newman, Shell, & Cheng, 2012). Students' different perceptions of task values influence their learning experience and achievement in PE. The results of one study found that Chinese boys need to strengthen cognitive learning and girls need to strengthen psychomotor skill development in PE (Ding, Sun, & Chen, 2011). The study was to identify the extent to which the task values along with gender and body size predicted students' performance on knowledge and physical skill tests. New studies show that the rise in economic prosperity has correlated with an increase in physical inactivity, poor dietary habits, and obesity in Asian countries (Chin, Yang, & Masterson, 2003).

Korea

Korean government policy focused historically on economic growth for the past several decades in an effort to improve. Parents who lived or matured during the previously poor economy of Korea think that teaching "core" academics intensively is vital to improving their child's financial future. This includes preparation for elite universities, which in turn may lead to a higher salaried career. As a result, PE is regarded as secondary or inferior when compared to more academic subjects such as Korean, mathematics, and English.

In an effort to solve these problems, The Korean National Curriculum for Physical Education (KNCPE) has undergone consistent periods of reform every 6–8 years, the most recent implemented in 2001 (Lee & Cho, 2014). Lee and Cho's study intended to reflect and analyze the historical change of the KNCPE over the past 60 years. Yet the study was inconclusive because PE is still regarded as a minor subject in comparison with other core academics. Second, the principles employed to construct the framework for activities are heavily based on Western concepts and approaches, which are not always popular with faculty or the community. The study did show that many students are still physically unfit and passive in their daily life, suggesting that the curriculum has not been effective. Lee and Cho suggested further change to refocus the PE curriculum, arguing that PE in Korea is at curriculum crossroads.

How that change could occur is difficult to imagine, for any society. A study of curriculum change from the viewpoint of a chairperson shows just how difficult it can be for PE especially. A self-study was conducted in order to make known a chairperson's experiences with the various obstacles in revising the national curriculum and to offer previously unseen insights afforded by the curriculum maker's personal reflections (You, 2011). Four challenges the national curriculum administrator (responsible for writing or revising said curriculum) encountered were: (a) personal obstacles encountered as a young female chairperson, (b) environmental obstacles encountered as a marginally positioned chairperson, (c) professional obstacles faced as an innovative chairperson, and (d) institutionalized obstacles related to being named the official chairperson. Such resistance to change based on the identity of an implementer show how difficult it can be to moderate change in education in Korea.

Other studies have shown the differences in PE depending on age group. A study demonstrated that elementary school PE classes exhibited more humanistic behaviors. In contrast, middle school classes were conducted with a great deal of teacher input and high school classes had a very structured atmosphere (Yu & Kim, 2010). Variety in health amongst students also occurs with economic, social, and environmental differences, particularly when facing obesity factors. In addition to lifestyle change, health programs for overweight and obese children should focus on psychological health, and consider social and environmental factors as well (Kim, Park, Ma, & Ham, 2013).

In Korea, interest of parents towards schooling has moved from public schooling to private education and foreign schooling to teach their children high academic knowledge not addressed in public school and mastery of a foreign language, resulting in a decline in support for public schooling (Lee & Cho, 2014). They strongly believe that teaching their children advanced academic courses and foreign language will help their children to obtain higher salary jobs and better reputations than those enrolled in public school in society. In order to achieve these goals determined by parents and society, it is difficult for students to participate in PE and physical activity and to sleep sufficiently. The allocated PE time is 3 times a week from third to eighth grade, and only 2 times a week from ninth to tenth grade. Furthermore, it is optional for PE to be involved in whole curriculum, which means that PE class could be implemented less than 2 times a week (Yoo & Kim, 2005). Insufficient sleep in adolescents is shown to be associated with a wide variety of adverse outcomes, from poor mental and physical health to behavioral problems and lower academic grades (Wheaton, Chapman, & Croft, 2016).

METHODS

This study is a qualitative ethnography comparing cultural concepts of PE and student health in three countries. This cultural portrait shows how each society views PE, where those views stem from historically, and how they result in today's programs and application.

Data collected was mostly obtained through observations of school environments. The first author took the role of both observer and participant in some situations, interacting with students and teachers. Interactions included playing with and speaking with children, and discussing methods and questions with staff. Data was recorded in a research journal during the course of the visit. This past June the first author had the privilege of going on a study abroad trip to Xi'an, China and Seoul, South Korea. The purpose of the trip was to observe education in these two countries, which was conducted by visiting several schools, and compare it to education in the United States. Participants saw a variety of schools and levels, from preschool to university. Throughout the trip, it was noted language, activities, and lessons centered on the health of the student. It went beyond the PE classes taken and seen by the observer as a child in America. It happened during regular classes, and went beyond motor activity and into theory, training, and life implementation.

All three authors have some personal observations and experiences guiding this discussion. The first author's experiences come from time in an American school system and as a student teacher while completing a BA in education. The second author grew up in a Chinese school system and is a professional in the field of education. The third author has experiences from childhood in a Korean school system and is a doctoral student in the field of education.

RESULTS

Observation by First Author

On one of the tours during a trip to China, we passed multiple groups doing various light physical activities by the city wall. Some were juggling, some doing forms of Tai Chi, or simply stretching. Our guide informed us that physical activity is highly valued in Chinese society for many reasons, but the principal being that going to a doctor is too expensive to waste on preventable conditions. Consistent exercise is linked to preventing many physical and mental health ailments, including arthritis, for example. Chinese adults, especially as they retire and get older, practice movement and mobility to keep limber and healthy in the face of their age. This is a trend that starts very young.

While still in China, one of the schools we visited was a preschool. We were invited to participate in a song and dance routine that the children have all memorized. This lasted about half an hour. We were astonished by how organized the routine was, and that clearly the teachers had to learn and perform it too. We were told this is a common type of exercise, to dance along to music by following the teachers' movements, even for adults. Then the children were given structured playtime by playing active games like duck duck goose, London Bridge, or similar games. Several of the schools visited had murals, projects hanging, or lessons centered on the health of the student and the body. The preschool even had a section on traditional Chinese medicine. The principal emphasized how they wanted to teach the children holistically through not only the mind, but as a citizen and as a person (in the physical sense). I felt this approach better integrated PE and practice than the system currently used in the United States, where only physical activity is used in this age group. Teaching health practices does not come until perhaps the seventh grade in the United States.

There was a strong devotion to outside school work witnessed in the private schools visited in Korea. The first author visited a private high school academy for languages, which showed us a brochure boasting that students slept an average of 6 hours a night. As previously mentioned, there is high pressure on students to perform academically (Lee & Cho, 2014). Students spend 1 hour of homework time to each of class time, resulting in a total of 10 hours of school study per day. There is no time built in for social or free

126 ▪ J. KAPOTA, H. QIU, and G. PARK

rest. Even when visiting the public schools, a devotion to studies outside of class time was apparent. This lack of time for relaxation, social development, or other activities is concerning in the light of holistic student health.

Comparative Analysis

School PE is an important part of school education, makes an important part in letting students fully develop, and also an important way to raise talents for the society. Physical education and education is a cultural phenomenon of human society, with the formation of human society, and with the progress of society. The United States is one of the first countries to attach great importance to PE classes in schools, and the government and the education sector has been the core curriculum of PE curriculum. Here are some comparisons where all countries could benefit from one another by studying, and areas to collaborate in common issues.

Commonalities

A huge consideration in the rise of childhood obesity in America is the average American diet. Is childhood obesity a problem in all of these countries? According to researchers in the field of child health, yes it is. All countries can connect their obesity rates to similar issues of technology, low income, and food choice. Food choice is associated with the lunches provided through the schools to students and the reality of which items students actually consume. Studies on food waste examine which foods students pass over most often, typically vegetables (Liu et al. 2016).

The United States and China share struggles in funding and equipment for PE because it is taken less seriously as an academic field. All three countries share that mind-set, which is one of the biggest hindrances to progress in the field. It seems more attention is given to extracurricular sports or after school programs than taught courses, possibly because students can then be expected to pay fees or have parents that express interest in them. Sports are potential distractions to education that will result in a financially steady career path, or at best an alternative career for the less successful. Only in the United States is it a path towards financial help in higher education, again for the benefit of a college degree and a good job.

Physical education objectives are essentially the same between all countries (with Korea perhaps with only to a lesser degree of emphasis), mainly reflected in the cultivation of lifelong sports awareness, individual socialization, health first, and so on. China's sports education is more focused on the mastery of student sports skills, while in the United States, the student's personality play and interest is more prominent. There are some variances between cultivating self-exercise and personal health (as in Asia) and individual interests and enthusiasm (as in the United States). The goal is through PE to promote students in the body, knowledge, social, and emotional development, to develop students for life-long participation in sports activities, awareness, interests, and habits.

By no means can it be said that one method of student PE is universally better than another. Chinese and American sports teaching objectives are basically the same, mainly reflected in the cultivation of lifelong sports awareness, individual socialization, "health first," and so on. China's sports education is more focused on the mastery of student sports skills, while in the United States, the student's personality play and interest is more prominent. But certain methods and motivations are certainly significant across all three of the countries examined. All three are concerned with the rise of childhood obesity, and all can potentially link this rise to the rise of technology which leads to a more sedentary lifestyle. All countries seek to implement national standards in public schools to address growing health concerns. And all recognize the importance of parental and community involvement for success.

Differences

One of the greatest challenges to student health is economic factors and the ability to see a doctor. Data has shown that low-income families can't afford healthier food choices and so are at higher risk of obesity and its associated health conditions (Ding et al., 2011; Kim et al., 2013; Edwards & Cheely, 2016). Those same families and children at risk for health issues cannot afford regularly seeing a doctor. Remarkably, in China this spurs physical activity in all ages as a prophylactic. The implementation in school is to introduce methods and supplement existing activities as the students age. The United States and Korea do not seem to share this dedication to physical activity in general, but only within schools as a remedy for the lack of PE outside of schools.

Who does society say is responsible for physical health? In the United States, it seems the brunt of PE and activity is on the school system and schedule. Korea is similar in this trend, though less observations or data show if outside school activities are high. Participation in activities like team sports improve when facilitated by the school, even if after hours. Both countries wish to involve parents and community, but don't seem to have much improvement in the area. In China, the burden of physical health is on the self, and such involves more education about being healthy and practices that can be done at any time. Community and parental involvement are much higher, as is support for curriculum change in education. China and Korea share a lack of time allotted to PE due to emphasis on academic burdens and future university preparation, as discussed in detail previously.

How the government mandates PE is vastly different between the United States and Asian countries. Political and philosophical roots account for much of the differences (Wang et al., 2015). In China and Korea, mandates are set at the national level and are very centralized, in part to cultural adherence to a single federal government. In contrast, the United States is more diverse in both cultures and political structures due to state vs. federal power. Asian cultures also grew from philosophies valuing an individual's contributions to society over the individual themselves (Wang et al., 2015). American education has religious roots and culturally values individual independence. Both have concern for improving society with an educated population, but the approach is different due to these philosophies.

There is an emphasis on familial involvement in their children's sports in the United States that is not as culturally strong elsewhere. Eighth grade American kids spend more than twice the amount of time on sports as Korean children of the same age (Ripley, 2013). Students in the school not only learn PE, but in secondary school also have a large variety of extracurricular exercise, and a variety of sports clubs, sports associations to meet the choice of different students interested. Family participation, support, and entertainment makes sports a culture. American kids expect to participate in school sports as a kind of rite of passage (Ripley, 2013). Parents lead their children and siblings to watch the game, support their favorite team, and cheer to encourage them.

DISCUSSION

Over the course of the last several decades, advances in the internet and social media have brought distant parts of the globe closer together. As this occurs, it is becoming increasingly possible for physical educators to learn from one another and to work collaboratively to advocate and build high-quality PE programs (Housner, 2005). The dedication to sports education, nutrition reform, or community assistance are successful models that can be shared across borders. By learning from one another we can improve PE past our cultural limitations or biases. Asian countries might observe and study more about successful technology integration on the individual student level from the United States. Americans can in turn recognize the importance of expansion of PE in all levels of school activity and home. Hopefully as nations continue to compare and learn from one another, student health concerns will improve globally.

REFERENCES

Chin, M., Yang, J., & Masterson, C. (2003). Connections between physical education and physical best in Hong Kong, China: An alternative new model of innovative teaching in health-related fitness in Asia. *ICHPER-SD Journal, 39*(3), 61–64.

Cummiskey, M. (2011). There's an app for that: Smartphone use in health and physical education. *Journal of Physical Education, Recreation & Dance, 82*(8), 24–29.

Ding, H., Li, Y., & Wu, X. (2014). A review of scholarly and research work in physical education in China during the first decade of the 21st century. *Quest, 66*(1), 117–133.

Ding, H., Sun, H., & Chen, A. (2011). Gender, BMI, values, and learning in physical education: A study on Chinese middle schoolers. *Learning and Individual Differences, 21*(6), 771–778.

Edwards, O. W., & Cheeley, T. (2016). Positive youth development and nutrition: Interdisciplinary strategies to enhance student outcomes. *Children & Schools, 38*(3), 170–177.

Housner, L. D. (2005). Introduction: Like the United States, Asian nations have grappled with the challenge of creating and using national physical education standards. *Journal of Physical Education, Recreation & Dance, 76*(6), 13.

Kehm, R., Davey, C. S., & Nanney, M. S. (2015). The role of family and community involvement in the development and implementation of school nutrition and physical activity policy. *Journal of School Health, 85*(2), 90–99.

Kim, H. S., Park, J., Ma, Y., & Ham, O. K. (2013). Factors influencing health-related quality of life of overweight and obese children in South Korea. *Journal of School Nursing, 29*(5), 361–369.

Lee, K., & Cho, S. (2014). The Korean national curriculum for physical education: A shift from edge to central subject. *Physical Education and Sport Pedagogy, 19*(5), 522–532.

Liang, G., Walls, R. T., & Lu, C. (2005). Standards and practice for physical education in China. *Journal of Physical Education, Recreation & Dance, 76*(6), 15.

Liu, Y., Cheng, S., Liu, X., Cao, X., Xue, L., & Liu, G. (2016). Plate waste in school lunch programs in Beijing, China. *Sustainability, 8*(12), 1288. https://doi.org/10.3390/su8121288

Perlman, D. J., & Pearson, P. (2012). Identifying diverse means for assessing physical activity. *Strategies: A Journal for Physical and Sport Educators, 25*(7), 22–24.

Qian, L., Newman, I. M., Shell, D. F., & Cheng, C. M. (2012). Reducing overweight and obesity among elementary students in Wuhan, China. *International Electronic Journal of Health Education, 15*, 62–71.

Ripley, A. (2013). The case against high school sports. *The Atlantic.* Retrieved from https://www.theatlantic.com/magazine/archive/2013/10/the-case-against-high-school-sports/309447/

Yoo, S. S., & Kim, H. Y., (2005). Standards and practice in Korean physical education: Six revisions of the national physical education curriculum have brought greater autonomy to schools and teachers, yet better teacher practices are still needed. *Journal of Physical Education, Recreation & Dance, 76*, 20–24.

Wang, C., Ma, W., & Martin, C. L. (2015). *Chinese education from the perspectives of American educators: Lessons learned from study-abroad experiences.* Charlotte, NC: Information Age.

Wheaton, A. G., Chapman, D. P., & Croft, J. B. (2016). School start times, sleep, behavioral, health, and academic outcomes: A review of the literature. *Journal of School Health, 86*(5), 363–381.

You, J. (2011). A self-study of a national curriculum maker in physical education: Challenges to curriculum change. *Journal of Curriculum Studies, 43*(1), 87–108.

Yu, J., & Kim, J. K. (2010). Patterns of interactions and behaviors: Physical education in Korean elementary, middle, and high schools. *ICHPER-SD Journal of Research, 5*(1), 26–32.

PART III
NEW PEDAGOGICAL FRAMEWORK AND PRACTICES

CHAPTER 9

CHINESE AND SOUTH KOREAN EDUCATION REFORMATIONS

Unrealistic Expectations in the Implementation of Western Pedagogy

Cory Alexander

Global market opportunities, as well as advancements in technology, continue to make diverse cultures more accessible to foreign societies, despite geographical distance. This interconnectedness has not only facilitated the meshing of languages and cultures across borders, but also led to the current movement of reformations and the sharing of policies and ideologies. Education, being one of the more prominent forces in any society's economic output, has therefore been heavily affected across the globe with this widespread trend (Lee, Wang, & Yin, 2014). In an effort to confront economic stagnation and bolster global presence, diverse countries have started to adopt pedagogies or policies that have been successfully implemented by others, despite differences in cultural context (Chua & Tan, 2015). The East—notably China and South Korea—known for strict

---

Educational Practices in China, Korea, and the United States, pages 133–147
Copyright © 2019 by Information Age Publishing
All rights of reproduction in any form reserved.

133

134 ▪ C. ALEXANDER

adherence to their own traditions, have uncharacteristically joined in on this game of "adopting and selling" educational policies (notably from the United States). Although purposefully done to prepare students to be more effective, like-minded, and active members of the worldwide community, these efforts have been regarded as largely ineffective (Chua & Tan, 2015). So, how can the same systems that are so widely accepted and successful in one environment be so ineffective and unsupported in another? Overall, the conclusion is drawn that tradition and culture are innately ingrained in any society's educational system and thus cannot be disregarded when it comes to revamping policies. It is argued that policies must instead align and adhere to the strengths of its own culture and history in order for any reformations to make a positive and lasting impact.

In order to better understand why Western pedagogies have yet to be effective in the East, it is important to examine the history of these cultures, and from which principles their educational systems were founded. This will help validate the reasoning that policies cannot be simply and effortlessly traded across borders without giving heed to contextual and cultural differences.

LITERATURE REVIEW

Western Theories and Pedagogies

Western educational systems are known for fostering creativity and are described as implementing student-centered teaching pedagogy that emphasizes independent learning, giving choices, and being process-oriented (Cheung, 2016). Furthermore, individualized scaffolding, motivation, evaluation, and feedback are all utilized to encourage divergent and critical thinking, interpersonal exchange, and teamwork (Cheung, 2016). When comparing effective educational policies within this society with key characteristics indicative of Western culture—namely that of the United States—many explicit parallels can be noted: the value of independence and independent thinking, uniqueness, and "democratic ideals" where there is a spirit of mutual trust, openness of communication, and diverse interpretations (Frush & Muetz, 2007). This is important to recognize in order to understand just how much any given society's culture and ideals truly play into the successful implementation of any policy—whether outside or inside school walls. A great example of the power and influence of tradition can be seen when recent legislative mandates, such as the No Child Left Behind Act (NCLB) in 2002, have been faced with enormous pushback from all constituents in the educational system: teachers, administrators, students, and parents alike. Initially implemented in an effort to advance American competitiveness by giving the federal government more control through mandating the use of standardized testing, these new policies have strayed from original American values and more closely mimicked Eastern educational practices. Overall, they have been widely criticized as stifling creativity and inadvertently putting performance goals ahead of learning goals (Klein, 2016). In short, by effectually bulking up the federal role in holding schools and teachers accountable for student outcomes, this trend intrinsically challenges the very roots on which Western pedagogies and theories have been built (Farenga, Ness, Johnson, & Johnson, 2010). As an answer, many current efforts are therefore being taken by local systems to reclaim autonomy and address educational redesign policies with their own methods (42 states have currently been granted waivers from the NCLB program as of 2016; Farenga et al., 2010; Klein, 2016). Overall, this recent movement towards a standardized curriculum in the West is proving to be both unsuccessful and unaccepted by the majority of local and state educational stakeholders.

Eastern Theories and Pedagogies

The Chinese education system, directly descending from the teachings of Chinese philosopher, Confucius (551–479 BC), is inherently recognized as the driving force behind Eastern pedagogy and will therefore be referenced as the prime representation of Eastern Educational Systems in this chapter (Niu, 2007). This philosophy places moral education and the fostering of benevolence as the definitive objectives of education. Furthermore, Confucianism is recognized for stressing the importance of community over the individual, acknowledgment of hierarchy, loyalty to duty and rules, and most importantly, the memorization of the classics (Niu, 2007; Rasmussen & Zou, 2014). This emphasis in memorization, as adopted by the traditional Chinese education system, naturally encourages rote learning methods in order to achieve a knowledgeable command of content. In summary, focus on teacher-centered pedagogy, conformity, extreme discipline, and obedience to authority are central to this system—inherently conflicting with the Western values of independence, creativity, and higher-thinking skills (Lee, Wang, & Yin, 2014). Overall, the Chinese education system has consistently been characterized by two overriding and codependent themes: high-stakes testing and the far-reaching control of the central government; these two themes will be broken down in the following sections.

Central Government Control and Standardized Testing

Formally established during the imperial era of the Zhou Dynasty in 11th century BC, the traditional educational system in China was intentionally

136 ▪ C. ALEXANDER

molded in the interest of the state administration in order to produce an elite and scholarly class and cultivate and train future state officials (Niu, 2007). The strict positioning of education around the elite continued to be the focal point of Chinese education and became even more concentrated around 13 centuries ago with the creation of the Imperial Test, or keju. Intrinsically based on how thoroughly a candidate understood the Confucian classics, success on this exam was the lone path that opened the door to a career as a government official—the embodiment of Chinese success (Niu, 2007). This specific emphasis led to what has been aptly coined "the examination culture" to describe the Chinese educational structure. In this system, all stakeholders in education place an extraordinary stress on students' results in public examinations. Therefore, as can be imagined, this intense emphasis drove teachers to explicitly teach to the college entrance exam (Lee et al., 2014). Overall, education and knowledge were clearly the primary means to attain any semblance of social and economic mobility and have been inherently linked to the advancement and success of the country (Wan, 2012).

Boiled down, this educational system was established on one curriculum, one set of textbooks, and one exam that determined students' fate. It was not until 1905 that Keju was ultimately abandoned as China faced its first wave of Western influence, brought on by a series of military aggressions from foreign powers. This, coupled with seeing technological and scientific advances from the West, stirred the Qing Dynasty (1868–1912) to explore ideas of incorporating Western learning into their traditional education system. They specifically attempted to release central power with the hope this would spur on economic growth (Niu, 2007). However, the enduring effects of keju and its deeply embedded tradition that lasted for 1,300 years are evident as the People's Republic came into power in 1949. This "new" government, a state-run system with complete control over the Ministry of Education (MOE), immediately reformed the old educational systems that had been established by the Nationalist government in order to reestablish a structure that would innately be non-Western in style (Rasmussen & Zou, 2014). Once again, China was back to being a centralized system where knowledge-based emphases were consistent with Chinese traditions (Niu, 2007). At this point, Chinese education under the first 30 years of the People's Republic continued to be identified as one of the most centrally controlled and politically stimulated educational systems in the world (Wan, 2012). Each school still used the same national-style curriculum and unified textbooks created by the central authority. Naturally, this type of scheme, once again, laid down fertile ground for the reimplementation of a centralized testing system that adhered to the government's aspirations; hence, the National College Entrance Exam (NCEE), or Gaokao, was instated by the MOE for the purpose of determining college admissions in 1952. Its inherent characteristics of being "knowledge-driven and inseparable from state interests," as well as still having the sole power to determine the future of a student, proves to be very much like its predecessor, the Imperial Exam (Niu, 2007, p. 82). And while the start of the Cultural Revolution in 1966 reveals an effort to discontinue the NCEE by establishing a model that is neither swayed by foreign or conventional Chinese educational systems, the power and influence of cultural traditions once again endure as the test was immediately reinstated after the Revolution (Wan, 2012).

All in all, numerous educational reforms have taken stage, most predominantly through the 19th and 20th centuries, but notable change is both scarce and sluggish. In order to better understand the context and reasoning behind why tradition and culture are so stubbornly enduring in the East, the prominent themes of the East's educational reformations will now be examined.

The East's Changes in Policies and Efforts to Improve Learning

Current educational reforms that are sweeping across both Western and Eastern countries have the same aspiration in mind: the desire to foster creativity in this rapidly advancing and knowledge-based economy (Cheung, 2016). By closely monitoring the present successes and outcomes of specific Western policies, the East has therefore centered on two underlying purposes in their most current strand of reformations: (a) the need to be more globally competitive, and (b) the need to cultivate innovation.

In order to meet these goals, as well as in an effort to revamp their old education system that has been deemed as "obsolete and examination-oriented," Eastern systems have recognized that two of the most heralded and traditional aspects of their education structure must be overhauled if they are to expect any type of change in their output (Lee et al., 2014). The revamping of these two aspects—the central control of the government and the college entrance exam—has become paramount to the future of Eastern educational policies and practices. It is these same deeply embedded traditions—although fervently followed—that have been holistically identified as the cause of the current economic stagnation and lack of innovation in today's Eastern societies (Lei, Zhang, & Zhao, 2012).

While there have been countless attempts throughout the 19th and 20th centuries aimed to revolutionize the traditional education system in China, only the most relevant and current actions will be addressed in the sections below. Understanding the themes behind these specifically listed reformations and policies will better illustrate as to where Eastern systems are

138 ▪ C. ALEXANDER

situated—both educationally and economically—in today's highly competitive and globalized economy.

Movement Toward Decentralization

In order to achieve the vision of "quality-oriented education" that was originally outlined in the 1985 Decision to Reform the Education System by the MOE, the Chinese government embarked on the pivotal process of decentralization by shifting responsibilities and authority from the central government to regional governments and other lower-level bodies, such as universities (Chua et al., 2015). The hope was to bolster the country's ability to foster innovation by allowing localized districts to specialize their educational policies to the needs of their students.

Beckett, Li, Guo, Guo, and Guo (2013) comprehensively outline the next successive step in reformations—the new curriculum reform that was launched by the MOE in June 2001. Described as an amendment of "basic education unparalleled in modern Chinese history" (p. 247), the wide-reaching implementation of the reform was illustrated in a recent report administered by the China Education and Research Network. In short, it has been implemented in all grade levels, involving more than 474,000 schools, 10 million teachers, and 200 million students since 2005. The aspirations underpinning the new curriculum intentionally aim for the development of each student and, therefore, call for radical changes in all areas of the Chinese education system, including educational philosophy, curricula, standards, pedagogy, assessment, and teacher education and development (Beckett et al., 2013). These required changes inherently illustrate a drastic departure from traditional Chinese education.

As can be imagined, the decentralization and revamping of a deeply embedded tradition is a very time-consuming and complicated process. In order to encourage and further along the effort to displace power and autonomy, additional educational directives continued to be administered by the MOE, most notably the Outline of China's National Plan for Medium- and Long-Term Education Reform and Development (2010–2020). Initially established in 2010 and considered to be the most comprehensive of educational policies to date, this plan specifically identifies additional university autonomy, as well as the reforming of the college admission process as the two key aspects of educational restructuring in the next decade (Lei et al., 2012). These specific efforts once again support the country's overarching acknowledgement that these two traditions must be addressed and revamped. Accordingly, this plan specifically calls for the government to continue to release central control and ultimately permit administrators and faculty to run their schools. The government's function is therefore expected to be restricted to providing services and funding, as well as creating and monitoring educational endeavors. Lastly, the plan also sets the goal of changing the one-exam-decides-all method to a thorough evaluation of a student as a whole person using multiple tests and factors for college admission (Lei et al., 2012). This therefore leads into the discussion of the National College Entrance Exam.

National College Entrance Exam

The NCEE (Gaokao) has been widely recognized as the leading cause of inhibiting innovation and creativity in China (Lei et al., 2012). This testing system, initially adopted in 1952, but very much comparable to its ancestor, the keju, has profoundly shaped Chinese education in respect to its function, content, objective, and value of education (Qiu & Zhao, 2012). And because it holistically determines the fate of a student's life, it has an enormous effect on all participants within the system: teachers, administrators, parents, and above all, students. For example, rather than focusing on fostering critical thinking, innovative skills, or the development of the student as a whole—all aspects which Western systems hold in high esteem—the NCEE renders these concepts innately insignificant by not including them in the exam. Instead, teachers, students, and administrators alike have been conditioned to dedicate every moment in the classroom towards learning HOW to take this test, rather than focusing on how to promote critical, innovative, and independent thinking. Hopper (2010) cites Margot Landman, the director of a teacher exchange program for the National Committee on United States–China Relations, in order to accurately illustrate this situation:

> Nothing else is considered in the college application process, so if you have a bad day or happen to be a person who doesn't test well, tough luck. That's a huge amount of pressure and it means that much of secondary is geared to that exam. The Chinese will say over and over that their education system doesn't allow creativity. (as cited in Hopper, 2010, "Parents Pay for Nursery School, Supplemental Classes," para. 4)

A study based on the effects that this type of high-stakes testing has had on China's educational and economic status in today's world draws similar conclusions:

> Using the Gaokao scores as the only indicator for college admission brutally boils students' multi-year learning experiences down to their performance in a number of exams in two days. There have been numerous endeavors to reform the Gaokao since it was reiterated in 1977 after the Cultural Revolution. However, none of the endeavors seem successful. We have to be aware

140 ▪ C. ALEXANDER

that the reform of the Gaokao will require a deeper shift in Chinese attitudes. (Lei et al., 2012, p. 269)

Hopper perhaps best summarizes this overall tension with a direct quote by Yong Zhao—a professor at Michigan State University and an expert on China's education system—as he considers obstacles confronting the innovation problem in Chinese education:

> It [gaokao] seems to be the only way to enable people with very limited means or power to have some sort of social mobility... The test itself is also a curse for which as China moves to an innovation-based economy, they are looking for more creative, diverse talent and that testing has constrained school systems to produce them. Can China truly free itself from such a long, time-honored device? (as cited in Hopper, 2010, "Creating Innovators in China," para. 2)

Zhao emphasizes that all Chinese educators continue to battle between two present truths: Knowing that their students' only hope of going to college comes from excelling at the test, and, recognizing that students need much more than the test to truly play a critical role in China's emergent economy (as cited in Hopper, 2010, "Creating Innovators in China," para. 2).

Overall, these statements lead to the following question: Is quality-oriented education compatible with exam-oriented? In short, despite the goal to replace exam-oriented education with quality-oriented education, the essence and heart of the public remains fixated on the exam and its promises for a better, more mobile future: "As long as high-stakes exams remain, the fierce competition among parents for high-performing schools and prestigious universities will remain. Given the prevailing realities in China, it is difficult for educators to promote student-centered learning in schools" (Chua & Tan, 2015, p. 697). In short, in this exam-driven culture, the priority of educational stakeholders "is for the students to ace the exams, especially the college entrance exam to qualify for a place in a prestigious university" (Chua & Tan, 2015, p. 691). Clearly, even if quality education is fully being promoted to both teachers and administrators, the reality and powerful tradition of the NCEE still reigns.

In accordance with the above synthesis, it is understandable as to why both central control and the NCEE have been considered the true culprits in China's failure to cultivate innovative talents. Both are recognized for placing an enormous emphasis on rote memorization as well as relying heavily on drill practice and repetition: techniques that can stifle both creativity and the desire for true and meaningful learning (Lei et al., 2012). It seems that it is unlikely that China will be able to achieve its dream of cultivating creativity and innovation unless these two customs are fundamentally altered. However, even amidst a long string of overhauls and restructurings specifically geared to adapt these two factors to more closely mimic its Western counterpart, an analysis of current educational practices in China reveal that these two aspects continue to endure, attesting to the true power of tradition. Overall, Chinese education is steeped in an environment that still deems success as the production of excellent test scores. Therefore, rather than forcing teachers, students, and administrators to juggle between two distinctly conflicting expectations and traditions, what is more important is to figure out a system that intrinsically works within the contexts and traditions of a society in which it has been built.

METHOD

In order to examine how a country's culture, history, and traditions inherently impact both the effects and types of policies utilized in that particular society's field of education, an ethnographic qualitative approach was utilized. A series of informal interviews were conducted during an educational trip to China and South Korea in June of 2016 in order to further understand—first-hand—thoughts, experiences, and reactions to the East's present and traditional education system. Participants included students, teachers, and administrators in one pre-K, two elementary schools, two middle schools, one high school, and two universities in several locations spanning across both countries. The informal interviews were mainly administered in focus group settings to encourage brainstorming and a more comfortable environment; interviews with administrators were conducted in a one-on-one setting. Personal input from both Chinese and South Korean tour guides are also incorporated. Furthermore, unstructured and reflective observations as a moderate participant were recorded into a daily journal and later transferred into descriptive field notes. Observations spanned from 30 minutes in some settings, to close to three hours in one of the schools. Lastly, data were also gathered from published works and articles.

RESULTS

Reception to Policy Reformations

A review of data, research, and feedback that have been both documented and personally witnessed about curricular, pedagogical, and test-related reformations simply point to the conclusion that they have not been effective. A survey administered by the Chinese MOE in 2007 to collect general public feedback on acceptance level of the new policies and reformations paints a realistic portrait. Although this examination was by no means an official and infallible assessment of public sentiment, a written source based

142 ▪ C. ALEXANDER

on this feedback details that the MOE acknowledged that, despite these efforts for change, the core of the education system in China seems to stubbornly remain the same as before the reforms:

> Although many educators seem to have accepted the concept of "quality education" and some teachers have changed their teaching practices, by and large the focus on the whole child remains lip service. Quality education is loudly spoken, but test-oriented education gets the real attention. (Qiu, 2012, p. 320)

Excerpts of informal interviews below provide further insight into how the current practices and overall culture of the education systems in China and South Korea are currently being received and viewed by teachers, students, and administrators respectively. Due to the repetitive nature of the responses, the below statements are synthesized in my own words in order to illustrate the general sentiment witnessed. All interviews were conducted during a study abroad experience to both countries in the Summer of 2016. Please note that names and schools have been protected for purposes of privacy:

- There is a well-known statement in China that says that "all students give their English back to their teachers when they graduate." (Tour guide—Xi'an, China, 6/18/2016, addressing how students do not learn English for communicative purposes and real-life application, but rather to "pass the test.")
- I prefer that our teacher just lecture the whole time. I know it is a good idea to work together in a group and discuss topics, but it is a waste of time and time is valuable. If the teacher is lecturing, at least I know all the information is important and will be on the test. (High School student—Xi'an, China, 6/20/16)
- We have no opportunity to practice with native English speakers, and that is what we want. Our teacher doesn't know English very well. I wish we could have more authentic and realistic conversations with people from the United States but it just doesn't seem to be important here. (Female college student—Xi'an, China, 6/21/16, stating how she wishes the classroom experience would change)
- We never learned English in high school. It was all about the test and learning how to answer the questions. Now that we are in college, we really want to learn English but we don't know how. We don't have any opportunities. (Male student—Xi'an, China, 6/20/16)
- No one in China knows English. In secondary school, it is all about the test, so we don't really learn anything. Something needs to change. (Male student—Xi'an, China, 6/20/16, reflecting on what students really are learning/retaining in the classroom)

- Students want the curriculum to change—they want to be immersed in more authentic environments where they learn applicable and useful information. The government recognizes this. There will be big changes in the next 10 years. (Administrator from Seoul, S. Korea, 6/23/16, noting the recent changes in student behavior toward the standardized curriculum)
- We face immense pressure all year round. It is all about grades and performance still. We feel it; the students feel it. I'm not sure if this will ever change. How can it? It's all we've known. (Male teacher from, Seoul, S. Korea, 6/23/16)

DISCUSSION

The Power of Context, Culture, and Tradition

After the above review on the history and traditions of both the Western and Eastern educational systems, as well as understanding how the new Western policies adopted by the East have been received, the next step is to examine "why" these practices have not been successful. The probable answer: It may exclusively have to do with the power of culture, tradition, and therefore, context. If a specific way of life has been instated and followed for more than 2,000 years (combining the traditions from both the keju and NCEE)—seldom with another viable option available—how can anyone or anything be expected to feasibly change? For example, with this most current round of reformations, teachers are being asked to follow Western models and pedagogies that categorically challenge how they view themselves in the classroom, as well as how they impart knowledge to their students. If this emphasis never existed before, how can educators be expected to change their habits and ways of life that inherently do not align with their established cultural values? For example: While Western culture demonstrates and lauds individualism, Chinese culture holds community and socialistic aspects in high esteem (Beckett et al., 2013; Chua & Tan, 2015). So, taking a policy or pedagogy that was explicitly bred in a Western environment, can it also effectively coexist and work in an Eastern environment where the context is starkly different? Quite simply, the East is confronted with a dilemma between traditional Confucian ethics and values, and new global values, such as decentralization, efficiency, and accountability. In other words:

Chinese administrators believe the new Western educational ideas are effective for democratic education, collaborative learning, and close teacher–student relationships. On the other hand, they see Chinese traditional education strengths as respect for teachers, emphasis on basic education, and high national and international examination scores. (Lee et al., 2014, p. 296)

These teachers grew up in a traditional learning environment and therefore tend to be fixed in their ways of thinking as well as in actions. Their own exam-driven culture and conventional ways completely contrast the new student-centered learning pedagogy that they are supposed to promote, intrinsically "handicapping" them between two opposing worlds. Although the curriculum reform has introduced a diverse syllabus with learner-centered pedagogies and alternative assessment, the reality is that success in the high-stakes exams is still most important (Chua & Tan, 2015).

Ultimately, these adopted Western policies have been ineffective as the East struggles to reconcile their own cultural significance and beliefs with those from a completely foreign context. So, just how significant is this gap between intentions and reality? Simply, the importance of context and tradition must be considered and weighed before any lasting decisions are made. Therefore, before importing educational policies from another culture, it is vital to be aware of that other nation's economical, cultural, and political background. If they contrast those of the importing nation's environment, most likely their policies will not be received in the same way, nor be as effective. In other words, it is very challenging to isolate educational reform from the cultural and contextual characteristics of the schools and societies from which it was originally derived with those to whom they are ultimately being transferred.

Overall, the argument is that there exist fundamental cultural differences between Western and Eastern perspectives that inherently make policy transfer in China challenging. Educational reformers must consider sociocultural norms and constraints in their own setting versus those from which they are importing their policies. For example, are there sufficient school resources and classroom conditions available to comply with a drastic change in pedagogy and deliverance of knowledge? How will teachers adapt and how will students adhere to these changes considering the atmosphere of high-stakes testing? Will there be teacher training/professional development to help close the gap (Yan, 2015)? All in all, these questions lead to a more pervasive question: Is it necessary for the importing society to change their own environment so that a new foreign policy will assimilate better? But what if specific adjustments are innately infeasible? An example comes from comparing the sizes of classrooms in the East from those of the West:

[Chinese academics/leadership] found many reform initiatives were feasible in small size classes common in Western developed countries, but much less so in a classroom crowded with an average of more than 50 students which is quite prevalent in cities in China. (Lee et al., 2014, p. 305)

Chinese and South Korean Education Reformations ▪ **145**

These types of crowded classrooms described above are consistent with what was witnessed during the study abroad trip to China and South Korea respectively, regardless of them being public or private schools, secondary or university-level schools.

A further example of trying to adopt policies that simply are not practical to the realities of a different context comes from examining the current curriculum initiatives; this new pedagogical push to cultivate students' all-around development—not just the familiar knowledge developed exclusively with the NCEE in mind—goes completely against Chinese tradition. With extreme competition persistently existing around students trying to get into college where there are less spots available than the amount of students applying, all efforts ultimately end up turning back to the NCEE since it is the only way to knowingly secure a university spot (Hopper, 2010). Hence, by trying to focus on students' all-around development is in direct contrast with the Chinese tradition of "learning to the exam": "since the college entrance exam [is] still the main means of achieving upward social mobility, school leaders [are] not sure whether they could ensure students' performance if public examination remained as high under these reforms" (Lee et al., 2014, p. 305).

Overall, these specific examples suggest the importance of implementing ideology that aligns with the cultural foundations of any given society.

CONCLUSION

Continual efforts to spur on innovation and improve the quality of education in the East by dually revamping the testing structure as well as decentralizing the traditional system simply have not produced desired results. Why? In short, Chinese and Eastern educational systems have been built on traditions and beliefs that root back to more than 2,000 years ago, and it is from these traditions that both the testing culture and central government control were founded. In essence, fundamental cultural norms carry a weight that cannot easily be dismissed. These two systems have always been heralded as central components to a system that has been embedded in a society for thousands of years. Although the format and the content of the NCEE are changing, the purposes of the test and its role in students' lives have not changed. So, when it comes to the essential question for implementation research, it should not simply be based on what generally works, but rather, what works for whom, where, when, and why. The process of adopting foreign policies cannot be considered context-free, but are undeniably influenced by local cultural conditions. Factors such as a country's national history, as well as its aspirations and political ideologies can all shape and contribute to a culture-specific education policy terrain of education policy making. In short, the culture of the school reflects the overall culture of that society (Chua & Tan, 2015). Thus, if China and South Korea are truly aiming to revamp their educational practices to ensure a more well-rounded and prepared student for a global society, they must look to implement and adhere to systems that align with their cultures, within their own contexts (Lee et al., 2014). In short, policies cannot simply be borrowed from other cultures if they are to be lasting and effective.

REFERENCES

Beckett, G., Li, Q., Guo, L., Guo, S., & Guo, Y. (2013) Changes in Chinese education under globalisation and market economy: Emerging issues and debates. *Compare: A Journal of Comparative & International Education, 43*(2), 244–264.

Cheung, R. H. P. (2016) The challenge of developing creativity in a Chinese context: The effectiveness of adapting Western creative pedagogy to inform creative practice. *Pedagogy, Culture & Society, 24*(1), 141–160.

Chua, C. S. K., & Tan, C. (2015). Education policy borrowing in China: Has the west wind overpowered the east wind? *Compare: A Journal of Comparative and International Education, 45*(5), 686–704.

Farenga, S. J., Ness, D., Johnson, B., & Johnson, D. D. (2010). *The importance of average: Playing the game of school to increase success and achievement.* Lanham, MD: Rowan & Littlefield.

Frush, K. L., & Muetz, K. G. (2007). Connecting early American values to the current practice of adult education. *Journal of Adult Education, 36*(1), 36–43.

Hopper, J. (2010, November 16). Is China's education system keeping up with growing superpower? *ABC News.* Retrieved from http://abcnews.go.com/WN/China/chinas-education-system-helping-hurting-superpowers-growing-economy/story?id=12152255

Klein, R. (2016). No child left behind: An overview. *Education Week.* Retrieved from http://www.edweek.org/ew/section/multimedia/no-child-left-behind-overview-definition-summary.html

Lee, J. C., Wang, W., & Yin, H. (2014) Dilemmas of leading national curriculum reform in a global era: A Chinese perspective. *Educational Management Administration & Leadership, 42*(2), 293–311.

Lei, J., Zhang, G., & Zhao, Y. (2012). Between a rock and a hard place: Higher education reform and innovation in China. *On the Horizon, 20*(4), 263–273.

Niu, W. (2007). Western influences on Chinese educational testing. *Comparative Education, 43*(1), 71–91.

Qiu, W., & Zhao, Y. (2012). Policy changes and educational reforms in China: Decentralization and marketization. *On the Horizon, 20*(4), 313–323.

Rasmussen, P., & Zou, Y. (2014). The development of educational accountability in China and Denmark. *Education Policy Analysis Archives, 22*(121).

Wan, G. (2012). The educational development in China: Perspectives from the West. *New Horizons in Education, 60*(2), 1–20.

Yan, C. (2015). We can't change much unless the exams change: Teachers' dilemmas in the curriculum reform in China. *Improving Schools, 18*(1), 5–19.

CHAPTER 10

HOW SMART LEARNING IS DEFINED

An Analysis of 27 Definitions by Korean Scholars

Kiran S. Budhrani

The clock struck noon and the classroom bell rang at an elementary school in Seoul, South Korea. Mr. Yoon, the social studies teacher, waded across the front of the classroom to settle down his cheery fifth graders in his comfortable school slippers paired with formal slacks and a long-sleeve shirt. The students followed the same shoe etiquette of removing their outdoor shoes and changing into school slippers upon entering the classroom. Because outdoor shoes are considered dirty in Korean culture, the tradition of wearing slippers is followed both at home and in school.

The young students settled in their seats comfortably with their shorts and breezy cotton T-shirts. Reluctant to dirty their school bags, they hung their bags on hooks screwed to the sides of their desks instead of placing them on the ground. We, visiting teachers and graduate students from the United States, stood at the back of the room, observing every detail of their

---

Educational Practices in China, Korea, and the United States, pages 149–174
Copyright © 2019 by Information Age Publishing
All rights of reproduction in any form reserved.

149

classroom, from the bulletin boards to the decorations. Mr. Yoon was more nervous of our presence than his students were. I even caught a naughty student seated in front joking with Mr. Yoon in the Korean language, implying that he had to speak to the visitors in straight English. This joke was half meant, knowing that speaking in straight English was uncommon, and his teacher would most likely struggle. Lessons at elementary schools were conducted in the Korean language, and speaking in straight English was greatly admired.

Mr. Yoon did not say much to the visitors. We did not have any idea what his lesson plan was for the next 45 minutes of class, but we watched him quickly turn on his Samsung computer and large screen Samsung TV and prompt the students to watch a video. The video played with Korean narration for a few minutes. Then, Mr. Yoon debriefed his key points with a slide show of newspaper clippings, graphs, charts, and images of Korea's current events.

The lesson quickly shifted from the teacher lecturing, to a group activity where students had to work together to create a "futuristic newspaper" poster. At this point, we had a better idea where the lesson was headed. All students came prepared with printed pictures of futuristic technologies such as solar-powered cars, modern buildings, and new forms of wind energy. Mr. Yoon handed each group a poster template and the students began to lay out their pictures and write news captions. By the end of the group activity, the students generated absolutely creative work, put together with neatness and meticulous precision.

Each group was asked to hang their newspaper posters on the board for discussion. As the first group was ready to present, Mr. Yoon brought out his Android smartphone, launched the Mobizen app, and initiated smart screen mirroring (Figure 10.1). This technique allowed him to share the screen of his Samsung smartphone onto the large screen Samsung TV through the personal computer to enhance the students' poster presentations.

Mr. Yoon mirrored his device through the built-in camera, allowing the students to hover over and enlarge sections of their poster while discussing (Figure 10.2). This increased visualization for the large class and facilitated a more focused presentation of student work. Mr. Yoon's story is just one

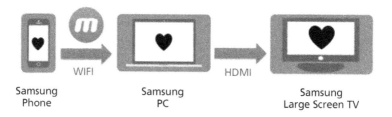

Figure 10.1 Smart screen mirroring device set-up.

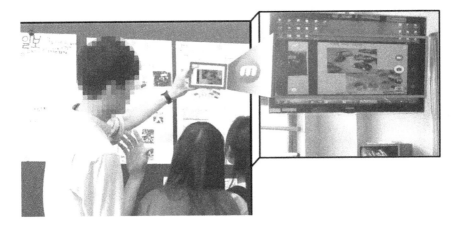

Figure 10.2 Mr. Yoon and his students screen mirroring with the Mobizen app.

anecdote to make the case of how teachers can effectively use smart technologies, like smartphones and tablets, to enhance learning in the classroom. This unique observation triggered an interest to explore the literature on South Korea's practices of using information and communication technologies (ICT) and smart mobile devices for education.

The mobile device is one of the fastest growing technologies in the last decade because it is handheld, multipurpose, and portable with Internet access (Ng, 2015). Amidst a population of 50 million in Korea, the number of mobile phone subscribers was 10 million in 2010, 20 million in 2011, and has risen to 30 million in 2012 (Kim, 2012; Lim, 2012). South Korea is at the forefront of broadband access, ICT, and mobile technology, producing an environment where educational policies and programs are largely interrelated with integrating technology (Gallagher, 2016).

One of the most widely recognized definitions of smart learning is that of the Korean Ministry of Education, Science and Technology or MEST who institutionalized "smart learning" as an education reform in 2011 and defined "smart" as self-directed, motivated, adaptive, resource-enriched, and technology-embedded learning (MEST, 2011). The reform was due to foreseen changes in the role of teachers and students, the advancement of teaching-learning methods amidst emerging educational environments, and the individualization and customization of learning to fit the levels of learning needs (MEST, 2011). The smart learning strategy is implemented in parallel with Korea's master plan for ICT in education, science, and technology to develop digital textbooks, introduce online classes and online assessment systems, improve copyright systems for free educational content, and to augment teachers' capabilities for implementing smart learning (MEST, 2011).

MEST's (2011) definition of smart learning as five characteristics was descriptive of a proposed learning paradigm or learning environment for the future, but it did not provide educators details on how to implement such. An earlier concept of smart learning was proposed by Kwak (2010), which emphasizes the individual learners over the technology and proposed that learning through such a technological infrastructure should be according to the learning needs of the individual (Gallagher, 2016; Kim, Cho, & Lee, 2013). Other researchers defined other characteristics of smart learning to include self-directed, real-time, and personalized learning (Kim 2010, as cited in Sung 2015, p. 117). Jang (2010) defined smart learning to be learner-centered, collaborative, flexible, interactive, self-directed, and realistic (as cited in Sung, 2015, p. 116).

Other definitions of smart learning traces back to how the concept emerged amidst similar terminologies like e-learning, m-learning, and u-learning. Noh (2011) claims that the concept of smart learning emerged as a response to the limitations of e-learning, as well as, a result of changes brought about by the advancement of smart devices and technologies. Existing definitions and characteristics of smart learning among Korean scholars show that it is an "evolved form of e-learning that included smarter educational environments" generally making use of smart phones to enhance the effectiveness of education based on new learning methods (i.e., participation, sharing, and customization), new pedagogies, smarter content, and smart devices (Jo, Yang, & Lim, 2012; Wikipedia, n.d.).

While Korean scholars have attempted to define and describe smart learning and its characteristics, no clear definition of smart learning exists to date (Jo et al., 2012; Kim et al., 2013; Lee, Kim, & Chung, 2013; Lee, Lim, & Um, 2015; Sung, 2015). To present a more organized understanding of the smart learning terminology beyond descriptive characteristics, Zhu, Yu, and Riezebos (2016) introduced the Smarter Education conceptual framework which describes smart learning to include three essential elements: (a) smart learning environments, (b) smart pedagogy, and (c) smart learners.

The purpose of this research is to conduct a content analysis of 27 smart learning definitions written by Korean authors, and in doing so, provide an empirical basis from which to further the discussions on this topic within the Korean context. The 27 definitions in this study were derived from a literature search of definitions that currently exist among Korean authors/scholars between 2010 to 2016, but is no way exhaustive of the myriad of definitions that are in use in other regions such as North America and China. It is not the purpose of the research to arrive at an explanation for why such variability occurs among smart learning definitions, nor is it the purpose to construct a definition representative of the attempts made thus far. This research aims to empirically examine the various elements of smart learning across the 27 definitions to surface how Korean authors have defined or described smart learning environments, smart pedagogies, and smart learners. Thus, the following research questions are posed:

1. How do Korean authors define or describe smart learning environments?
2. How do Korean scholars define or describe smart pedagogy?
3. How do Korean scholars define or describe smart learners?

This chapter is organized in four major sections: review of the literature, methodology, results and discussion, and implications. The first section on the review of the literature provides a background on the evolving concept of smart learning from e-learning, m-learning, and u-learning, and on the three elements of the Smarter Education framework (Zhu, Yu, & Riezebos, 2016) which include smart learning environments, smart pedagogies, and smart learners. The second section on the methodology describes the research design, data sources, data collection methods, data analysis methods. The third section highlights the results and discussion emphasizing keyword analyses among smart learning elements. The last section discusses the implications of the research findings, with emphasis on the changes foreseen in students, pedagogy, learning environments, culture, and governance.

REVIEW OF THE LITERATURE

Evolving Concept of Smart Learning

Technology progress has been regarded as a solution for improving the quality of education (Kim et al., 2013). The concept of smart learning (Figure 10.3) sprung from online learning concepts of e-learning, m-learning, and u-learning (Kim, 2012; Kim et al., 2013; Lee & Son, 2013; Lim, 2012; Zhu et al., 2016). E-learning is electronically supported learning that uses ICT to enable radio and broadcasting technology, computer-based instruction (CBI), or web-based instructions (Kim et al., 2013; Lee & Son, 2013; Lim, 2012). Mobile learning (m-Learning) was driven by the advancement in the ease-of-use of mobile and wireless devices (Kim et al., 2013). It improved e-learning by adding flexibility in learning time, location, and cost, as well as, mobility of the learner, which was not supported in traditional educational modes (Kim et al., 2013). Ubiquitous or u-learning is a more high-tech educational environment that allows learning anytime and anywhere through more improved technologies like sensors, augmented and virtual reality. It moved the learning style where learning can take place

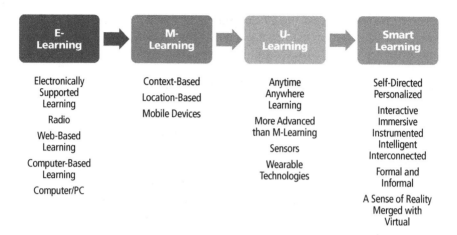

Figure 10.3 Evolution of online learning to smart learning.

anytime and anywhere without the limitations of time, locations, or environments (Kim et al., 2013).

Smart learning expands how e-learning, m-learning, and u-learning is implemented to combine real and virtual, formal and informal learning environments. Smart learning began from the lack of authenticity in e-learning and mobile learning (Hwang, Tsai, & Yang, 2008; Zhu et al., 2016). The importance and necessity of authentic learning activities where learners work with real-life, real-world problems triggered the need to now design learning that combine both real and virtual learning environments seamlessly, merging aspects of mobile learning and ubiquitous learning. While learning should happen anytime, anywhere, learners should be able to transfer learning in formal and informal learning scenarios, and individual and social learning scenarios through smart devices (Chan et al., 2006; Zhu et al., 2016). Thus, smart learning is not a new education paradigm; it has the characteristics of current online learning models but attempts to add authenticity (Kwon et al., 2013).

South Korea's Smart Learning Paradigm

Duk-hoon Kwak, CEO of Educational Broadcasting System (EBS) in Korea and Chairman of the Korean Smart Learning Forum, is known to be the pioneer of smart learning who helped the country learn more about its vision and significance (Kim, 2012). Korea's IT Times (Kim, 2012) highlights Dr. Kwak's long interest in combining IT with education to provide high quality education for students who could not afford access. The Korean MEST defined "SMART" as self-directed, motivated, adaptive, resource-enriched, and technology-embedded learning methods (MEST, 2011). Smart learning is described as:

- S: Self-Directed, which means that the education system is progressing toward a self-learning system more than ever. Students' roles transition from knowledge adopters to knowledge creators. Also, teachers become facilitators of learning.
- M: Motivated means education becomes experience centered and involves learning by doing; creative problem solving and individualized assessment are pursued.
- A: Adaptive means strengthening of the education system's flexibility and tailoring learning for individual preference and future careers.
- R: Resource-enriched means that smart learning utilizes rich content based on open market, cloud education services from both public and private sectors. In other words, it expands the scope of learning resources to include collective intelligence, social learning.
- T: Technology-embedded means that in the smart learning education environment, students can learn anywhere, any time through advanced technologies. (Kim et al., 2013, p. 172)

MEST (2011) also highlights that "smart education is a feature of future education, which means expansion of time, space, learning materials and learning methods, which overcome the limits of conventional classroom lectures" (p. 17). Smart learning underscores a shift in education to foster 21st century skills, particularly on the 7Cs of critical thinking and problem-solving, creativity and innovation, collaboration and leadership, cross-cultural understanding, communication, ICT literacy, career and life skills (MEST, 2011).

Smart Learning Environments

Noh et al. (2011) as cited in J.-E. Lee et al. (2015) lists examples of smart environments to include cloud computing, networks, servers, smart devices, and embedded devices. But within a broader framework, smart learning bases its foundations on the capabilities of smart devices and intelligent technologies (Kim, Song, & Yoon, 2011; Lee, Zo, & Lee, 2014; Zhu et al., 2016).

Smart Devices

Low and O'Connell (2006) describe today's smartphones as a convergence of many tools into one or the "Swiss army knife" of this century (p. 79). The portability and ease of use of the smartphone may seem to replace the previously pressing need for personal computers and laptops, however researchers have started to believe that mobile phones support formal and informal learning, and complete the process of learning via computers (Taki & Khazaei, 2011).

Smartphones appeared in the early 2000s featuring high-level graphic interfaces, touchscreen capability, built-in Wi-Fi, GPS capability, built-in storage, and Internet access (Minges, 2012), which promoted the download and use of "apps" to carry out specific functions. The strength lying in the capabilities of smartphones and the highly personalized nature of mobile devices provides an excellent platform for the development of personalized, learner-centric educational experiences (Low & O'Connell, 2006; Ng, 2015).

The smartphone features portability (small size and weight), social interactivity (enabling collaboration and data exchange), context sensitivity (capacity to respond to current location, time and environment), connectivity (ability to create a shared network), and individuality (personalization and ownership of learning; Klopfer, Squire, & Jenkins, 2002). Similarly, Lee and Son (2013) identify that mobile internet provides for ubiquity (real-time information from anywhere), reach (access from access from anywhere without the constraints of time and space), security, convergence, localization (to identify a specific point in time where the user's current location is unknown), instant connectivity (to navigate the necessary information within a short time), and personalization.

Intelligent Technologies

Intelligent technologies, such as cloud computing, learning analytics, big data, Internet of things (IoT), sensors, wearable technology and so forth, promote the emergence of smart learning to be personalized and adaptive (Zhu et al., 2016). The Internet of things is now a common buzzword used by technology advocates. It refers to the number of "things" connected to the Internet, where things go beyond mobile phones and tablets, to consumer devices or household appliances such as watches, eyeglasses, cars, refrigerators, and more. Connection to the Internet is supported by sensors that collect and transfer without direct human input (Horowitz, 2015). For example, a home temperature system can have a noise sensor that detects how many people are at home and can adjust the thermostat accordingly. Cisco predicts that there will be 50 billion devices connected to the Internet by 2020; Morgan Stanley predicts this number at 75 billion and claims that there are 200 unique consumer devices or equipment that have potential to connect to the Internet (Danova, 2013).

Smart Pedagogies

Compared to m-learning or u-learning, which focus on the devices or Internet technologies, smart learning strongly emphasizes the pedagogy needed when integrating technology. This section gives insight on the instructional strategies and opportunities promoted by using mobile devices as a pedagogical tool, as well as, the requirements and factors for smart learning.

Mobile devices as pedagogical tools. The pedagogy of bring-your-own-device (BYOD) has gained interest in primary schools and higher education with its focus on student learning interventions. However, in the elementary classroom, it is understandable that young children do not bring their own smart mobile devices to school. Thus often, classrooms that are "smart" come equipped with iPads or tablets for young students to use. In contrast, Ng (2015) highlights a more important aspect relevant to elementary schools, which is the teacher and how they use smartphones as a pedagogical tool. The following key points are important to note when considering how teachers can use technology as a pedagogical tool:

> Mobile devices blur the boundaries between formal (i.e., planned, structured, school-based, and facilitated) and informal (unplanned, opportunistic, non-facilitated, out-of-school, interest/learner driven) learning, enabling continuity in learning between contexts; it is through the ability to use devices across contexts that seamless learning spaces are created. (Ng, 2015, p. 8)

Seamless learning spaces can be forged by using mobile and web apps in the classroom for (a) collaboration activities (i.e., peer assessment, peer-editing, brainstorming, shared notes, collaborative bookmarking, collaborative reading); (b) communication activities (i.e., posting comments, voice-calls, back-channeling, translation, sending reminders); and (c) creation activities (i.e., collaborative writing/blogging, mini-presentations, playlists, how-to guides; Hardison, 2013). Mobile or web apps also allow activities for students to acquire information, make meaning, and promote knowledge transfer (Schwartz, 2015). As seen in the anecdote of Mr. Yoon at the beginning of the chapter, mobile devices bring about new opportunities in the classroom such as: (a) increased visualization for students; (b) enhanced student presentation, discussion, and focus; (c) efficient use of time-in-class; (d) increased student-student, student-teacher, student-technology, teacher-technology interactivity; (e) relevant, up-to-date learning; and (f) the transfer of learning towards and outside of the classroom.

Requirements and Factors for Smart Learning

The concept of seamless learning is evidently a strong factor in making smart education possible. Seamless learning is strongly related to ubiquitous learning. Ng (2015) and Ogata and Yano (2004) identified six requirements for ubiquitous learning that promote smart learning and continuity between virtual and real learning environments. The list is provided below (Ng, 2015, p. 8):

1. permanency, where learners never lose their work unless it is deleted on purpose;
2. accessibility, where learners are able to access their files, documents, and data from anywhere;
3. immediacy, where learners are able to obtain information immediately;
4. interactivity, where learners are able to interact with teachers, peers, or experts through synchronous or asynchronous communication, enabling knowledge development and transformation to occur more readily;
5. situating of instructional activities, such that learning is embedded in the learners' daily lives and across different contexts; and
6. adaptability, where learners can get the right information at the right place in the right way.

Furthermore, Kwon et al. (2013, p. 12) identifies the six important factors of smart learning to be: self-directed learning, interaction, learning management systems (LMS), knowledge-building community, use of social networking sites (SNS), use of smart devices.

Smart Learners

The smart era in South Korea peaked in 2012 with the establishment of a prototype Smart School in the city of Sejong (Choi, 2012), where students are experiencing high-tech learning experience, most of which students around the world can only dream of. At Sejong, all students have tablets with full wireless network and Internet coverage; there is automatic checking of attendance using an e-identification card; lectures from teachers are synchronized with students' tablets; students can review class material freely after school with their tablet and PC; notes on whiteboards are recorded for easy review; security systems check students' location; and teachers can check security status by area of the school (Lee, n.d.). Other practices in smart schools include digital tracking of attendance (roll call), digital note-taking (Espiritu, 2016), smart screen mirroring, and VR technologies for video (MobileScout, 2016).

Smart devices will evolve to intelligent technologies in schools. A study (Uzelac, Gligoric, & Krco, 2015) from the University of Belgrade used sensors to measure different aspects of the classroom environment (temperature, humidity, and carbon dioxide levels) through sensors and attempted to link these factors to student focus. The lecturer wore a headset to collect data on the lecturer's voice and a microphone on a smartphone collected data on the overall noise level in the room. While the results of this study were preliminary, it showed that with sensors, strong analytical programs, and cloud storage, a "smart" classroom could exist that collects, analyzes, and packages data for teachers to use and improve the way they conduct instruction (Horowitz, 2015).

Smart learning puts emphasis on developing a "smarter learner" with the technologies that seamlessly integrate to their day-to-day activities like attendance, lectures, testing, lessons reviews, and so forth. As reflected in the examples in the previous paragraphs, smart learners have increased access to information, data trackers, and integration of technology into their study habits. It is expected that as learners begin to adapt advanced technologies, they will exhibit collaboration, creativity, convergence, and problem-solving skills (Lee et al., 2015).

Various Korean scholars have attempted to define and describe smart learning and its characteristics, there is a breadth of terminology being mentioned or cited in each definition that makes it difficult to form a clear understanding of what smart learning really means or how it is described as an educational paradigm. Further analysis and synthesis is necessary to surface the essential concepts, key words, characteristics, or terminologies commonly used among these definitions. The purpose of this research is to employ a directed approach to content analysis (Hsieh & Shannon, 2005) of 27 smart learning definitions derived from literature by Korean authors/scholars between 2010 to 2016 in an attempt to better understand how they define or describe smart learning environments, smart pedagogies, and smart learners.

METHODOLOGY

Research Design

This research employs a directed approach to content analysis (Hsieh & Shannon, 2005) to validate or extend conceptually the Smarter Education framework of Zhu et al. (2016) utilizing smart learning environments, smart pedagogies, and smart learners as three predetermined coding categories. Using key words as a unit of analysis, 27 smart learning definitions were scanned for keywords that represent any of the three elements. Keywords that were relevant were tallied for rank order and comparisons of frequency.

Data Sources

Google Scholar was primarily used to conduct the search for smart learning definitions. Key words used for the search included "smart learning" or "smart education." Data sources included in the study required that: (a) one or more definitions or characteristics of smart learning included, presented, or published by Korean authors/scholars; and (b) it had text written in English. Using this criteria, eleven sources had one or more smart learning definitions written by Korean authors/scholars (Table 10.1). Journal articles, proceedings, conference papers, and book chapters often had multiple authors and their definitions cited, particularly in the Introduction section or Review of Literature section of the paper. Consequently, reviewing the 11 data sources, 16 unique author/s were found to have contributed to the compiled 27 definitions of smart learning for this study (Table 10.2). Among the 27 definitions, four definitions were presented by the author/s themselves, while the other 24 definitions were cited from secondary sources. Data sources written in Korean text were excluded from the study. However, Korean authors that were cited in English in secondary sources were included (Table 10.3). It was evident in Google Scholar that several smart learning studies were published by American and Chinese scholars; however, these were excluded from the analysis because they diverted from the Korean context.

Data Collection

The 11 data sources included in this study were examined for smart learning definitions. As a result, Table 10.4 summarizes the 27 definitions

TABLE 10.1 Descriptive Summary of Selected Sources

Korean authors with proposed smart learning definitions	16
Sources with one or more smart learning definitions	11
Journal	6
Proceedings	1
Conference presentation	1
Conference paper	1
Report	1
Book chapter	1
Number of definitions collected from primary and secondary sources	27
Definitions from primary source	4
Definitions from secondary source	23

How Smart Learning Is Defined ▪ **161**

TABLE 10.2 Korean Authors With One or More Smart Learning Definitions

Source	Research/Topic	Type
Hwang, D. J. (2011)	Smart innovation in education and learning	Conference presentation
Korean MEST (2011)	Adapting education to the information age	Report
Koo, D.-H. (2012)	Trends and revitalization of smart-learning in elementary and middle schools	Journal
Kwon et al. (2013)	The framework of the smart learning infrastructure in South Korea: Focus on agriculture education system	Conference paper
Jo et al. (2012)	Design of a structured plug-in smart education system	Book chapter
Jo, Park, Lee, & Lim (2014)	An integrated teaching and learning assistance system meeting requirements for smart education	Journal
Jo, Park, Ji, Yang, & Lim (2016)	A study on factor analysis to support knowledge based decisions for a smart class	Journal
J.-A. Lee et al. 2013	Study on communication of characteristics smart learning from UX perspective	Journal
J.-E. Lee et al. (2015)	A cyber engineering education strategy based on smart learning	Journal
M.-S. Lee & Son (2013)	Development of BYOD strategy learning system with smart learning supporting	Journal
Sung, M. (2015)	A study of adults' perception and needs for smart learning	Proceedings
Total: 11		

that were collected and organized by year, author, and definition, most of which were taken from a secondary source because the original definition was either inaccessible, could not be found through a web search, or written in Korean text. Each definition was mapped with a reference code (e.g., D1) to aid data analysis and presentation of results in subsequent sections of this chapter.

Data Analysis

The 27 smart learning definitions examined had multiple key words that were easily coded to describe either smart learning environments, smart pedagogies, or smart learners. A table for each smart learning element was created to show the list of key words identified that descriptive of the element, a tally of definition sources (indicated as a list of reference codes)

TABLE 10.3 Korean Authors With Definitions Cited in Primary and Secondary Sources

Author	Source of Definition
Hwang, D. J. (2011)	Primary source
Jang, S. (2010)	Cited in Sung (2015)
Kang, J.-H. (2011)	Cited in Kwon et al. (2013)
KERIS (2011)	Cited in Koo (2012)
Kim, D. (2010)	Cited in J.-A. Lee et al. (2013)
Koo, D.-H. (2012)	Primary source
Korean MEST (2011)	Primary source
Kwak, D.-H. (2010)	Cited in J.-A. Lee et al. (2013); Sung (2015)
Lee, J. (2011)	Cited in Jo, Park, Ji, Yang, & Lim (2016); Jo, Park, Lee, & Lim (2014)
Lee, S.-H. (2010)	Cited in D.-W. Lee & Lee (2012)
D.-W. Lee & Lee (2012)	Cited in J.-E. Lee et al. (2015)
Noh, K.-S. (2011)	Cited in Sung (2015)
Noh, K., Ju, S., & Jung, J. T. (2011)	Cited in Kwon et al. (2013); J.-E. Lee et al. (2015); Sung (2015)
Park, C. (2011)	Cited in Sung (2015)
Sung, M. (2015)	Primary source
Wikipedia (Korea)	Cited in Jo et al. (2012)
Total: 16	

that included such key words, and the frequency and percentage of how often the key word occurred among the 27 definitions.

A componential analysis (see Table 10.8) of the 27 smart learning definitions was tabulated to gain a larger picture of how many definitions had all three smart learning elements "present" (i.e., indicated as "+") and how many definitions had at least one or more of the smart elements "absent" (i.e., indicated as "−"). Results from this analysis informs or validates the Smarter Education framework of Zhu et al. (2016) which proposes that smart learning should include the three elements of smart learning environments, smart pedagogies, and smart learners.

RESULTS AND DISCUSSION

Table 10.5 shows a summary of 14 unique key words that describe smart learning environments. The most frequently occurring key word refers to the use of smart technology (52%) such as mobile devices, ICT, or computers in smart learning environments. But clearly, the definitions show that smart learning environments are not limited to just the use of smart

TABLE 10.4 27 Definitions or Characteristics of Smart Learning by Korean Authors

Year	Author	Definition or Characteristic of Smart Learning
2010	Kwak, D-H.	D1: A learner-centered humanistic learning system that provides easy access to learning sources and enhances interaction among learners and between learners and an instructor, and supports a self-directed learning environment (Kwak 2010, cited in Sung 2015, p. 116)*
		D2: Intelligent and adaptive learning that considers many learning types and abilities and enables learners to foster thinking, communication, and problem solving skills using various smart devices (Kwak 2010, cited in Sung 2015, p. 116)*
		D3: Effective learning that is intelligent customized focusing on learners, based on advanced ICT, human beings, and contents rather than devices. It considers various learning types of learners, increases thinking, communication, and problem solving skills, and creates opportunities for cooperative and individual learning, which makes learning more exciting (Kwak 2010, cited in J.-A. Lee et al. 2013, p.62)*
2010	Kim, D.	D4: Motivational, self-directed, real-time, and personalized (Kim 2010, cited in Sung 2015, p. 117)*
		D5: Motivation, self-directed, real-time, learning management, individualization (Kim 2010, cited in J.-A. Lee et al. 2013, p. 63)*
2010	Jang, S.	D6: Learner-centered, collaborative, flexible, interactive, self-directed and realistic (Jang 2010, cited in Sung 2015, p. 116)*
2010	Lee, S-H.	D7: Smart learning is realistic, engaging, informal, and creative. Smart learning increases a sense of reality and engagement, diminishes the boundary between play and learning, and enhances cognitive and creative abilities (Lee 2010, cited in Sung 2015, p. 116)*
		D8: Sense of reality, immersive, informal learning, cognitive (learning) support system, creative thinking (Lee 2010, cited in J.-A. Lee et al. 2013, p. 63)*
2011	Hwang, D.J.	D9: A flexible environment for education/learning where competence of learners to be intensified based on changes in student's behavior through open access to Open Educational Resource, smart IT, and international standards (slide 19)
2011	Kang, J.H.	D10: Learner-directed learning, learner-learner, learner-professor, learner-learning programs interaction, the implementation of technology (training, equipment, transfer of knowledge, content development, technology, etc.), and smart e-learning system (SNS-based collaborative learning) (Kang 2011, cited in Kwon et al. 2013, p. 12)*

(continued)

TABLE 10.4   27 Definitions or Characteristics of Smart Learning by Korean Authors (continued)

Year	Author	Definition or Characteristic of Smart Learning
2011	KERIS (Korea Education and Research Information Service)	D11: Smart learning is based on learners' smartness in addition to a smart device and the individualization of learning service (KERIS 2011, cited in Koo, 2012, p. 160)[*] D12: A learning method which the learner develops self-initiated and creative learning capability while he/she utilizes smart devices and social networks to examine his/her needs and establish a learning process to achieve optimal results (KERIS 2011, cited in Koo, 2012, p. 161)[*]
2011	Lee, J.	D13: Integrated educational environment in which cooperative, interactive, participative, sharing, and intelligent learning are available through new forms of teaching–learning content, environment, and ICT (Lee 2011, cited in Jo, Park, Lee, & Lim, 2014, p. 2455)[*] D14: Intelligent customized teaching–learning support system intended to lead changes in entire education systems such as the new pedagogy, curriculums, assessment, and the teachers required in an information- and technology-centric society in the twentyfirst century; a form of learning made by grafting adaptive learning onto human-oriented social learning (Lee 2011, cited in Jo, Park, Ji, Yang, & Lim, 2016, p. 45)[*]
2011	Noh, K-S.	D15: Achieved through smart ways of personalized, intelligent, and integrated approaches, social learning, and collective intelligence (Noh 2011, cited in Sung 2015, p. 116)[*]
2011	Noh, Ju, & Jung	D16: The important factors of smart learning is learner-centered learning environment and the learning effect, the maximum utilization of the state-of-the-art information and communication technology, and supporting effective interaction effect (Noh et al. 2011, cited in Kwon et al. 2013, p. 12)[*] D17: Combination of smart information and communication technologies that makes it easy to access the source of information on the learning, support learners, and learner-instructor interaction effectively, and learner-driven human-centered learning methods (Noh et al. 2011, cited in Kwon et al. 2013, p. 12)[*] D18: Student-centered, self-directed, interaction, intelligent, informal learning, and a sense of reality, etc. (Noh et al. 2011, cited in M.-S. Lee & Son 2013, p. 260)[*] D19: E-learning entails smart infrastructures, and training methods; smart infrastructures denote cloud computing, networks, servers, smart devices and embedded devices; smart ways include customization, intelligence, convergence, social learning, and collective intelligence (Noh et al. 2011, cited in J.-E. Lee et al. 2015, p. 1169)[*]

(continued)

Year	Author	Definition or Characteristic of Smart Learning
		D20: A human-centered and self-directed learning method which connects the smart information communication technology to the learning environment (Noh et al. 2011, cited in Sung 2015, p. 116)*
		D21: Is carried out based on the smart infrastructure of cloud computing, networks, servers, smart devices, and other embedded devices (Noh et al. 2011, cited in Sung 2015, p. 116)*
2011	Park, C.J.	D22: Smart learning is mobile device attached, intelligently applicable, customizing according to levels, collaborative through social networks, and inclusive of formal and informal learning (Park 2012, cited in Sung 2015, p. 117)*
2011	Korean MEST	D23: Self-directed, motivated, adaptive, resource-enriched, and technology-embedded (p. 17)
2012	Koo, D-H.	D24: A practical self-conducted learning which utilizes convenient mobile computers based on wireless networks to overcome the limit of time and space and instantly fulfill individual or cooperative learning activities (p. 162)
2012	D-W. Lee & Lee	D25: The application of smart technology to e-learning and smart technology exhibits and embodies sensing, intelligence, mobility, elasticity, and integration (D.-W. Lee and Lee 2012, cited in Lee et al., 2015)*
2015	Sung, M.	D26: A humanistic approach to learning that offers hands-on and personalized opportunities to acquire information, manage knowledge, interact, and collaborate with peers and instructors so that learners can apply their knowledge and skills to solve problems and achieve goals in an authentic context (p. 116)
n.d.	Wikipedia (Korea)	D27: Learning that makes use of smart phones, and furthermore, as an overall approach that enhances the effectiveness of education based on new learning methods which include characteristics such as participation, sharing, and customization, by introducing smart teaching methods, smart contents, and smart devices (Wikipedia n.d., cited in Jo et al., 2012, p. 893)*

* Definition was cited from one or more secondary source because the original definition was either inaccessible, could not be found through a web search, or written in Korean text.

TABLE 10.5 Keywords Describing Smart Learning Environments

Keyword	Definition Source	Frequency	Percentage (n = 27)
Smart technology (i.e., mobile devices, ICT, computers)	D2, D3, D9, D11, D12, D16, D17, D19, D20, D21, D22, D24, D25, D27	14	52%
Intelligent/intelligence	D2, D3, D13, D14, D15, D18, D19, D22, D25	9	33%
Smart infrastructure (i.e., sensors, cloud computing)	D19, D21, D25	3	11%
Networks (i.e., wireless networks, servers)	D19, D21, D24	3	11%
Adaptive	D2, D14, D23	3	11%
Technology-embedded	D19, D21, D23	3	11%
Social networks	D10, D12, D22	3	11%
Teaching–learning support system	D8, D14, D17	3	11%
Integrated	D13, D15, D25	3	11%
Learning system	D1, D16	2	7%
E-learning systems	D10, D25	2	7%
Mobility	D25	1	4%
Elasticity	D25	1	4%
Convergence	D19	1	4%
Total number of keywords: 14			

technology like smartphones or tablets (Kim et al., 2013). They also include the use of smart infrastructure, networks, social networks, e-learning, and a teaching-learning support system, reflecting the characteristics of being intelligent, adaptive, integrated, and a technology-embedded learning system. Intelligent as a characteristic stands out as a frequently occurring key word in 9 out of 27 definitions.

Among the three elements of smart learning analyzed, smart pedagogies garnered the most number of key words reflecting a large range of proposed pedagogies for a smart learning implementation (Table 10.6). The top six most frequently cited pedagogies among the 27 definitions describe smart learning to be individualized, interactive, human-centered, real-time, customized, and student-centered. However, the fact that there were 22 unique pedagogical strategies identified cannot be overlooked. This is significant in that while most authors have described pedagogical strategies that are generally more constructive and fitting to the 21st century notion of education, it also shows that smart learning does not adopt a one-size-fits-all cookie-cutter strategies or characteristics. It promotes both formal and

How Smart Learning Is Defined ▪ 167

TABLE 10.6 Keywords Describing Smart Pedagogies

Keyword	Definition Source	Frequency	Percentage (n = 27)
Individualized/individualization/ personalized/personal needs	D3, D4, D5, D11, D12, D15, D24, D26	8	30%
Interaction/interactive (i.e., learner–instructor interaction, learner–learner interaction)	D1, D6, D10, D13, D16, D17, D18, D26	8	30%
Humanistic/human-centered/ human-oriented	D1, D14, D17, D21, D20, D26	6	22%
Sense of reality/realistic/real-time	D4, D5, D6, D7, D8, D18	6	22%
Customized/customization	D3, D14, D19, D22, D27	5	19%
Student-centered/learner-centered/student focused	D1, D3, D6, D16, D18	5	19%
Collaboration/collaborative learning	D6, D10, D22, D26	4	15%
Informal learning	D7, D8, D18, D22	4	15%
Social learning	D14, D15, D19	3	11%
Cooperative	D3, D13, D24	3	11%
Collective intelligence	D15, D19	2	7%
Participative/participation	D13, D27	2	7%
Sharing	D13, D27	2	7%
Flexible	D6, D9	2	7%
Formal learning	D22	1	4%
Authentic	D26	1	4%
Practical	D24	1	4%
Hands-on	D26	1	4%
Immersive	D8	1	4%
Engaging	D7	1	4%
Exciting	D3	1	4%
Multiple learning styles	D2	1	4%
Total number of keywords: 22			

informal learning. It describes a social, practical, and authentic learning. It encourages futuristic ideas of immersive, real-time, and flexible learning.

Note that similar keywords were grouped in the table but listed explicitly. While some pedagogical keywords may be perceived as similar while coding, some keywords may be used differently in context to the learning environment or learner (e.g., sense of reality vs. real-time; interaction vs.

interactive). For example an "interactive learning system" may denote that a learner is interacting with the learning system's functions or navigation buttons. In contrast, "interactive learning" may denote that a learner is engaging in interaction strategies with the teacher or with other learners (i.e., learner–learner interaction, learner–instructor interaction).

Table 10.7 shows a summary of eight unique keywords that describe smart learners. Results show that smart learning proposes to develop learning skills such as problem-solving, ability to access information, creativity, communication, motivation, and ability to manage learning. The most frequently occurring key word among the 27 definitions describe learners as being self-directed (37%). This result is notably unique among the top key words of Tables 10.5, 10.6, and 10.7 in that it was the only element among the three smart learning elements where the top keyword align directly to the widely-recognized government initiated "SMART" learning definition from MEST (2011; i.e., self-directed, motivated, adaptive, resource-enriched, technology-embedded).

It is apparent however, that a componential analysis of smart learning definitions in Table 10.8 shows that only a third of the 27 definitions included in the study reflected the three elements of Zhu et al. (2016). Results show that 25 out of 27 definitions had at least one or more keywords associated to pedagogy; 22 out of 27 definitions had at least one or more keywords describing learning environments; and 15 out of 27 definitions had at least one or more keywords about learners and their skills. While eight important learner skills were tallied from the 27 definitions, it is the least described among the three elements. This results contrasts to the original

TABLE 10.7 Keywords Describing Smart Learners

Keyword	Definition Source	Frequency	Percentage (*n* = 27)
Self-directed/self-initiated/self-conducted/learner-directed/learner-driven	D1, D4, D5, D6, D10, D12, D17, D20, D23, D24	10	37%
Acquire/access information	D1, D17, D26	3	11%
Problem solving/solve problems	D2, D3, D26	3	11%
Motivated	D4, D5, D23	3	11%
Creativity	D7, D8, D12	3	11%
Thinking skills	D2, D3	2	7%
Communication	D2, D3	2	7%
Learning management/manage knowledge/manage learning	D5, D26	2	7%
Total number of keywords: 8			

How Smart Learning Is Defined ▪ **169**

TABLE 10.8 Componential Analysis of Smart Learning Elements by Source

Definition (n = 27)	Smart Environments	Smart Pedagogies	Smart Learners
D1	+	+	+
D2	+	+	+
D3	+	+	+
D4	–	+	+
D5	–	+	+
D6	–	+	+
D7	–	+	+
D8	+	+	+
D9	+	+	–
D10	+	+	+
D11	+	+	–
D12	+	+	+
D13	+	+	–
D14	+	+	–
D15	+	+	–
D16	+	+	–
D17	+	+	+
D18	+	+	–
D19	+	+	–
D20	+	+	+
D21	+	+	–
D22	+	+	–
D23	+	–	+
D24	+	+	+
D25	+	–	–
D26	–	+	+
D27	+	+	–
Total	22 (83%)	25 (93%)	15 (56%)

concept of smart learning proposed by Kwak (2010), which emphasizes the individual learners over the technology (Gallagher, 2016). Evidently, the content analysis reveals that the definitions of smart learning currently existing among Korean authors/scholars have placed more emphasis on smart learning environments and pedagogy over the skills associated to smart learners.

The smarter education framework of Zhu et al. (2016) includes elements of smart learning environments, pedagogy, and learners, but it did not include "smart content." Four definitions (i.e., D9, D11, D27, D23) made mention of keywords pertaining to content such as "smart content," "resource-enriched," and "open educational resources." This is not surprising because the earlier government initiated definition by MEST (2011) highlighted the need for learning environments to be resource enriched. However, results from this study showed that smart learning definitions emphasized smart technologies and smart pedagogies more than smart learners or smart content. It is interesting to note that only one definition made mention of "smart standards" (D9). The smarter education framework of Zhu et al. (2016) did not include "smart content" or "smart standards." These two additional elements added to smart learners, smart pedagogy, and smart environments can frame a larger systems view of adopting or implementing a smart education framework. Future studies may consider defining and including these elements in future research.

IMPLICATIONS

Smart learning definitions have manifested the use of more advanced, intelligent, and adaptive IT infrastructure, but also puts focus on greater personalized and self-directed instructional strategies to foster thinking, communication, and problem-solving skills using various smart devices (Kwak, 2010, as cited in Sung, 2015, p. 116). Smart learning describes the ideal type of learning expected in a digital age where teachers and students utilize smart devices through wireless networks to access digital resources and personalize learning seamlessly.

A recent report suggested that "adding 21st century technologies to 20th century teaching practices is just diluting the effectiveness of teaching" (OECD, 2015, as cited in Parmar, 2016, para. 2) and that teachers and schools have yet to understand the kind of technological pedagogies required to make the best use of it in the classrooms. Korea's smart education framework encourages technology to be well integrated into the student learning experience, which requires rethinking of the pedagogic workflow. Parmar (2016, para. 4) describes this to be:

1. The disappearance of walls and enclosed structure of the classroom, in which both the teacher and student can communicate seamlessly through various digital channels and in which they become co-learners.

2. It is the facilitation and instruction of learning processes from teacher to student within a collaborative and mutually beneficial manner, and in which the student becomes their own teacher.
3. Importantly, it is the pedagogic interactions that takes place between the two participants in which the "killer app" is still the teacher.

Parmar (2016) stresses well that the role of the teacher does not fade away with the integration of technology, but rather just becomes even more essential in the teaching learning process. However, there is a strong emphasis on student-centered, self-directed learning where the student becomes his or her own teacher at some point. Most importantly, the idea of again, seamless communication through digital channels allows the teacher and student to quite nicely become co-learners.

Espiritu (2016) recommends that in the current era of educational change, "the entire society must realize that informal, lifelong, technology-supported, and connectivist learning is here to stay." Major stakeholders including the students, teachers, administrators, parents, employers, and government must be involved (Espiritu, 2016). The growth in learning technologies often lead faculty and their teaching practices to struggle over the complexity brought about by new technologies. Beyond textbooks, blackboards, and tests, student learning is technology-supported by electronic media, the Internet, e-books, learning apps, and instructional videos. New ICT have their advantages and attractiveness, but the problems of education are always more complex than solutions provided by technology alone (Gunawardena, 2014). In order to teach and learn with mobile devices, teachers and students need to acquire technical knowledge of the device that they are using and understand its limitations.

There is much we can learn from Korea's implementation of Smart Learning. Government stakeholders need to become aware, get onboard, adapt and ultimately commit to making a change in our education system and ICT capabilities (Espiritu, 2016). Korea's government policy of smart education promoted the shift in learning culture for all other stakeholders including students, teachers, administrators, parents, and employers. The vision of a futuristic education is seen to be one with smart learning environments, smart pedagogy, and smarter learners. Mr. Yoon is a young elementary school educator, but inspires all educators either in the elementary, high school, higher education, and vocational sectors to become smarter users of technology to provide smarter learning experiences to students.

REFERENCES

Chan, T.-W., Roschelle, J., Hsi, S., Kinshuk, Sharples, M., Brown, T., & Norris, C. (2006). One-to-one technology-enhanced learning: An opportunity for global research collaboration. *Research and Practice in Technology Enhanced Learning, 1*(1), 3–29.

Choi, J. S. (2012). Sejong city to have Korea's first smart school. Retrieved from http://www.korea.net/NewsFocus/Sci-Tech/view?articleId=99412

Danova, T. (2013). Morgan Stanley: 75 billion devices will be connected to the internet of things by 2020. Retrieved from http://www.businessinsider.com/75-billion-devices-will-be-connected-to-the-internet-by-2020-2013-10

Espiritu, J. L. (2016, September). *Cultivating an e-learning culture.* Paper presented at the National Conference on Technology in Education, SMX Mall of Asia, Manila, Philippines.

Gallagher, M. S. (2016). *Charting trajectories on the peripheries of community practice: Mobile learning for the humanities in South Korea* (Doctoral dissertation). Bloomsbury, England: University College London.

Gunawardena, C. N. (2014). Globalization, culture, and online distance learning. In T. Anderson & D. Wiley (Eds.), *Online distance education: Towards a research agenda* (pp. 75–107). Alberta, Canada: Athabasca University.

Hardison, J. (2013, January 7). Part 1: 44 smart ways to use smartphones in class. Retrieved from http://gettingsmart.com/2013/01/part-1-44-smart-ways-to-use-smartphones-in-class/

Horowitz, E. (2015, August 11). A peek at a "smart" classroom powered by the internet of things. Retrieved from https://www.edsurge.com/news/2015-08-11-a-peek-at-a-smart-classroom-powered-by-the-internet-of-things

Hsieh, H.-F., & Shannon, S. E. (2005). Three approaches to qualitative content analysis. *Qualitative Health Research, 15*(9), 1277–1288.

Hwang, D. J. (2011, January). *Smart innovation in education and learning.* Paper presented at the International E-Learning Conference, Bangkok, Thailand.

Hwang, G.-J., Tsai, C.-C., & Yang, S. J. H. (2008). Criteria, strategies and research issues of context-aware ubiquitous learning. *Journal of Educational Technology & Society, 11*(2), 81–91.

Jo, J., Park, J., Ji, H., Yang, Y., & Lim, H. (2016). A study on factor analysis to support knowledge based decisions for a smart class. *Information Technology and Management, 17*(1), 43–56.

Jo, J., Park, K., Lee, D., & Lim, H. (2014). An integrated teaching and learning assistance system meeting requirements for smart education. *Wireless Personal Communications, 79*(4), 2453–2467.

Jo, J., Yang, Y., & Lim, H. (2012). Design of a structured plug-in smart education system. In S. Yes, Y. Pan, Y. Lee, & H. Chang (Eds.), *Computer Science and its Applications* (Vol. 203, pp. 891–901). *Lecture Notes in Electrical Engineering.* Dordrecht, The Netherlands: Springer.

Kim, S-M. (2012). Along with e-learning and cloud computing, comes the advancement of smart learning: EBS, the heart of smart learning and lifelong education. *Korea IT Times, 91,* 18–20.

Kim, T., Cho, J. Y., & Lee, B. G. (2013). Evolution to smart learning in public education: A case study of korean public education. In T. Ley, M. Laanpere, & A. Tatnall (Eds.), *Open and social technologies for networked learning* (Vol. 395, pp. 170–178). Berlin, Heidelberg: Springer. Retrieved from http://link.springer.com/10.1007/978-3-642-37285-8_18

Kim, S., Song, S.-M., & Yoon, Y.-I. (2011). Smart learning services based on smart cloud computing. *Sensors, 11*(8), 7835–7850.

Klopfer, E., Squire, K., & Jenkins, H. (2002). *Environmental detectives: PDAs as a window into a virtual simulated world.* Presented at the Wireless and Mobile Technologies in Education, 2002. Proceedings. IEEE International Workshop on, IEEE.

Kwak, D-H. (2010). *Meaning and prospect for smart learning.* In Proceedings from the seminar for Korea e-learning industry association.

Kwon, H-I., Kim, D-J., Ryu, G-J., Kang, J-H., Park, J-S., & Joo, H. (2013). *The framework of the smart learning infrastructure in South Korea: Focus on agriculture education system* (pp. 10–14). Presented at the Free and Open Source Software Conference (FOSSC-13), Muscat, Oman.

Lee, A. J. (n.d.). *Smart learning in Korea.*

Lee, J-A., Kim, T-H., & Chung, J-H. (2013). Study on communication of characteristics smart learning from UX perspective. *International Journal of Smart Home, 7*(6), 59–72.

Lee, J-E., Lim, D., & Um, G. (2015). A cyber engineering education strategy based on smart learning. *International Information Institute (Tokyo), 18*(4), 1169.

Lee, J., Zo, H., & Lee, H. (2014). Smart learning adoption in employees and HRD managers. *British Journal of Educational Technology, 45*(6), 1082–1096.

Lee, M-S., & Son, Y-E. (2013). Development of BYOD strategy learning system with smart learning supporting. *International Journal of Software Engineering and Its Applications, 7*(3), 259–268.

Lim, K. (2012). "SMART" learning trends in Korea. Presented at the Innovative ICT Practices in Teaching and Learning: A Regional Seminar, Sejong Hotel, Seoul, Korea. Retrieved from http://www.unescobkk.org/fileadmin/user_upload/ict/Workshops/regionalseminar2012/ppt/Keol_Lim_SK_Telecom.pdf

Low, L., & O'Connell, M. (2006). *Learner-centric design of digital mobile learning.* Presented at the Proceedings of the OLT Conference.

MEST: Ministry of Education, Science, and Technology of the Republic of Korea. (2011). *Adapting education to the information age.* Korea Education and Research Information Service (KERIS).

Minges, M. (2012). *Chapter 1: Overview.* In Information and communications for development 2012: Maximizing mobile (pp. 11–30). Retrieved from http://siteresources.worldbank.org/EXTINFORMATIONANDCOMMUNICATIONANDTECHNOLOGIES/Resources/IC4D-2012-Report.pdf

MobileScout. (2016). *Samsung Smart School helped to connect elementary students from Portugal and South Korea.* Mobilescout.com. Retrieved from http://www.mobilescout.com/samsung/news/n69687/Samsung-Smart-School-connect-elementary-students.html

Ng, W. (2015). Mobile learning: BYOD and personalised learning. In W. Ng (Ed.), *New digital technology in education: Conceptualizing professional learning for educators* (pp. 171–189). Cham, Switzerland: Springer International. Retrieved from http://dx.doi.org/10.1007/978-3-319-05822-1_8

Noh, K-S. (2011, May). *Smart learning and future education.* Presented at the education information Wednesday forum. Korea Education and Research Information Service.

Ogata, H., & Yano, Y. (2004). Context-aware support for computer-supported ubiquitous learning. In *Wireless and mobile technologies in education, 2004.* Proceedings. The 2nd IEEE International Workshop on (pp. 27–34). IEEE.

Parmar, N. (2016). *3 tips for mobile pedagogy in the classroom.* Retrieved from http://asia.blog.terrapinn.com/edutech/2016/06/10/223/?utm_campaign=8603%20EduTECH%20Asia%202016%20-%20Blog%20Newsletter%20-%20June%2013_NON%20SG&utm_medium=email&utm_source=Eloqua

Schwartz, K. (2015). *Teacher recommended: 50 favorite classroom apps.* Retrieved from https://ww2.kqed.org/mindshift/2015/07/29/teacher-recommended-50-favorite-teaching-apps/

Sung, M. (2015). A study of adults' perception and needs for smart learning. *Procedia-Social and Behavioral Sciences, 191,* 115–120.

Taki, S., & Khazaei, S. (2011). Learning vocabulary via mobile phone: Persian EFL learners in focus. *Journal of Language Teaching and Research, 2*(6), 1252–1258.

Uzelac, A., Gligoric, N., & Krco, S. (2015). A comprehensive study of parameters in physical environment that impact students' focus during lecture using Internet of things. *Computers in Human Behavior, 53,* 427–434. https://doi.org/10.1016/j.chb.2015.07.023

Wikipedia. (n.d.). 스마트러닝. Retrieved from http://ko.wikipedia.org/wiki/스마트러닝

Zhu, Z-T., Yu, M-H., & Riezebos, P. (2016). A research framework of smart education. *Smart Learning Environments, 3*(1). https://doi.org/10.1186/s40561-016-0026-2

CHAPTER 11

21st CENTURY CLASSROOM
Finding the Right Balance

Florence Martin

If we teach today's students as we taught yesterday's, we rob them of tomorrow.
—John Dewey

This quote has been instrumental to me as an educator. I was born in India and completed my K–12 and undergraduate education there before moving to the United States for graduate school. Visiting K–12 schools and universities in China this summer was a reminder of my school days in India. During my 10-day visit to China, I had the opportunity to visit two elementary schools, one middle school, one high school and three universities in Chengdu and Xi'an. This chapter is based on my observations, informal interviews with educators and students in China, and follow-up conversations with my Chinese colleagues in the United States.

Being in American educational institutions for the last 15 years, first as a graduate student and then as a faculty member, I have learned and also taught in numerous classrooms in face-to-face, hybrid, and online formats. As an international student, adapting to the education system in the United States was a big change initially. I quickly learned that the student-centered,

Educational Practices in China, Korea, and the United States, pages 175–188
Copyright © 2019 by Information Age Publishing
All rights of reproduction in any form reserved.

interactive teaching strategies were more exciting and motivating than the teacher-centered, lecture-driven, and exam-focused teaching strategies that I grew up with.

The previous edition of this book has a chapter by Lambert (2015) on 21st century classrooms, comparing the East and West and finding a middle ground. As a follow-up to that chapter, I have reviewed the characteristics of 21st century learners and classrooms in the United States and in China and recommend 21st century skills that are essential to prepare 21st century learners.

LITERATURE REVIEW

21st Century Learners

The 21st century learners comprise of the millennials which include both Generation Y and Generation Z learners. The millennials were born between the early 1980s and the early 2000s and some of their characteristics include multitasking, tech savvy, a preference for instant gratification and recognition, connectedness, and collaboration. Lancaster and Stillman (2002) describe the Generation Y members as confident and technologically advanced, with a sense of entitlement. Rothman (2016) describes Generation Z learners as "first generation born into an integrated and globally connected world where the Internet has always been available" (p. 2).

Table 11.1 provides a comparison of the characteristics of the Generation Y and Generation Z learners, both considered 21st century learners (Smalley, 2014).

Overall, 21st century learners are technology literate, media savvy, flexible, dynamic, multitaskers, communicators, collaborators, interactive, networked, reflective, creative, adaptive, student centric, lifelong learners, anywhere anytime learners, and have multimodal learning styles.

TABLE 11.1 Characteristics of 21st Century Learners (Generation Y and Generation Z Learners)	
Generation Y (Born 1981 to 1994)	Generation Z (Born 1995 to 2010)
Raised on the web	Raised on social web
Communicate with text	Communicate with images
Share things	Create things
Present-focused	Future-focused
Digital-savvy	Digital-centric

21st Century Classrooms in the United States

With 21st century learners in the classrooms, it is important that the classrooms are designed and implemented to be 21st century classrooms. Some key characteristics that the 21st century classrooms in the United States strive for include student-centered, technology-enhanced, performance-based assessments, and collaborative learning (see Figure 11.1). Not all classrooms in the United States include these elements, but several schools and universities are striving to be 21st century classrooms.

Student-Centered Classroom

In student-centered classrooms, we move away from traditional teaching practices and focus on collaboration, project-based learning, and technology integration (Barnes, 2013). Barnes' (2013) characteristics of the student-centered classroom include creating ongoing projects to attain mastery and demonstrate learning, replacing homework with engaging in-class activities, and involving students in the evaluation of their work. Student-centered classrooms promote collaboration, so arranging desks as

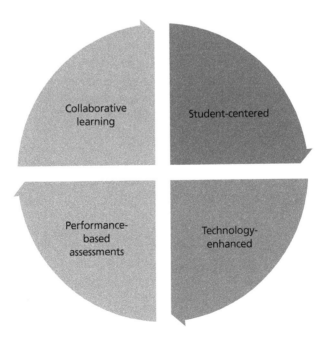

Figure 11.1 Characteristics of a 21st century classroom in the United States.

to enhance communication and collaboration is key rather than arranging desks facing a teacher lectern or desk. Teachers become facilitators in the classroom. However, turning control over to the students does not mean that teachers are losing control in this setting.

In student-centered classrooms, active learning strategies are used to engage students. When students are engaged through hands-on projects, they develop a strong connection with the subject. Slunt and Giancarlo (2004) see student-learning instruction as a positive and effective method to direct learners toward having control over their learning, accept the responsibility, and get involved in their learning process actively instead of being passive and just receive information from lectures. Having independent minds and the ability to make educated decisions are both outcomes of student-centered strategies (Brown, 2008).

Technology-Enhanced Learning

With rapid changes in technology, the 21st century classroom has become more powerful. The goal of the student-centered classroom is "to immerse learners in rich experiences, using various tools, resources, and activities with which to augment or extend thinking" (Hannafin, Hill, & Land, 1997, p. 97). Student-centered learning and instructional technology go hand in hand as the technology enables active, self-directed, and collaborative learning. There are gadgets such as iPads which even kindergartners can navigate with ease. More and more classrooms are pursuing to be 1:1 so that each student has the use of a device without having to share. Technology can be distracting and expensive, but has its benefits if it is effectively integrated in the classroom.

Armstrong (2014) in her study calls upon teachers to use technology to engage and empower learners by putting students at the center and empowering them to take control of their own learning by providing flexibility. Polly and Hannafin (2010) state there is a need to enhance teachers' professional development programs in order to have technology-rich and learner-centered instruction for students. Teachers need to go through well-developed training programs to enhance their skills and understanding of their content area. Kopcha (2010) introduces a mentoring model of technology integration that moves teachers through four specific stages of technology adoption to support student-centered learning. The model consists of (a) analyzing teacher's needs, (b) preparing teachers to use technology in student-centered ways, (c) increasing teachers' experiences with pedagogy, and (d) mentoring teachers to become technology leaders for their school.

Performance-Based Assessments

Traditional testing requires students to answer questions in a multiple choice test or an essay exam. However, some essay questions that include constructive response questions can also be performance assessments. Performance assessment requires students to demonstrate knowledge and skills and measures how well students can apply or use what they know, often in real-world situations. Some of the performance-based assessments may include projects, presentations, and portfolios, which are usually graded with a rubric. Performance-based assessments are able to tap into and measure students' higher-order thinking skills, including Bloom's higher level measuring verbs such as evaluate, create, apply, synthesize, and integrate information (Bloom, 1956). Some of the performance-based assessments expect students to evaluate the reliability of sources of information, synthesize information to draw conclusions, or use deductive/inductive reasoning to solve a problem (Wei, 2008).

Weimer (2002) insists on learning as the main goal of student-centered methodology and expects assessment to enhance the learning experience. Critical thinking skills will be developed in this process as students learn to evaluate their peers' work as well as their own work, which creates opportunities for learners to put into practice their knowledge and skills. Weimer (2002) also believes that such approaches in assessment decrease exam anxiety and cheating temptation significantly.

Collaborative Learning

The final characteristic that is highlighted in a 21st century classroom is collaborative learning. Collaborative learning occurs when two or more people learn or attempt to learn something together. Collaborative learning results in an active exchange of ideas within small groups. Gokhale (1995) found that collaborative learning fosters the development of critical thinking through discussion, clarification of ideas, and evaluation of others' ideas. Laal and Ghodsi (2012) state that collaborative learning is an approach in education which brings learners together, as they work to solve a problem, create a product, or complete a task.

Collaboration learning consists of a variety of benefits including academic, social, and psychological. Smith, Sheppard, Johnson, and Johnson (2005) state involvement is a necessary part of a meaningful learning process. Collaborative learning results in actual facilitation of learning by designing meaningful learning experiences for learners rather than just transferring knowledge by the teacher.

180 ▪ F. MARTIN

METHODS

In the following section, the author of this chapter presents findings from data collected during a study tour to China.

Observations: I had the opportunity to visit two elementary schools, one middle school, one high school, and three universities in Chengdu and Xi'an.

Informal Interviews: During the trip, I was also able to conduct informal interviews with several students and teachers at each of these schools.

Follow up Interviews: After the trip, I was able to conduct informal interviews with colleagues from China who currently live and teach in the United States.

Data sources were analyzed inductively to identify frequently occurring themes.

RESULTS

Chinese Classrooms

This is not a generalization of all Chinese classrooms or a research-based finding, but my individual perception from visiting two elementary schools, one middle school, one high school, and three universities in Chengdu and Xi'an in China. This chapter is based on my observations, informal interviews with educators and students in China and conversations with my Chinese colleagues. I have been told that the classrooms in international schools in China which I did not visit are drastically different from the public and private schools that I visited.

Some key elements I noticed in the Chinese classrooms are seen in Figure 11.2.

Teacher-Centered Classroom

Being a teacher seems to be a much valued profession in China. Teachers are considered authoritative and much respected. Students stand up to greet a teacher when he or she walks into the classroom. The classes are very teacher-centered and lecture-based. The classrooms are usually set up in a traditional manner with the desks facing the teacher. In three of the classrooms that I visited, there were interactive activities and all three were

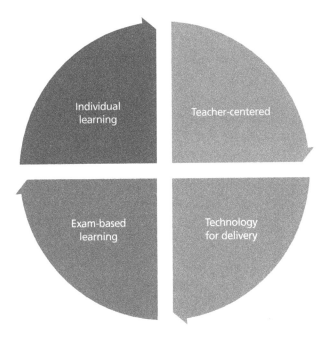

Figure 11.2 Characteristics of a 21st century classroom in China.

classrooms where students were learning English. It was interesting to note that one of the students commented that this particular day was the most engaging class in the entire year.

Wu and Huang (2007) state that the difference in student-centered and teacher-centered classes is based on experience opportunities provided by each method. The researchers reported that in a teacher-centered classroom, less engagement and fewer learning opportunities occur whereas student-centered classes are more interactive with student-initiated questions. The researchers reported that students explored difficult concepts under the teacher's guidance in a student-centered classroom. Simulations were used to display the content in teacher-centered classrooms and were followed with questions that were initiated by students, and provided an opportunity for students to visualize phenomena. In the student-centered classroom, "simulations were used to negotiate meanings, clarify confusions, examine predictions, and reinforce concepts developed during previous activities" (p. 746). The student interactions were video recorded and later analyzed.

In their study, Wu and Huang (2007) also reported improvement in low-achieving students similar to the level of high-achieving students in teacher-centered classrooms. On the other hand, medium- and high-achieving students in student-centered classrooms performed significantly higher than low-achieving students. Low-achieving students in student-centered classes showed high levels of disengagement that negatively influenced their learning. This study showed that different instructional approaches might be necessary for different types of students with different achievement levels.

Technology for Delivery but Not for Learning

Being an instructional technologist, I was curious about the use of technology in the classroom. Almost every classroom I visited had an LCD display to project from the computer. The teachers had built-in PowerPoints that they used for instruction. All the classrooms had only one computer for the teacher; students were mere listeners. I was told that if students had to do activities on the computer, it would disrupt the class setting. Hence, teachers prefer to take students to a lab to access the computer while enforcing discipline.

Researchers have found that using technology in the classroom and engaging students with it has a positive impact on their motivation and learning outcomes (Ng, 2012). Moreover, technology integration in classrooms increases students' cognitive ability and helps them with self-management skills (Webb, 2005). Ertmer (2005) states that technology integration is closely related to teachers' beliefs regarding using technology in the classroom and it leads to the teachers' decision whether to use or not to use technology. Plomp, Anderson, Law, and Quale (2003) believe that the teachers' decisions regarding integrating technology in a classroom are shaped by their view of 21st century skills that students should have.

Exam-Based Learning

In every high school classroom or university classroom I visited, there was talk about the GaoKao or the high school entrance exam. Students in high schools worked very long hours, from 8:00 a.m. to 9:00 p.m., to study for the entrance exam. The exam-based learning and entrance exam concept was designed more than a thousand years ago to move common people into government positions. The exam still exists to date. High school students are asked to cut down extracurricular activities to focus on the exam. This also has resulted in students focusing more on theory and subject knowledge instead of learning practical and problem-solving skills.

Liu and Wu (2006) found that the development of the GaoKao college entrance exam in China has been influenced by the country's political and social development as well as traditional culture. GaoKao is used as a tool to influence the pursuit of higher education as well as to select qualified students. It is also believed that this entrance exam can help promote mobility and equity in Chinese society since it allows college entrance based on factors other than political relations or connections. However, the Gao-Kao unified national admission test has negatively affected education and students' health. Liu and Wu (2006) discuss the negative influence of this entrance exam on allocating the curriculum and efforts of entire schools toward high college acceptance rate in this exam. The college admissions test has led to similarities among schools, without room for creativity. At very young ages, students focus on getting ready for the exam; consequently physical activities and subjects that are not exam-related do not get adequate attention. To keep the college entrance exam competitive, the difficulty of the entrance exam has been increased each year. Criticism and suggestions regarding this national higher education entrance examination, ranges from cheating on exams, illegal GaoKao migration to less populated areas where the passing score is lower than the metropolitan areas, teenage suicide rates, and teacher stress. GaoKao has been criticized for inhibiting innovative thinking but appears to provide an equitable way for Chinese students to get into universities.

Individual Learning

Classes in China are designed for individual learning especially at the high school level. While there might be some discussion-based activities in the classroom, the focus is on individual learning and how well each individual is prepared for the entrance exam at the end of their high school years. Chinese culture values education, and the traditional focus on education has an important role in Chinese society. Individuals with higher education levels are associated with a higher social class, while those with low educational background are considered a shame for the individual, families, and the country (Davey, De Lian, & Higgins, 2007). Success in education is related to successfully passing the national higher education entrance examination mentioned (Liu & Wu, 2006). Since the university entrance exam is important in Chinese society, the sole effort of the school, teachers, and parents is to make sure students are able to pass it successfully. The focus of instruction is at the individual level and not on collaborative learning to achieve course goals. Moreover, competitiveness is valued and this has caused psychological pressure for students. Due to the large population of China, university spaces are fewer than the number of applicants and, as a result, this creates a fierce competition to be admitted to top ranked universities (Dai, Chen, & Davey, 2007). Since secondary schools are evaluated according to the number of the students who have passed the college entrance exam successfully (Liu & Wu, 2006), the main goal has

184 ▪ F. MARTIN

TABLE 11.2 Comparison of the 21st Century Classrooms and Classrooms I Visited

21st Century Classroom	Classrooms I visited in China
Student Centered	Teacher Centered
Technology Enhanced	Technology for delivery
Performance based	Exam driven
Collaborative	Individual focused

become to prepare individual students for the entrance exam and nothing more (Dai, Chen, & Davey, 2007).

As a review, here is a quick comparison of the 21st century classrooms in the United States and in China (see Table 11.2).

While I don't want to come to a conclusion that one model is better than the other, it is commonly known that Chinese students are productive and hardworking and have been successful in a lot of disciplines. While the 21st century skills are essential, maybe the United States educational system needs to address some of the important elements that still work in Chinese schools. It is my hope that the teaching profession is valued in the United States as much as in China and that the American students work as hard as the Chinese students.

DISCUSSION

Comprehensive Frameworks of 21st Century Learning Skills

In the above sections, I reviewed the characteristics of the 21st century learners and classrooms in the United States and in China. There have been global initiatives on creating comprehensive frameworks for 21st century learning skills both in the United States and across the world. Below follows a review of four 21st century learning skills frameworks.

- In the United States, the National Education Association (2015) proposed the four Cs (creativity, critical thinking, communication, and collaboration) as shown in Figure 11.3. This organization helped establish the Partnership for 21st Century Skills in 2002 and developed a Framework for 21st Century Learning in 2012 (P21 Skills, 2013).
- The European Union has identified eight areas of 21st century key competencies for lifelong learning, which include: learning to learn; communication; mathematical, scientific, and technological

competence; digital competence; cultural; social; and civic competences; and a sense of initiative and entrepreneurship (Gordon et al., 2009).
- The Organization for Economic Co-operation and Development (OECD), which includes 35 countries, has formulated 21st century skills and competencies which include: communication, ethics, and social impact dimension of communication (Ananiadou & Claro, 2009).
- Finally, a large group of researchers defined 21st century skills as ways of thinking, ways of working, tools for working, and living in the world in a project titled "Assessment & Teaching of 21st Century Skills" (ATC21S; Binkley et al., 2012).

I would like to end this chapter with a quote from the former president of the United States, Barack Obama (Montopoli, 2009), in his address to the Hispanic Chamber of Commerce: "I'm calling on our nation's governors and state education chiefs to develop standards and assessments that don't simply measure whether students can fill in a bubble on a test, but whether they possess 21st century skills like problem-solving and critical thinking and entrepreneurship and creativity" (Montopoli, 2009, p. 5). The "Three Rs," reading, writing, and arithmetic, are not sufficient for this current generation of students. If today's students want to compete in this

Figure 11.3 The four Cs essential for the 21st century classroom.

global society they are expected to exhibit proficiency as described by the "Four Cs": communicators, creators, critical thinkers, and collaborators (see Figure 11.3).

In the end, mere acquisition of knowledge and skills does not make students into competent thinkers, collaborative workers, or problem solvers. It is essential that the students do not just receive information but are able to interpret it, reflect on it, and construct knowledge from it. Educators must strive to prepare 21st century learners who learn more than content knowledge, but are also creative, critical thinkers, communicative, and collaborative. I hope we prepare students to not only demonstrate mathematical, scientific and technological competence, digital competence, cultural, social, and civic competences, but also to be equipped with ways of thinking, ways of working, tools for working, and for living in the world.

REFERENCES

Ananiadou, K., & Claro, M. (2009). *21st century skills and competences for new millennium learners in OECD countries.* Paris, France: Organization for Economic Cooperation and Development.

Armstrong, A. (2014). Technology in the classroom: It's not a matter of 'if' but 'when' and 'how'. *The Education Digest, 79*(5), 39.

Barnes, M. (2013). *Five steps to create a progressive, student-centered classroom.* Retrieved from http://inservice.ascd.org/five-steps-to-create-a-progressive-student-centered-classroom/

Binkley, M., Erstad, O., Herman, J., Raizen, S., Ripley, M., Miller-Ricci, M., & Rumble, M. (2012). Defining twenty-first century skills. In P. Griffin, B. McGaw, & E. Care (Eds.), *Assessment and teaching of 21st century skills* (pp. 17–66). New York, NY: Springer.

Bloom, B. S. (Ed.). (1956). *Taxonomy of educational objectives. Handbook 1: Cognitive domain.* White Plains, NY: Longman.

Brown, J. K. (2008). Student-centered instruction: Involving students in their own education. *Music Educators Journal, 94*(5), 30–35.

Dai, M., Chen, Z., & Davey, G. (2007, July). Mental health implications of the Chinese university entrance exam. *Proceedings of the Conference on Psychology in Mental Health: Prospects and Challenges,* Bangalore, India.

Davey, G., De Lian, C., & Higgins, L. (2007). The university entrance examination system in China. *Journal of Further and Higher Education, 31*(4), 385–396. https://doi.org/10.1080/03098770701625761

Ertmer, P. A. (2005). Teacher pedagogical beliefs: The final frontier in our quest for technology integration? *Educational technology research and development, 53*(4), 25–39.

Gokhale, A. A. (1995). Collaborative learning enhances critical thinking. *Journal of Technology Education, 7*(1), 22–30.

Gordon, J., Halász, G., Krawczyk, M., Leney, T., Michel, A., Pepper, D., & Wiśniewski, J. (2009). *Key competences in Europe: Opening doors for lifelong learners across the school curriculum and teacher education* (CASE Network Reports No. 87). Warsaw, Poland: Center for Social and Economic Research.

Hannafin, M. J., Hill, J. R., & Land, S. M. (1997). Student centered learning and interactive multimedia: Status, issues, and implications. *Contemporary Education, 68*(2), 94–99.

Kopcha, T. J. (2010). A systems-based approach to technology integration using mentoring and communities of practice. *Educational Technology Research and Development, 58*(2), 175–190.

Laal, M., & Ghodsi, S. M. (2012). Benefits of collaborative learning. *Procedia-Social and Behavioral Sciences, 31*, 486–490.

Lambert, R. (2015). Preparing students with 21st century life skills in an age of globalization: In search of middle ground between east and west. In C. Wang, W. Ma, & C. L. Martin, (Eds.), *Chinese education from the perspectives of American Educators* (pp. 165–178). Charlotte, NC: Information Age.

Lancaster, L. C., & Stillman. D. (2002). *When generations collide: Who they are, why they clash, how to solve the generational puzzle at work.* New York, NY: Harper Collins.

Liu, H., & Wu, Q. (2006). Consequences of college entrance exams in China and the reform challenges. *KEDI Journal of Educational Policy, 3*(1), 7–21.

Polly, D., & Hannafin, M. J. (2010). Reexamining technology's role in learner-centered professional development. *Educational Technology Research and Development, 58*(5), 557–571.

P21 Skills. (2013). Partnership for 21st century skills. *Battelle for Kids.* Retrieved from http://www.p21.org/about-us/p21-framework

National Education Association. (2015). *Preparing 21st century students for a global society: An educator's guide to the "four Cs."* Retrieved from the National Education Association http://www.nea.org/assets/docs/A-Guide-to-Four-Cs.pdf

Ng, W. (2012). Can we teach digital natives digital literacy? *Computers & Education, 59*(3), 1065–1078.

Montopoli, B. (2009, March 10). Obama's remarks on education. *CBS News.* Retrieved from http://www.cbsnews.com/8301-503544_162-4855902-503544.html

Plomp, T., Anderson, R. E., Law, N., & Quale, A. (Eds.). (2003). *Cross-national information and communication: Technology policy and practices in education.* Charlotte, NC: Information Age.

Rothman, D. (2016). A tsunami of learners called Generation Z. *Maryland Public Safety Online Journal, 1*(1). Retrieved from https://mdle.net/Journal/A_Tsunami_of_Learners_Called_Generation_Z.pdf

Slunt, K. M., & Giancarlo, L. C. (2004). Student-centered learning: A comparison of two different methods of instruction. *Journal of Chemical Education, 81*(7), 985–988.

Smalley, K. (2014). The abcs of gens y and z and their attitudes to work. *Randstad.* Retrieved from https://www.randstad.ca/workforce360-trends/archives/comparing-and-contrasting-millennials-and-gen-z_488/

Smith, K. A., Sheppard, S. D., Johnson, D. W., & Johnson, R. T. (2005). Pedagogies of engagement: Classroom-based practices. *Journal of engineering education, 94*(1), 87–101.

Webb, M. E. (2005). Affordances of ICT in science learning: Implications for an integrated pedagogy. *International journal of science education, 27*(6), 705–735.

Wei, C. (2008). What is performance based assessment? *Stanford SRN*. Retrieved from https://edpolicy.stanford.edu/sites/default/files/events/materials/2011-06-linked-learning-performance-based-assessment.pdf

Weimer, M. (2002). *Learner-centered teaching: Five key changes to practice*. San Francisco, CA: Wiley.

Wu, H. K., & Huang, Y. L. (2007). Ninth-grade student engagement in teacher-centered and student-centered technology-enhanced learning environments. *Science Education, 91*(5), 727–749.

CHAPTER 12

CULTURALLY SPEAKING

Comparing Culturally Relevant Pedagogy in Chinese, Korean, and American Classrooms

Lori J. Williams

China, Korea, and the United States are three separate and distinct countries. While these three countries share some similarities and differences, they are becoming more diverse and interconnected due to our increasingly globalized economy. The educational systems in China, Korea, and the United States are not completely insulated from globalization and other changes that occur in the broader society. As will be discussed in this chapter, globalization and other societal phenomena, such as war, immigration, and government legislation, have trickled down into the schools. In some respects, these phenomena have influenced the teaching pedagogies of K–16 educators. Culturally relevant pedagogy, which is the subject of this chapter, is an example of a teaching pedagogy that has been developed and undergone changes due to broader societal issues such as those mentioned above.

While the definition of culturally relevant pedagogy will be further explained in the following section, at this point it is sufficient to say that it is

Educational Practices in China, Korea, and the United States, pages 189–205
Copyright © 2019 by Information Age Publishing
All rights of reproduction in any form reserved.

190 ▪ L. J. WILLIAMS

a teaching pedagogy that seeks to recognize and utilize the home culture of the students in the classroom to help improve their academic success in school. The question this chapter seeks to address is whether culturally relevant pedagogy really matters within the context of K–16 classrooms. Moreover, does the answer change when comparing educational systems in different countries? This chapter attempts to explore these issues by answering the following guiding questions specific to classrooms in China, Korea, and the United States:

1. What is culturally relevant pedagogy?
2. What factors influence the use of culturally relevant pedagogy in the classroom?
3. What impact does culturally relevant pedagogy have on student learning?
4. How does culturally relevant pedagogy influence parental and community involvement?

We cannot begin to fully discuss these issues without first defining the term *culture*, which is the critical root word within the phrase, "culturally relevant pedagogy." Culture has been the subject of much discussion by various researchers (Damen, 1987; Hofstede, 1984; Lederach, 1995; Trumbull, 2005; Useem, Useem, & Donoghue, 1963). For purposes of this chapter, however, I adopted the definition provided by Kuper, a well-known anthropologist (as cited in Banks & Banks, 2010, p. 8):

> The essence of a culture is not its artifacts, tools, or other cultural elements but how the members of the group interpret, use, and perceive them. It is the values, symbols, interpretations, and perspectives that distinguish one people from another in modernized societies; it is not material objects and other tangible aspects of human societies.

Ladson-Billings (1995) and several other researchers recognize culture as being a crucial component of culturally relevant pedagogy (Durden, Escalante, & Blitch, 2015; Gay, 2000; 2013; Paris, 2012; Sleeter, 2012; Wyngaard, 2007).

The overarching question mentioned above is whether culturally relevant pedagogy really matters within the context of K–16 classrooms. However, an important but underlying question is whether *culture* really matters within the context of K–16 classrooms. Both questions will be explored throughout the following sections of this chapter and then specifically revisited in the final section. Implications of the results of this research are also presented. First, we will undertake a review of the literature.

REVIEW OF THE LITERATURE

Culturally Relevant Pedagogy Defined

Over the past 20 years, researchers have assigned several different names to the teaching pedagogy originally referred to as culturally relevant pedagogy. Other names have included culturally responsive teaching (Chung & Kang, 2013; Gay, 2000; Zhang & Wang, 2016); culturally responsive pedagogy (Sleeter, 2012), and more recently, culturally sustaining pedagogy (Paris, 2012).

A seminal study in this area is the work of Ladson-Billings (1994). Ladson-Billings found that the academic achievement of the African American students in her study was suffering, in part due to the failure of educators to appreciate the students' culture and their desire to treat them as objects rather than as a source of knowledge. In 2014, Ladson-Billings revisited this issue, noting that "the secret behind culturally relevant pedagogy is the ability to link principles of learning with a deep understanding and appreciation for culture" (Ladson-Billings, 2014, p. 77). She expressed concern that many researchers had strayed too far away from the original concept she had proposed several years earlier. She stated that her vision of culturally relevant pedagogy was becoming unrecognizable in some instances as some educators had reduced the pedagogy to "adding some books about people of color, having a classroom Kwanzaa celebration, or posting 'diverse' images" (Ladson-Billings, 2014, p. 82).

More recent attention in the literature has focused on expanding the use of culturally relevant pedagogy (Paris, 2012). Paris (2012) argued that the terms "culturally relevant pedagogy" and "culturally responsive pedagogy" do not go far enough to describe the teaching and research related to students who are marginalized due to systemic inequalities. In fact, he noted that the current climate in terms of policies and practices, tends to encompass two goals which explicitly set out to create a monolingual and mono-cultural society (Paris, 2012, p. 95). In response, he posited that researchers and teachers need to embrace cultural pluralism and cultural equality. In doing so, they can present some resistance to combat these negative policies and practices. His decision to offer a new term, "culturally sustaining pedagogy," was predicated on the belief that this alternative term was more encompassing and more realistically reflected the teaching and research concerning these marginalized students (Paris, 2012, p. 95). In his view, the term culturally sustaining pedagogy better reflects the important ideals of valuing and maintaining the language, literacies, and other cultural practices of these students as they continue to learn the language, literacies, and other cultural practices of the dominant culture (Paris, 2012, p. 95). In 2014, Ladson-Billings praised researchers such as Paris for their

Factors Influencing the Use of Culturally Relevant Pedagogy in China, Korea, and the United States

At least two main factors have influenced the use of culturally relevant pedagogy in the United States: changing demographics in the schools and the passage of certain government legislation. Historically, school demographics nationwide have predominantly consisted of Caucasian students, and to a lesser extent, African American students. Other minority groups were present but at much lower percentages. The demographics began to change dramatically over the past several years. The number of English learners in U.S. public schools was approximately 3.5 million during the 1997–1998 school year. By the 2007–2008 school year, this number reached 5.3 million. This represented a 53.25% increase in the English learner student population over the preceding 10 year period (The U.S. Department of Education, 2011). School enrollment figures now reflect increasingly diverse student bodies. The changing composition of the student populations enrolled in the public schools of the United States has resulted in a higher percentage of students whose language, culture, and ethnic background fall outside of the mainstream population. According to U.S. government statistics, there were 4.6 million English language learners in American schools during the 2014–2015 school year as compared to 4.3 million during the 2004–2005 school year (U.S. Department of Education, 2017). The English learner population is projected to continue its growth over the next several years. In fact, English learners are expected to account for one-fourth of the total student population in U.S. schools by 2025 (National Clearinghouse for English Language Acquisition, 2007).

Information recorded by the U.S. Department of Education reveals that public school students in the United States speak a variety of languages including Arabic, Vietnamese, Hmong, Russian, Haitian, Somali, and Tagalog, to name a few. While Spanish was the home language for more than 77% of all English language learners during the 2014–2015 school year, Chinese and Korean also fell within the top 11 home languages for English language learners, representing 109,000 and 28,500 students respectively (U.S. Department of Education, 2017). The statistics further reveal that English language learners graduated at a rate of 62.6% during the 2013–2014 school year. While this rate was 5.6% higher than that of the 2010–2011 school year, the graduation rate for English language learners still falls below the national average of 83% for all students enrolled in public schools in the United States (U.S. Department of Education, 2017).

The change in demographics placed many educators in the precarious position of not knowing how to effectively educate this influx of students whose background, cultures, and sometimes languages were quite different from the mainstream students in the majority population. Many schools across the country were already facing a widening achievement gap between Caucasian and African American students. Problematizing the matter was the prevailing narrative proposed by many educators and others in society that these students, by holding onto their native language and culture, were hindering their own chance to achieve academic success. This deficit-laden thinking caused many of these students to feel unworthy and devalued in the classroom. Over the years, legislation such as Proposition 227 in California and the federal No Child Left Behind Act (NCLB) of 2002 also contributed to the problem. Proposition 227, enacted in 1999, dismantled most bilingual education in the state of California. The NCLB (2002) brought about an intense focus on having every student achieve academic success in the classroom. While the intent of the law was admirable, there were negative ramifications. If students did not perform well on the standardized tests, individual schools, teachers, and administrators could be penalized.

In the face of these high-stakes tests and the possible repercussions for low-performing students, many teachers focused less on meeting the needs of the students and more on teaching to the test. This turn of events in the educational arena negatively impacted the use of culturally relevant pedagogy in classrooms across the country. The prevailing view in the era of high-stakes testing was that culturally relevant pedagogy was not a priority within the context of NCLB.

Several educators and scholars, dissatisfied with this deficit-laden narrative and the negative effects associated with high-stakes testing, supported the idea of using culturally relevant pedagogy, the same pedagogy originally promulgated by Ladson-Billings in 1994. They highlighted the importance of using culturally relevant pedagogy to educate diverse students in their pursuit of academic success, equal to the achievements of students in the mainstream culture (Gay, 2000; Sleeter, 2012; Wlodkowski & Ginsberg, 1995).

One major factor that has influenced the use of culturally relevant pedagogy in China and Korea is the countries' presence and involvement in a globalized society. The rapid expansion of the Chinese and Korean economies has ushered in western businesses, new visitors and residents, in addition to outside influences which have had some impact on the Asian traditional way of life. The strong desire to educate the population after the Six-Two-Five conflict of 1950 is another factor which has influenced the use of culturally relevant pedagogy in Korea. This conflict goes by several different names. In the United States it is often referred to as the Korean War. The increasing number of after-school private tutoring services for Korean children, otherwise known as hagwons, have also played a role in the use of culturally relevant pedagogy. The governments of both China and Korea have instituted educational reforms to keep up with the fast-paced societal changes. Some of the changes mentioned above are considered threats to the Confucian ideals which are embedded in Chinese and Korean cultures. Educational reforms in both countries call for the inclusion of character and culture into school curriculums. These types of reforms are in agreement with Confucian thought. This has prompted some educators in China and Korea to include culturally relevant teaching pedagogy into their teaching practice.

Impact on Student Achievement

Some Korean educators are using culturally responsive pedagogy in their attempt to increase the academic achievement of their students (Chung & Kang, 2013). While not all researchers agree with the effectiveness of culturally relevant pedagogy, there is a body of research that argues for its positive impact on student achievement in the United States (Gay, 2000; Ladson-Billings, 2014; Paris, 2012). In a recent comparative study of how two schools in China used culturally responsive teaching, Chinese-based researchers Zhang and Wang (2016) acknowledged that a similar body of knowledge had not yet materialized in their country. They concluded that more research should be done in order to explore the effectiveness of culturally responsive teaching in China (Zhang & Wang, 2016, p. 68).

How Culturally Responsive Pedagogy Influences Parental and Community Involvement

The concept of culturally relevant pedagogy encompasses the notion that teachers will find meaningful ways to incorporate the home culture of students and their families into lessons and activities. Accordingly, the cultural knowledge and lived experiences of the students' parents and other family members can be a significant benefit to the school and to the educational success of the students in the classroom. Research shows that parents in China and Korea are often very involved with their children's education (Huang & Gove, 2015; You, Lim, No, & Dong, 2016). The terms tiger mom and tiger parent have been used to describe the intense involvement that many Asian parents demonstrate concerning their children's education. China's one child policy introduced in 1979 (and abolished in 2016), gave this concept added significance because many Chinese parents are keenly interested in giving a significant amount of attention to their only child. It is a widely held belief that children will become successful in life when they receive a lot of attention and support from their parents. In the United States, more parental and community involvement within the schools was recommended through the NCLB Reauthorization Act in 2007 (NCLB Reauthorization, 2007). During a hearing before the 110th Congress of the United States discussion focused on effective strategies for engaging parents and communities in schools. Since that time, schools have enjoyed varying levels of success in increasing parental involvement. Many schools are looking for ways to get communities involved as collaborating with parents and communities is a way to create partnerships that will benefit the students.

In recent years, there has been an increasing interest in finding ways to help students achieve higher levels of academic achievement in K–16 schools. This remains a valid issue due to the achievement gaps that in many cases continue to exist between culturally and linguistically diverse students and their counterparts in the mainstream society. In the past years, culturally relevant pedagogy has attracted much attention as a viable pedagogy to help students increase their academic performance in school. While a number of researchers have studied this issue, there exists a gap in literature using a cross comparative framework. This work attempts to contribute to this body of research by specifically exploring the reasons for and manner in which culturally relevant pedagogy is used in K–16 classrooms in the United States, China, and South Korea. Examining these issues within this context will provide insight for educators and contribute to their pedagogical knowledge and teaching practice, particularly as they work with diverse student populations.

DATA COLLECTION AND ANALYSIS

The findings in this chapter are informed by data collected and analyzed during my study tour to China and Korea in June 2016. I had several opportunities to engage in conversations and conduct informal interviews with students, faculty, and administrators in China and Korea. The schools included elementary, middle, high, and universities. Additional data was obtained from many personal observations, as well as information acquired during the presentations given by our tour guide in China. Artifacts were accumulated from school personnel and other sites I visited as part of a study group. Throughout the trip, I also reflected on each day's events and entered my reflections into a journal. This data was supplemented by the field notes that I took while visiting schools, cultural and historic sites around Xi'an, China and Seoul, South Korea. Finally, I took many pictures and recorded videos to document the places I had visited and the people that I met. The pictures and videos were very instrumental in helping me further reflect on what had occurred during the visits to China and Korea.

RESULTS

Culturally Relevant Pedagogy

The purpose of the trip to China and Korea included visits to several schools and cultural sites in both countries. During the school visits, I had many opportunities to observe teachers using culturally relevant pedagogy in their classrooms. While common activities often associated with culturally relevant pedagogy were present, the teaching pedagogies varied among and within the schools and classrooms. The teachers incorporated several aspects of their students' home cultures into the lessons. This was represented through readings, videos, music, dance, skits, traditional clothing, classroom presentations, and other culturally related items and discussions.

During the first full day in Xi'an, my group and I visited kindergarten students in an elementary school. The students were three to four years old, as kindergarten in China is equivalent to preschool in the United States. We were greeted warmly by the principal, other administrators, and teachers. The principal provided us with an overview of the school's history leading up to the present day. His oral presentation was supplemented with a video about the school. He emphasized the importance that culture played in the school. He made clear that culture was a crucial component of the curriculum and a crucial part of the vision for the school. In his words: "culture is life."

The principal explained what he described as the ten tenets of culture that were deeply embedded within the school curriculum. The tenets included: (a) Chinese etiquette, (b) Chinese holidays/festivals, (c) Chinese taste (preferences), (d) Chinese children, (e) Chinese New Year, (f) Chinese style, (g) Chinese love (of family), (h) Chinese tea, (i) Chinese calligraphy, and (j) Chinese dragon. He also outlined other ways culture was being incorporated into the students' education. He informed us that there is a growing concern within the Chinese government that Chinese youth prefer American culture over their own culture. This concern prompted the Ministry of Education to request that schools incorporate the ten tenets into the curriculum. The ten tenets were to be implemented in the five broad areas of health, society, language, science, and art. According to the principal, the students should have a solid foundation of Chinese culture by the time they graduate kindergarten.

During this school visit, I had an opportunity to observe the students in their regular class setting. I ate a traditional lunch in the classroom and participated in group physical exercises with students and teachers during the morning recess break. Chinese culture in the form of artwork, writings, and hand carvings was prominently on display throughout the school. The students and teachers presented us with handmade gifts before we left. From my own personal perspective, the principal's words set the tone for the rest of the visit to China and Korea. The information that I received from this first school helped provide a framework for my research.

During the remainder of the trip I visited several other schools at the middle school, high school, and university levels. The school visits were informative and revealing of Asian culture. During the visits, I was able to observe and speak to teachers, administrators, and students. I watched the students perform skits, sing songs, play traditional musical instruments, and do readings in English, Korean, and Chinese. I also gleaned additional information as I listened to and asked questions during panel discussions presented by students, teachers, and administrators.

In addition to the school visits, I also visited historical and cultural sites. The demilitarized zone in Korea was one of the highlights of the trip. My visit to this site caused me to reflect on the Korean War and the lasting effects it has on Korean society in general and the Korean school system in particular. The intense focus on education by parents, students, and educators is a prime example of how Korean society has changed in the years following the Korean War. Prior to the Korean War, a high percentage of the population was illiterate and education was not a priority for the majority of Koreans. Today, there is a high premium placed on obtaining a good education so that one can graduate from a key university, get a good job and be successful in life.

I also visited sites within walking distance of the hotel such as local markets and shopping centers. Throughout our stay in China, we were accompanied by a Chinese tour guide who was full of passion and knowledge regarding her native country. She was born and raised in Xi'an, China, and was obviously excited about sharing her knowledge with our group. She provided us with information whenever we travelled to and from the schools, restaurants, and sightseeing tours. The combination of these activities enabled me to get a snapshot of the educational systems in both countries.

What Factors Influence the Use of Culturally Relevant Pedagogy?

During our visit to Korea, we participated in a panel discussion with the faculty and staff of a foreign language high school. The school had a population of 640 students and 100 faculty members. The panel discussion touched on several topics such as the school's history, general information about the student body, the curriculum, and the faculty and staff's desire to foster creative, independent, and critical thinkers. One of the school's main goals is to create global talent, as their students have a choice of studying one of five languages and cultures (Chinese, Japanese, Russian, French, or English). Because of the global focus, there were many ways that the school embedded culture into their program. For example, there were displays in the hallways relating to cultural traditions, clothing, and literature. There were also specific rooms to hold traditional musical instruments. The students play these instruments during music classes.

In response to my question about the use of culturally relevant pedagogy in the classroom, one faculty member stated that similar to schools in the United States, he does incorporate the students' home culture into the lessons and activities as a bridge to help students access new material. This faculty member was an American teaching English in a Korean school. I thought his response was interesting because he was knowledgeable about the teaching practices in the United States and Korea. He acknowledged that he does not use this teaching method every day, but said it was part of his teaching practice. From his perspective, including the students' home culture into the lessons often makes it easier for them to grasp new material. He elaborated further about why he incorporates their home culture into the lessons:

> I incorporate Korean culture to latch onto what the students already know (their schema). The students appreciate that I took the time to learn about their culture. This is a foreign language school and culture is a big part of learning a language. I use videos, songs, PowerPoint presentations and different types of media.

A discussion with a fifth-grade elementary school teacher in Korea rendered a similar response. She said it was helpful for her students to learn English by discussing it within the context of their own culture. During my observation in her class, the students were practicing their listening, speaking, and writing skills in English by interviewing their classmates and classroom visitors such as myself. The interviews were conducted in English after the students had viewed a video and then participated in a class discussion about the video in their native language. Their use of English during the interviews was based on information they acquired in their native language. Prior to conducting the interviews, the students provided oral and written responses to questions posed by the teacher. The teacher facilitated the class discussion through primarily speaking in Korean. The students were asked to respond to the oral questions in Korean but were encouraged to write their responses in English. The teacher allowed the students to respond in their native language if they had difficulty writing their answers in English. As a homework assignment, the students were required to work in groups to learn a chant in English. The chant was related to the interview questions the students practiced with their classmates and members of the study tour during the lesson. The groups would receive extra credit if they created a dance to reflect what they had learned.

On my last full day in Xi'an, I had an opportunity to conduct an informal interview with a local college student. Through this exchange I was able to obtain a student perspective on the use of culture and culturally relevant pedagogy in the classroom. The student was enrolled at a large urban university. She relayed her personal experiences from her time in high school and college:

> In high school, my teachers helped us learn Chinese and American culture. By contrasting, they made it clear to us. As a college student, my teachers included Chinese or American culture to help us learn. Teachers will tell us some differences and similarities to help us. In high school, they mainly use culture by narrating and giving examples. In college, they do this by showing videos and movies, or by speeches from foreigners, and through cultural exchange meetings. I like different things about Chinese and American culture.

What Impact Does Culturally Relevant Pedagogy Have on Student Learning?

My visit to various classrooms in China and Korea allowed me to see the impact that culturally relevant pedagogy had on student learning. This included students at all grade levels from kindergarten to university. The level of engagement of the students in the first kindergarten class in China, coupled with their responses to the questions being asked by their teachers, was indicative that there was a positive impact on student learning. The students and teachers were primarily speaking Chinese. The teachers had incorporated culture into the lessons and the students responded enthusiastically to the given assignments. I watched as the teacher infused art into the lesson to explain about nature, an important topic in the students' home country of China.

In a visit to a middle school in China, seventh-grade students put on a skit. The skit was another example of how the teachers wove the students' home culture into their lesson as a base from which the class would learn and use English. This skit encompassed many aspects of the Chinese culture, including history, geography, food, drink, music, and traditional dress. The students played traditional musical instruments as part of the skit and shared traditional food and drinks with us. The skit was presented entirely in English. While the presentation enabled the students to practice their English language skills, it was also a way for them to share Chinese culture with visitors in a language that they could understand. The fifth-grade class that I had visited in Korea also demonstrated the impact that culturally relevant pedagogy had on student learning. It was evident that the students felt more comfortable conducting the interviews in English after making personal connections with the video. The video, a visual representation of their own culture, was based on Korean characters and a Korean-based storyline.

How Does Culturally Relevant Pedagogy Influence Parental and Community Involvement?

Parental Involvement

Parental and community involvement in the schools was present in China and Korea. Throughout my conversations with different students, administrators, and faculty members, it was obvious that parental involvement was frequent. Community involvement was evident in both countries but to a lesser extent.

During the first school visit in China, the principal and teachers discussed the vital role that parents played in the schools. The parents were an integral part of the school and often participated in different activities. In fact, some of the handmade gifts that were presented to our group had been made by parents. Faculty, administrators, and students at the other schools visited in Xi'an, China also emphasized the importance of parental involvement. A class assignment in a translation class at one of the universities in Xi'an demonstrated the importance of this topic. The assignment specifically focused on the type of influence parents had over their children's lives in terms of making decisions about their education. The students were asked to translate a paragraph which highlighted the importance that parents placed on obtaining a good education. The assignment noted that parents generally require their children to study hard and get high scores so that they can attend prestigious universities. This issue also arose in a panel discussion at one of the universities in Xi'an. During this discussion, the students gave the following types of responses when asked about their parents' involvement in their lives and their decisions regarding school:

> Kim said her parents were college educated. They told her that education was not only a way for success, but it was very important. Her parents always support her.

> Tom said his parents did not have a good education. They told him education is important and that he needs to study hard. They also told him that what kind of life he has is his choice and with an education, he will have a better chance to get a better job. His parents help him do his best.

> Beth said her parents supported her and encouraged her to go to a good university. Her uncle and aunt are alumni of the university.

Barbara said her parents started talking to her about working hard when she was in kindergarten. Her classmates have also had an influence on her.

While visiting a public middle school in Xi'an, some of the teachers told us that the school had a lot of parental involvement. For example, parents donate books and volunteer their time. Some of the parents also provide consulting and technical assistance.

During the panel discussion at the foreign language high school in Korea, one staff member said students, teachers, and parents contribute equally to the success of the school. The other panel members agreed with this statement. These educators stated that they had continuous interaction with parents through phone calls, emails, attendance at open houses, social festivals, and open classes twice a year. The parents also participate in school management of the dorms and serve as representatives on the Parent Teacher Association committees.

While traveling in Xi'an, our tour guide often provided her own insights about daily life in China. During one of these conversations, she spoke about the involvement of parents in the education of their children. Her views on this topic were very consistent with the views expressed by many of the students:

> The parents feel that if their children do not go to university, they have no future. The kids cannot get a good job if this happens. The kids' success is the parents' success.

Community Involvement

Faculty members and administrators discussed community involvement at some of the schools in China and Korea. For example, community organizations and members participate in different activities related to the various cultures being studied at the foreign language high school in Korea. During a tour of the school, I observed notes from foreign dignitaries such as country ambassadors written to students and displayed on the walls. Two of the middle schools in Xi'an also enjoy some level of community involvement. The schools receive a lot of resources because they are located in high-tech areas of the city. As a result, the schools have received funding from the local government and other assistance from community partners to bolster their technological capabilities.

DISCUSSION

This study abroad trip allowed me to see firsthand how some Chinese and Korean schools compare to schools in the United States. During the visit, I had many opportunities to observe the culture of students enrolled in Chinese and Korean schools. Culture was evident everywhere we went, including in the schools and cultural sites.

I also had opportunities to observe the Chinese and Korean teachers' use of culturally responsive pedagogy in the classroom. The teachers used a variety of methods and activities in their classrooms, such as small group and pair work, music, art, dance, poems, stories, role play, oral presentations, and videos. Their incorporation of the students' home culture into the curriculum as a way to facilitate access to the material was similar to methods that I use in my own ESL classes. Similar to schools in the United States, the use of culturally relevant pedagogy was often dependent on the specific class and the specific teacher involved.

Two ideas associated with Confucianism, harmony and collective work, were evident in some of the classrooms that I visited. For example, as the younger students travelled through the hallway and to the playground outside, they held onto the person in front of them, in order to form an unbroken chain. These human chains displayed the cooperative nature of their classroom and society. The hospitable treatment that was extended to me in both countries also revealed an important part of the Chinese and Korean cultures.

Three broad themes emerged from my analysis of the data. First, it became clear that culture is an integral part of Chinese and Korean society. My observations of the adults and students at all grade levels brought to life how important culture really is in their daily lives. Another theme that emerged from my conversations with several of the participants involved the increasing access students take advantage of in their learning about other countries and cultures on the internet and social media. This theme came up for example in discussions about music, movies, and fashion. The students were very curious about American culture during our conversations but showed pride in their own culture. A recurrent theme in the informal interviews was the belief among interviewees that Asian parents have a strong desire to see their children succeed not just in school, but in life as well. This theme arose in the panel discussions and in other conversations with students, teachers, administrators, and the tour guide.

Finally, the visits to the historical and cultural sites took on added significance beyond the mere sightseeing aspect of the trip. These excursions provided a culturally rich experience and helped place the information gained during the school visits in context. While a longer visit would have been preferable to obtain a more in-depth view of China and Korea, this short trip allowed me to experience things I could not have possibly experienced while at home or at work in North Carolina.

IMPLICATIONS AND RECOMMENDATIONS

Returning to the questions posed at the beginning of this study, it is now possible to state that culture and culturally relevant pedagogy do matter within the context of the K–16 schools in China and Korea, at least with respect to the schools that I visited. This finding is consistent with the research presented. The participants' voices coupled with my own observations and analysis of the data provide further evidence that leads me to this conclusion. I believe this type of pedagogy is not only representative of good teaching (Ladson-Billings, 1994), but its ongoing use in the classroom allows educators to engage the students in ways which enable the students to draw on their own cultural backgrounds to become sources and resources of information (Ladson-Billings, 2014).

The findings of this study have important implications for future practice. As teaching professionals, our teaching practice should reflect and align with the professional teaching standards set forth by the policymakers in our respective jurisdictions. According to the North Carolina Professional Teaching Standards, "Teachers should facilitate learning for their students and establish a respectful environment for a diverse population of students." Additionally, educators should continually reflect on their teaching practice to determine whether the selected pedagogical tools are effectively working for the students in their class.

The role of teachers encompasses many responsibilities. Two important responsibilities that come to mind for teachers of diverse students include being a teacher-researcher and a teacher-leader. First, teacher-researchers must be willing to learn who their students are beyond demographic information. Teachers must take steps to understand history and culture. Once teachers determine their own knowledge gaps, they should make a concerted effort to inquire and incorporate that information into their teaching practice.

Teachers also have an obligation to take on the role of teacher-leaders in schools. In doing so, other educators and administrators may be promoted and encouraged to operationalize a culturally sustaining practice schoolwide, rather than one limited to individual classrooms. Class resources, activities, curricula, school programs and policies can all be positively impacted by the adoption of a culturally relevant pedagogy. This includes inviting parents and community members to collaborate with the school. Parental and community involvement in the schools presents meaningful opportunities for family members and community stakeholders as a way to contribute human and cultural capital for the benefit of the students and school-wide community. These three-way collaborations can help improve the academic lives of all students. My observations in the United States, China, and Korea revealed that positive benefits can result if schools are willing to adopt culturally relevant pedagogy.

REFERENCES

Banks, J. A., & Banks, C. A. M. (2010). *Multicultural education: Issues and perspectives, (7th ed.)*. Hoboken, NJ: Wiley.

Cammarota, J. (2007). A social justice approach to achievement: Guiding Latina/o students toward educational attainment with a challenging, socially relevant curriculum. *Equity and Excellence in Education, 40,* 87–96.

Chang, B., & Lee, J. H. (2012). "Community-based?" Asian American students, parents, and teachers in the shifting Chinatowns of New York and Los Angeles. *AAPI Nexus, 12,* 18–36.

Chung, C., & Kang, K. (2013). The development of science education program based on culturally responsive teaching. *Journal of the Korean Association for Science Education, 33,* 626–638.

Damen, L. (1987). *Culture learning: The fifth dimension on the language classroom.* Reading, MA: Addison-Wesley.

Durden, T., Escalante, E., & Blitch, K. (2015). Start with us! Culturally relevant pedagogy in the preschool classroom. *Early Childhood Educational Journal, 43.* http://digitalcommons.unl.edu/cyfsfacpub/86

Gay, G. (2000). *Culturally responsive teaching: Theory, research, and practice.* New York, NY: Teachers College Press.

Gay, G. (2013). Teaching to and through cultural diversity. *Curriculum Inquiry, 43,* 48–70.

Hofstede, G. (1984). National cultures and corporate cultures. In L. A. Samovar & R. E. Porter (Eds.), *Communication between cultures* (pp. 51). Belmont, CA: Wadsworth.

Huang, G. H., & Gove, M. (2015). Confucianism, Chinese families, and academic achievement: Exploring how Confucianism and Asian descendant parenting practices influence children's academic achievement. In M. S. Kline (Ed.), *Science education in East Asia pedagogical innovations and research-informed practices* (pp. 41–66). Basel, Switzerland: Springer.

Ladson-Billings, G. (1994). *The dreamkeepers: Successful teachers of African-American children.* San Francisco, CA: Jossey-Bass.

Ladson-Billings, G. (1995). Toward a theory of culturally relevant pedagogy. *American Educational Research Journal, 32,* 465–491.

Ladson-Billings, G. (2014). Culturally relevant pedagogy 2.0: Aka the remix. *Harvard Educational Review, 84,* 74–84.

Lederach, J. P. (1995). *Preparing for peace: Conflict transformation across cultures.* Syracuse, NY: Syracuse University Press.

NCLB Reauthorization: Effective strategies for engaging parents and communities in schools: Hearing of the committee on health, education, labor, and pensions, 110th Cong. (2007). Retrieved from https://www.govinfo.gov/content/pkg/CHRG-110shrg34476/html/CHRG-110shrg34476.htm

No Child Left Behind Act of 2001, Pub. L. No. 107–110, 20 U. S. C. § 6319 (2002).

Paris, D. (2012). Culturally sustaining pedagogy: A needed change in stance, terminology, and practice. *Educational Researcher, 41,* 93–97.

Sleeter, C. (2012). Confronting the marginalization of culturally responsive pedagogy. *Urban Education, 47,* 562–584.

The National Clearinghouse for English Language Acquisition and Language Instruction Educational Programs (NCELA), 2007. Retrieved from https://ncela.ed.gov/

The U.S. Department of Education (2011). *The growing numbers of English learner students*, 1998/99–2008/09. Washington, DC: National Clearinghouse for English Language Acquisition.

Trumbull, E. (2005). Language, culture, and society. In E. Trumbull & B. Farr (Eds.), *Language and learning: What teachers need to know* (pp. 33–72). Norwood, MA: Christopher-Gordon.

Useem, J., Useem, R., & Donoghue, J. (1963). Men in the middle of the third culture: The roles of American and non-Western people in cross-cultural administration. *Human Organization, 22,* 169–179.

Wlodkowski, R. J., & Ginsberg, M. B. (1995). *Diversity and motivation: Culturally responsive teaching.* San Francisco, CA: Jossey Bass.

Wyngaard, M.V. (2007). Culturally responsive pedagogies: African American high school students' perspectives. In J. L. Kincheloe & K. Hayes (Eds.), *Teaching city kids: Understanding and appreciating them* (pp. 121–129). New York, NY: Peter Lang.

You, S., Lim, S. A., No, U., & Dong, M. (2016). Multidimensional aspects of parental involvement in Korean adolescents' schooling: A mediating role of general and domain-specific self-efficacy. *Educational Psychology, 36,* 916–934.

Zhang, L., & Wang, Y. (2016). Culturally responsive teaching in China: Instructional strategy and teachers' attitudes. *Intercultural Education, 27,* 54–69.

PART IV

CONCLUSION

CHAPTER 13

CONCLUSION

Implications for Teacher Education

Lan Kolano, Chuang Wang, Michelle Pazzula, and Do-Hong Kim

In this edited book, the authors of these chapters explored different issues such as equity, pedagogy, curriculum, and policies and practices in China and South Korea. Some of the participants examined gender, parental involvement, teacher quality, and family socioeconomic status as well as the impact of their access to resources and career opportunities for students when they finish school. In their exploration of these themes and ideas, these authors experienced growth in their understanding of the culture and educational systems in China and Korea. They completed this experience with a deeper appreciation for the cultural differences that exist between western and eastern systems of education while formulating many more questions waiting to be explored.

Site visits to schools in both countries provided the authors insight into the role of how resources affect student access to the type of education they receive. Since most of the authors work in U.S. schools that are low income and high needs, observations in the most elite and well-resourced

Educational Practices in China, Korea, and the United States, pages 209–219
Copyright © 2019 by Information Age Publishing
All rights of reproduction in any form reserved.

209

schools in China and South Korea left many questions unanswered. Specifically, many wanted to explore the schools that they did not see, and find out how students in China and South Korea were supported if parents' involvement were limited by socioeconomic status, educational attainment level, work demands, and language barriers. Other authors were able to focus on the teaching and learning in the three countries. Authors explored how adopted educational textbooks provided a strong platform to engage students in cultural dialogue. In addition, the U.S. teachers were able to compare the usage of these strategies in their own classrooms and in the classrooms observed in China. The experience provided data that allowed them to compare the strategies used for successful development of second language acquisition. The school visits allowed the U.S. teachers to see how different foreign language pedagogical approaches compared with those in the United States.

The twelve chapters included in this edited book provide educators and stakeholders a glimpse into the education systems of China, South Korea, and the United States through the perspectives of U.S. teachers' experiences abroad, and the conclusion answers the following question, "What was the impact of this experience for teachers and teacher educators?" We also discuss how the experience abroad for these teachers can help to inform teacher education programs. This conclusion summarizes the ways in which the school site visits allowed U.S. teachers to learn about the similarities and differences in educational theories, teaching practices, learning styles, and educational policies in China, South Korea, and the United States. More importantly, it provides the reader insight into how this experience shaped U.S. teachers' and teacher educators' view of education in two countries that differ greatly from education in the United States.

STUDY ABROAD, TEACHER PREPARATION, AND PEDAGOGICAL PRACTICE

There has been a great deal of research in the past decade focused on the role of study abroad in teacher education (Addleman, Nava, Cevallos, Brazo, & Dixon, 2014; Hamel, Chikamori, Ono, & Williams, 2010; He, Lundgren, & Pynes, 2017; Jochum, Rawlings, & Tejada, 2017; Marx & Moss, 2011; Phillion, Malewski, Sharma, & Wang, 2009; Pilonieta, Medina, & Hathaway; 2017; Shiveley & Misco, 2015; Trilokekar & Kukar, 2011). Teachers and teacher candidates reported feelings of empathy for minorities (Phillion et al., 2009; Pilonieta et al., 2017; Smolcic & Katunich, 2017; Trilokekar & Kukar, 2011), disorientation (Addleman et al., 2014; Hamel et al., 2010; Pilonieta, et al., 2017; Trilokekar & Kukar, 2011), increased intercultural competence/global perspectives (He et al., 2017; Shiveley & Misco, 2015;

Smolcic & Katunich, 2017), and pedagogical and professional implications of their study abroad experiences (He et al., 2017; Pilonieta et al., 2017; Phillion et al., 2009; Shiveley & Misco, 2015).

We examined the findings from each chapter individually and the notes from teachers collected over the experiences. We primarily used reflections in the form of reflective responses from the China/Korea study abroad participants to understand the lens in which the teachers and teacher educators viewed their experiences. Several critical themes emerged from their reflections. Teachers and future teacher educators reported feelings of empathy for their current or future students. Not only did participants believe this experience would increase their compassion toward Asian students, but to all students who are immigrants or who come from immigrant families. Similarly, many teachers recognized the importance of this experience being cross-cultural. They respected the differences they had among themselves and the people and institutions they interacted with abroad, knowing that experiencing these differences was very relevant to their work or future work in education. Many post-travel responses also included the importance of reflection and the growth that occurred personally. These teachers challenged their presumptions of the visited nations and their cultures and returned with more open minds. These reflections echo the sentiments of many of the aforementioned authors and support the transformative learning theory (Taylor, 2008). Other important commonalities contributors to this book mentioned were walking in the shoes of others, being outside of their own cultural comfort zones, and having such experiences first-hand versus reading about them in textbooks. Furthermore, teachers felt this study abroad better prepared them to facilitate culturally responsive learning in their classrooms. They stressed the importance of communication and additional language building, positive classroom environment, nurturing the maintenance of native culture and language, and overall engagement and awareness of the needs of their international students.

One of the most prevalent themes of study abroad research is the self-awareness and feelings of empathy for minorities that teachers and teacher candidates gain while being a cultural, linguistic, and ethnic outsider during their time abroad. In Phillion et al.'s (2009) study, practicing teachers recalled their feelings of exclusion and isolation while being ethnic and language minority teachers in Honduras. Similarly, Pilonieta et al.'s (2017) participants reported sentiments of empathy related to being outsiders while teaching and learning in German schools. These feelings of empathy can assist teachers in relating to and better serving minority students in their U.S. schools.

Several authors reported feelings of disorientation or disequilibrium. Addleman et al. (2014) reported events that were disorienting to their participants. This disequilibrium was triggered by interactions that were unfamiliar or outside of the norms they would experience in their home cultures. Hamel et al. (2010) found participants encountered various kinds of cultural disequilibrium, such as food shock, social interactions, and language inability. The top responses to these disorienting situations included the student reframing his/her perspective and managing emotions to avoid feeling overwhelmed. Disorienting experiences were also coded as distancing elements (Pilonieta et al., 2017). These cultural, linguistic, and ethnic differences led preservice teachers to change their frames of reference. Trilokekar and Kukar (2011) studied the disorienting experiences of preservice teachers during study abroad participation in Hong Kong, Dublin, Ireland, and Jiangmen, China. These challenging experiences were reported to be the first step in transformation of perspective (Mezirow, 1978; Taylor, 2008).

While gaining heightened global perspectives and intercultural competence is a goal of interdisciplinary study abroad programs, it seems to be a central tenet of those specifically preparing teachers for culturally and linguistically responsive classrooms. He et al. (2017) utilized the Intercultural Development Inventory (IDI) to collect pre- and post-trip data on 12 full-time K–12 teachers from various disciplines. These inservice teachers traveled to China to interact with students and teachers. The majority of teacher participants increased their orientation on the IDI post-assessment. While reporting on the long-term impacts of study abroad on teachers, Shively and Misco (2015) surveyed practicing teachers who had studied in Luxembourg, Austria and Switzerland. Participants contended that their teacher preparation courses overseas increased their perspectives and made them more cross-culturally aware. Smolcic and Katunich (2017) further contributed to this theme in their review of a variety cultural immersion field experiences. They defined the term of interculturality as the capacity to work across cultures. These authors suggest that this interculturality, gained via cultural immersion programs such as study abroad, is a necessity for teachers in diverse schools.

Building on the intercultural interactions, participants in He et al.'s (2017) study developed curriculum for their classrooms based on their study abroad adventures. These teachers found ways to integrate Chinese language and culture into their instruction. When thinking of the ELs in their classrooms, participants who had traveled to Germany planned curriculum and accommodations that would be equitable, patient and supportive of the social, emotional, and instructional needs of these language minority students (Pilonieta et al., 2017). In the same manner, Phillion et al. (2009) maintained that study abroad has pedagogical implications for multicultural teacher education preparation. Those participants who had spent time in Central America disclosed desires to challenge reductionist representations of language, culture, race, and ethnic diversity. Beyond classroom conventions and

Conclusion ▪ **213**

pedagogy, practicing teachers who had previously studied abroad found their experiences central to their employability as open-minded and well-rounded teacher candidates (Shiveley & Misco, 2015).

SUMMARY OF CONCLUSIONS

Together, this edited text offers insight into the educational policies and practices in China and Korea from the perspective of U.S. educators. These teachers and teacher educators explored issues that intersected all three countries and included topics such as culture, gender, parental involvement, economy, curriculum, student fitness, English as a second/foreign language, smart learning, and education reformations. Through the eyes of these American educators, these chapters connected the classroom practices and innovations and identified broader theoretical/pedagogical issues among three distinct education systems in China, South Korea, and the United States. As a whole, the text offers educators analyses of the similarities and differences within epistemologies, enactment of pedagogical principles and classroom practices in China, South Korea, and the United States with a careful examination of the learners and learning in three diverse countries. The chapters challenge educators to think about ways that education is conceptualized, what cultural nuances inform it, and how teachers transform classrooms to provide students with experiences that challenge their ideas. The chapters bridge and transform seemingly opposing perspectives with evidence from field notes, observations, and interviews with teachers and students in the schools they visited. These perspectives, which would otherwise be lost to assumptions and stereotypes are important in the broadening of our ideologies of teaching and learning. This conclusion is organized in three sections that follow the structure of the chapters. In their exploration of issues, U.S. educators shared their observations and analyses in "Part I: Influence of Culture, Parental Involvement and Economy," "Part II: Teaching and Learning," and "Part III: New Pedagogical Framework and Practices."

Part I: Influence of Culture, Parental Involvement and Economy

The first part of the book captures different equity issues that exist in China, South Korea and the United States. The contributors of this book explored differences in educational resources and career opportunity with respect to gender, parental involvement, teacher quality, and family socioeconomic status. In the exploration of these topics, these U.S. educators reported positive feelings from the trip and deepened learning about culture and equity in these countries.

The trip to another country enhanced participants' appreciation for cultural differences and values. These U.S. educators reported that they learned different aspects of Chinese and South Korean life and education during their stay, for example one teacher stated:

> This trip allowed me a closer look at the nuances of two educational systems in East Asia, while concentrating on a more specific topic. It was fascinating to see the effects of philosophy and cultural beliefs on the system of education in different countries. (Teacher 17)

Some teachers spoke of the excitement of sharing their experiences with others, for example:

> I have a greater appreciation for seeing through others' eyes and going to experience something for myself. I hope that I am able to help others gain an appreciation for other styles of education and culture when I share about this trip in the future. (Teacher 10)

The teachers also shared that they gained a deeper understanding of teaching culturally and linguistically diverse students. They developed a better understanding of different perspectives, teaching approaches, and lifestyles. The teachers also expressed eagerness to use what they have learned in the future classrooms. One of the teachers stated:

> I have learned about many things that I will take into my classroom including cross-cultural sensitivity and awareness, the appropriate use of L1 in the classroom, and creating a positive classroom culture and environment. (Teacher 6)

Part II: Teaching and Learning

Part II showcases the observations with teaching and learning in the three countries. These chapters examine how texts were selected in the textbooks to provide a platform for students to engage in cultural dialogues. Topics included in this part also includes research-based teaching methods used frequently to teach English as a second language as well as physical education. What stood out in the reflections that the teachers wrote in their exploration of teaching and learning is how they changed in their ideas in these two countries. These U.S. teachers also described what they learned about their own teaching and learning practices through the intense observations and interviews with teachers and students in China and Korea.

It was through these experiences where they found the greatest space for change about their own ideas and beliefs.

These U.S. teachers shared that the trip was an eye-opening and positive experience and admitted that they had a limited understanding of other cultures prior to their travel. Thus, this trip exposed them to new experiences, broadened their horizons, and ultimately encouraged them to be more open-minded to cultural differences. One teacher stated:

> The China and South Korea trip was an eye-opening, thought-provoking, and short-lived experience, to say the least. Going into the trip, my knowledge of Asian countries as a whole was pretty limited. Although I knew some surface level things—the location, languages spoken, popular food dishes—my actual understanding of the people, sights, cultures, and schools was essentially non-existent. I was a blank slate, with the exception of assumptions I'd made and stereotypes I'd heard. (Teacher 24)

Another theme that emerged relates to challenging assumptions, biases, and misconceptions participants hold about culture. One of the participants shared her dispositions about Chinese and Korean cultures:

> As I reflect on my initial assumptions, without even being aware, I realize I initially approached China/Korea as if they were inherently weaker, worse off than we are/were, only because they were different. I assumed that our educational policies and pedagogies were the ONLY way, and THE correct solution. I did not even take into account China's history, culture, and traditions; I had merely drawn these conclusions only after reading articles and the opinions of others' experiences. (Teacher 3)

The teachers also expressed a profound transformation in their thinking. This experience encouraged them to reflect on their own educational experiences and perspectives. The quote below illustrates such transformation:

> Overall, this transformative experience abroad has forced me to rethink initial presumptions of others, and has simply encouraged personal growth, and ultimately challenged and inspired the development of my perspective—both individually (personally) and globally. In short, I have been confronted with the realization that I/we cannot suitably/fairly judge anything from afar under the guise that our opinions will be fair, realistic, untainted, and flexible. Instead, we must have these experiences ourselves, first-hand, in order to be able to draw accurate, personal, and fulfilling conclusions—all with the intent to better serve and interact with them. (Teacher 8)

Part III: New Pedagogical Framework and Practices

Finally, Part III presents a discussion of new pedagogies, classroom practices, and learning strategies in China, South Korea and the United States. All described the ways that they learned more about the education, life, and cultures of China and South Korea from visiting the school sites, interacting with the teachers and students there. They also described the ways that they connected with their colleagues who participated in the experience and formed deep friendships and professional connections with one another as a result. The major themes that emerged include how they developed a deeper appreciation for culture and an understanding of others. In thinking about their own pedagogical practices, they described their development empathy and about the importance of early exposure to language and culture for U.S. students. Most importantly, teachers described how their eyes were "opened," and assumptions were challenged, and how they were transformed in their thinking of themselves and their pedagogy from the experience.

This experience inspired participants to be more empathetic and caring teachers who address the needs of culturally and linguistically diverse students. For example,

As a future ESL teacher, I feel that this trip was very beneficial in understanding the Chinese culture because I will be able to empathize, with not only my Chinese students, but students from similar Asian countries. This will be very helpful in my efforts to communicate properly with them and understand their needs and learning preferences. (Teacher 4)

The travel abroad also enriched these teachers professionally and personally, for example:

My time abroad was an unforgettable experience. My memories and experiences in China and South Korea were "for the books." I was able to experience a new culture and learn about my profession in another country. This not only helped me grow professionally but also personally. (Teacher 20)

Teachers also shared that the trip to another country had a positive impact on their understanding of second language acquisition. One participant reported:

Of all the educational topics we discussed with the educators overseas, one I think that is the most important to discuss with American educators is the need for increased emphasis on second language acquisition in American schools. Despite the fact that English is a language that is mostly understood throughout the world, it is necessary for American citizens, and for English speakers in general, to be exposed to foreign languages at an early age in order to generate interest and to increase the potential for greater second language proficiency. (Teacher 12)

IMPLICATIONS FOR TEACHER EDUCATION

Experiences such as this one to China and South Korea can address the needs to help teachers develop multicultural teacher efficacy so they are better prepared to work with students from diverse communities. Social inequalities in the classroom (Levine-Rasky, 2000; Nieto, 1994; Smith, 2000) can be better addressed by teachers with increased global perspective gained through study abroad (He et al., 2017; Shiveley & Misco, 2015; Smolcic & Katunich, 2017). This, in part, can be achieved by increased feelings of empathy for minorities (Phillion et al., 2009; Pilonieta et al., 2017; Trilokekar & Kukar, 2011; Smolcic & Katunich, 2017). Furthermore, teachers, teacher candidates, and teacher educators can all benefit from pedagogical and professional impacts attained through focused international travel (He et al., 2017; Pilonieta et al., 2017; Phillion et al., 2009; Shiveley & Misco, 2015).

The experience at the school sites in China and Korea helped to affect teacher beliefs in positive ways. Through the analyses of their final reflections and documentation of their experiences (as presented in these individual book chapters), we found this short-term study abroad experience in China and Korea to be meaningful for teachers and teacher educators in several ways. The assumptions that were challenged for many was a result of the direct interaction the participants had with teachers and students in both countries. Through this experience, they learned to appreciate diversity and language in ways they had not experienced before. The teachers were honest in sharing the many assumptions they had about China and South Korea prior to travel. As a result of working with the students, observing the teachers, and interacting with schools in meaningful ways, these U.S. teachers began to understand the cultural beliefs that informed education in these two different countries in Asia. By working with the students in small groups in these schools and interviews with teachers, these U.S. educators learned about their motivations and pressures to achieve. While many were not sure how well they would be able to communicate with the students, they found the students' conversational English skills to be impressive. The school sites we visited were well organized and had a professional staff that worked as a cohesive unit. As a result of working with the students and their teachers abroad, these teachers came back to the United States with different perspectives on the students in China and South Korea. They described them as "impressive" and "amazing." Some indicated

218 ▪ L. KOLANO et al.

how "nervous" and "anxious" they were prior to starting, but were relieved once they had the chance to interact within these diverse school settings. Participants developed greater multicultural teacher efficacy and became more empathetic to the issues faced by English language learners in the United States. For some, this experience worked to disconfirm many of the stereotypes they held at the beginning of the experience.

The chapters provide the reader with summaries and analyses of the similarities and differences in epistemologies, pedagogical principles and classroom practices in China and South Korea as compared to U.S. classrooms. Together, these chapters contribute to a better understanding of not only the differences and similarities in educational thinking and practices in the three countries, but also examines the context in which educational decisions are made. As such, this book may help the educational community in all three countries better understand the cultural and sociopolitical contexts in which education is designed and implemented in these diverse countries. More importantly, the testimonials provided by the study participants underscore the importance of exposing U.S. teachers to diverse experiences abroad. Through the purposeful school site visits and focused interactions with teachers and students in China and South Korea, U.S. educators challenged their assumptions of others, deepened their understanding of educational policies and practices, and developed an appreciation for difference.

REFERENCES

Addleman, R., Nava, R., Cevallos, T., Brazo, C., & Dixon, K. (2014). Preparing teacher candidates to serve students from diverse backgrounds: Triggering transformative learning through short-term cultural immersion. *International Journal of Intercultural Relations, 43*(B), 189–200. https://doi.org/10.1016/j.ijintrel.2014.08.005

Hamel, F., Chikamori, K., Ono, Y., & Williams, J. (2010). First contact: Initial responses to cultural disequilibrium in a short-term teaching exchange program. *International Journal of Intercultural Relations, 34*(6), 600–614. https://doi.org/10.1016/j.ijintrel.2010.05.005

He, Y., Lundgren, K., & Pynes, P. (2017). Impact of short-term study abroad program: Inservice teachers' development of intercultural competence and pedagogical beliefs. *Teaching and Teacher Education, 66*, 147–157. https://doi.org/10.1016/j.tate.2017.04.012

Jochum, C., Rawlings, J. R., & Tejada, A. M. (2017). The effects of study abroad on Spanish teachers' self-efficacy: A multiple case study. *The Interdisciplinary Journal of Study Abroad, 29*(1), 28–45. Retrieved from http://www.frontiersjournal.com/

Levine-Rasky, C. (2000). Framing whiteness: Working through the tensions in introducing whiteness to educators. *Race, Ethnicity, and Education 3*, 271–292.

Marx, H., & Moss, D. M. (2011). Please mind the culture gap: Intercultural development during a teacher education study abroad program. *Journal of Teacher Education, 62*(1), 35–47.

Mezirow, J. (1978). Perspective transformation. *Adult Education, 28*, 100–110.

Nieto, S. (1994). Lessons from students on creating a chance to dream. *Harvard Educational Review, 64*, 392–427.

Phillion, J., Malewski, E. L., Sharma, S., & Wang, Y. (2009). Reimagining the curriculum: Future teachers and study abroad. *Frontiers: The interdisciplinary journal of study abroad, 18*, 323–339.

Pilonieta, P., Medina, A. L., & Hathaway, J. I. (2017). The impact of a study abroad experience on preservice teachers' dispositions and plans for teaching english language learners. *The Teacher Educator, 52*(1), 22–38.

Shively, J., & Misco, T. (2015). Long-term impacts of short-term study abroad: Teacher perceptions of preservice study abroad experiences. *Frontiers: The Interdisciplinary Journal of Study Abroad, 26*, 107–120.

Smith, R. (2000). The influence of teacher background on the inclusion of multicultural education: A case study of two contrasts. *The Urban Review, 32*, 155–176.

Smolcic, E., & Katunich, J. (2017). Teachers crossing borders: A review of the research into cultural immersion field experience for teachers. *Teaching and Teacher Education, 62*, 47–59. https://doi.org/10.1016/j.tate.2016.11.002

Taylor, E. W. (2008). Transformative learning theory. *New Directions for Adult and Continuing Education, 119*, 5–15.

Trilokekar, R., & Kukar, P. (2011). Disorienting experiences during study abroad: Reflections of pre-service teacher candidates. *Teaching and Teacher Education: An International Journal of Research and Studies, 27*, 1141–1150. https://doi.org/10.1016/j.tate.2011.06.002

ABOUT THE CONTRIBUTORS

Cory Alexander holds a Bachelor of Arts in business marketing, a minor in Biblical studies, a graduate certificate in TESOL (teaching English to speakers of other languages) and a master's degree in teaching from the University of North Carolina at Charlotte. She is currently teaching English II to English language learners at Garinger High School, one of the Charlotte Mecklenburg Schools in North Carolina. Email: zanderbrazil@gmail.com

Taylor Allen is a high school English language (EL) instructor at a large public school in North Carolina. He holds a master's degree from UNC Charlotte in teaching with a focus on teaching English to speakers of other languages (TESOL); he also holds a bachelor's degree from Michigan State University in political theory and globalization. He has an interest in tracking how educational outcomes effect domestic economies, which includes researching ways to improve educational practices to fulfill the educational mandate of training and equipping students to be productive and participatory members of their community—a need that is especially immediate and rewarding for minority language speakers in the United States. Email: taylorm.allen@cms.k12.nc.us

Kelsey Alvarez is currently an elementary teacher in Charlotte, North Carolina. She has her teaching certification in K–6 elementary education and special education. Kelsey received her master's degree in teaching English as a second language. Her passion is teaching in Title 1 schools. Email: KelseyAlvarez37@gmail.com

---

Educational Practices in China, Korea, and the United States, pages 221–225
Copyright © 2019 by Information Age Publishing
All rights of reproduction in any form reserved.

222 ■ About the Contributors

Kiran Budhrani is an instructional designer for online and blended learning at the Center for Teaching and Learning at the University of North Carolina at Charlotte. She is also a doctoral candidate in educational leadership at UNC Charlotte. She obtained her master's in computer applications and instructional systems technology from De La Salle University–Manila. Her research interests include: visual course mapping, course design epistemology, online teaching, and e-learning technologies in international settings. Email: kbudhran@uncc.edu

Michelle Chen completed her master's in teaching English as a second language in 2016 at the University of North Carolina at Charlotte. She is a Chinese and global studies teacher at Harris Road Middle School in Concord, North Carolina. She enjoys guiding students in acquiring language, with the goal of communication and understanding. She is interested in the methodology of comprehensible input and seeks continuous improvement in implementing this style of language education in her classroom. Email: michelle.chen@cabarrus.k12.nc.us

Laurie Dymes is a PhD candidate in curriculum and instruction with a focus on literacy and TESOL. She holds NC licensure in elementary education and ESL and has taught middle grades English language arts and social studies for 14 years. In addition, Laurie is National Board Certified in Literacy for Early Adolescent and Young Adults. Her research interests include adolescent literacy, implemented canons, and authentic reading experiences. Email: Laurie@Dymes.net

Jennifer Adamian James is a UNCC graduate who currently teaches English as a new language in Charlotte, North Carolina. Her areas of interest include working with linguistically and culturally diverse students with exceptionalities, language immersion magnet schools in the United States, and English as a foreign language education abroad. E-mail: jennyadamian@gmail.com

Peter Johnson received a bachelor's degree in mathematics at Salisbury University. After completing a graduate certification in TESL and a master's degree from the University of North Carolina at Charlotte, he became a math & ESL teacher at East Mecklenburg High School. Email: pete.johnson@live.com

Jessica Kapota is an instructional designer in the Center for Teaching and Learning with a BA in education and MA in history. Her interests include impostor phenomenon, new faculty training, and online learning. She is currently working on her EdD in educational leadership. Email: jkapota@uncc.edu

About the Contributors ▪ **223**

Yolanda Kennedy-Dounebaine is a doctoral candidate at the University of North Carolina at Charlotte. She currently holds a Master of Science in educational research measurement and statistics. Her research interests include underrepresented minority groups in STEM fields, comparative education, and racial inequities within education. Email: ylkenned@gmail.com

Dr. Do-Hong Kim is professor in the College of Education, Department of Advanced Studies & Innovation at Augusta University, Georgia. Dr. Kim earned her PhD in educational psychology and research from the University of South Carolina, with emphasis on quantitative methods and measurement theory. Her research interests include the application of psychometric and quantitative methods to issues in educational and psychological assessment. Email: dkim3@augusta.edu

Dr. Lan Kolano is a professor of education at the University of North Carolina at Charlotte. Her research focuses on the academic, language, and identity of immigrant learners, and in the development of the critical multicultural efficacy of teachers. She teaches undergraduate and graduate level courses that focus on issues of equity and education, immigration, and the education of English learners in urban school contexts. Email: Lan.Kolano@uncc.edu

Elizabeth Landon received a bachelor's degree in music performance at Northwestern University and a master's degree from Rice University. After completing a graduate certification in TESL and a master's degree in teaching from the University of North Carolina at Charlotte, she became an instructor of adult ESL at Rowan-Cabarrus Community College while maintaining a private flute studio. www.elizabethlandon.com, Email: lizlandonesl@gmail.com

Jessie Lay is a preschool teacher (Pre-K) at Virginia Chance School in Louisville, Kentucky. She received a Master of Education in teaching English as a second language from the University of North Carolina at Charlotte, where she is originally from, and received a Bachelor of Science in elementary education from Western Carolina University. Her favorite things to do are spending time with her cats, traveling, hiking, and cheering on the Louisville City FC at soccer games with her husband, Ben. Email: jessiel.lay@gmail.com

Dr. Florence Martin is a professor of learning, design, and technology at the University of North Carolina at Charlotte. She engages in research focusing on the effective design of instruction and integration of digital technology to improve learning and performance. Email: Florence.Martin@uncc.edu

224 ▪ About the Contributors

Gwitaek Park is a doctoral student in special education at the University of North Carolina at Charlotte. He is interested in not only teacher and parent education but also developing instructional interventions for positive outcome of students with low incidence disabilities. Email: gpark6@uncc.edu

Michelle Pazzula Jimenez is an ESOL teacher in York County, SC. She is seeking a PhD in curriculum and instruction from the University of North Carolina at Charlotte. Her research interests include study abroad for content teachers and the intersectionality of ESOL and SPED services in diverse schools. Email: mpazzula@uncc.edu

Hongjun Qiu is an associate professor of physical education at Xi'an Jiaotong University in China. He was a visiting scholar at the University of North Carolina at Charlotte during the 2014–2015 academic year. His research interests include the history of physical education in China. Email: qhongjun2009@126.com

Lauren Schmidt is an English as a new language teacher at Hopewell High School in Charlotte, North Carolina. Her expertise includes differentiating instruction for English language learners and the effect trauma can have on language acquisition. Email: laurenschmidt24@gmail.com

Dr. April Smith is the THRIVE program coordinator at the College and Community Fellowship based in New York, NY. Her research interest includes the educational advancement of marginalized populations of criminal justice impacted persons, especially Black, African American, or Brown women of color. Email: smithapril121212@gmail.com

Dr. Chuang Wang is a professor of educational research measurement and evaluation at the University of North Carolina at Charlotte. His expertise includes educational statistics and English language learner's self-efficacy beliefs. He is also interested in comparative education, especially Chinese and American education. Email: cwang15@uncc.edu

Kathryn Wagner is a doctoral candidate in Urban Education with a concentration in urban literacies at the University of North Carolina at Charlotte. Her research interests include the equitable education of English learners in public schools, critical pedagogy and classroom teachers, and the experiences of immigrant and refugee students in school. Email: kwagne20@uncc.edu

Lori J. Williams currently serves as an assistant attorney general for the Pohnpei State Attorney General's Office in the Federated States of Micronesia. She has a Master of Arts in teaching English as a second language and was previously employed as an English as a second language teacher in the Iredell-Statesville School District in North Carolina. She is interested in writing multicultural and STEM-related books for K–12 English language learners. Email: ljanet19@hotmail.com